# THE
# IMPROBABLE
# VOYAGE

# THE IMPROBABLE VOYAGE

## TRISTAN JONES

**S**

SHERIDAN HOUSE

First paperback edition
published 1998 by
Sheridan House Inc.
145 Palisade Street
Dobbs Ferry, New York 10522

First published 1986 by The Bodley Head Ltd, England.

*Library of Congress Cataloging-in-Publication Data*

Jones, Tristan, 1924-1995
   The improbable voyage of the yacht Outward Leg into,
through, and out of the heart of Europe.
   1. Rhine River—Description and travel. 2. Danube River—
Description and travel. 3. Jones, Tristan, 1924-1995.
Journeys—Rhine River. 4. Jones, Tristan—Journeys—Danube
River. 5. Sailing—Rhine River. 6. Sailing—Danube River.
7. *Outward Leg* (Yacht) I. Title.
DD801.R74J66   1986      914.3'404878      86-31833

Printed in the United States of America

ISBN 1-57409-062-3

*To Clare Francis, a brave lady*
*and*
*To Wally Herbert, a brave gentleman*

"Ceffyl da yw ewyllys"
"Where there's a will, there's a way"

—Old Welsh proverb

# Contents

PART THREE: OUT

# *Foreword*

This is a true yarn written by a sailor for, among others, fellow sailors. Some of these fellow sailors may, I hope, make this voyage with greater ease in the future. I have included in the story some information on things that matter to voyagers: depths of water, berthing, supplies and freshwater sources, and suchlike. I know that these matters will interest my fellow voyagers. I trust that they will not tire the general reader.

This is the story of one boat's extraordinary voyage, not a book about land travel through countries or cities. Here you will find little about art galleries or museums, or even history. Here you will find mainly the view from an oceangoing vessel's deck as she makes one of the most onerous and wonderful small-craft voyages of recent times.

I can only hope that the references to the needs of voyagers and to the knowledge they may need will serve to add to the "novelty" and "strangeness" of the whole real-life venture.

My voyage was made against the advice of most of the world's foremost authorities on exploration, river navigation and ocean voyaging. Only two persons among them thought it might be possible. For the rest, they washed their hands of me and wished me well (and probably good riddance). To those two people I dedicate this book.

On board *Outward Leg*
Meghisti,
Nisos Kastellorizo,
Greece

September–October 1985

# THE
# IMPROBABLE
# VOYAGE

# PART ONE

## *Into*

River Danube, called Donau in Germany, Duna in Austria, Dunaj in Czecho-slovakia, Dunav in Yugoslavia, Dunarea in Rumania and Dunay in U.S.S.R., the largest river in Europe except the Volga . . . debouches through a delta into the Black Sea after a course of about 1,750 miles.

Between Neustadt and Regensburg the river forces its way through a narrow, cliffy defile nearly one mile in length. At the eastern end of the defile is Kelheim . . . and as the Ludwig canal connects River Altmühl with River Main in Bamberg, *it is possible to traverse the European continent, by water, from the North Sea to the Black Sea.*

*The Black Sea Pilot, 1969*
British Hydrographic Department,
Ministry of Defence.

*Scheisse!*                                    Unknown German official, Ludwig
                                               Kanal 1944.

Bloody hell!                                   The author when he saw why the
                                               German official had cursed in 1944.

                                               5 December 1984

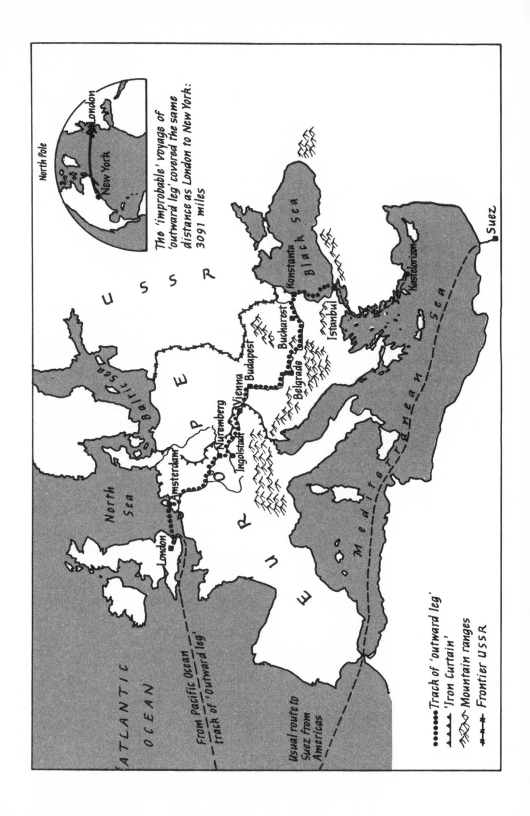

North Pole

London

New York

The 'improbable' voyage of 'outward leg' covered the same distance as London to New York: 3091 miles

ATLANTIC OCEAN

North Sea

London

Amsterdam

Baltic Sea

U   S   S   R

Black Sea

Konstanta

Bucharest

Belgrade

Budapest

Vienna

Nuremberg

Ingolstadt

E   U   R   O   P   E

Istanbul

Kusfalanzan

Mediterranean Sea

Suez

From Pacific Ocean track of 'outward leg'

Usual route to Suez from Americas

•••••• Track of 'outward leg'
▲▲▲▲ 'Iron Curtain'
⋀⋀⋀⋀ Mountain ranges
━╋━╋━ Frontier USSR

# 1

# *On Pioneering*

What I'm writing now is an amalgam of my thoughts as they were in St. Katharine's Dock at the prospect ahead, and my conclusions now in Kastellorizo after the fact, a year and three thousand miles later. For the average small-craft voyager three things are certain: if he waits until his boat is one hundred percent ready, or if he waits until he has enough money for the whole voyage, or if he listens to most "sensible" people, he'll never get away from the dock.

It's different if the voyage is sponsored, of course; then some "sensible" people, with money invested by the barrel load, and anxious for a return on the investment, will push the poor sod out to sea as quickly as possible, whether his boat's ready or not. But they won't do it for the "impossible" voyages. They won't touch those with a barge pole. It doesn't suit their landsmen's views.

That's a good thing for the "impossible" voyager. It leaves him short of money; most of the time chronically short, and his boat is rarely wholly shipshape, but if he's worth his own salt he does get away from the dock. He might come a cropper in short order, but at least he makes a start, even though he might have no idea of how the voyage will carry on in the later stages. If the voyage doesn't start, then it was just a dream anyway and for him it is better for it to die than for the "sensible" people to lay hands on it. Money, although it helps, doesn't make real dreams come true; only faith, hope and compassion can do that, and patience; but the voyager can't be too patient or time will erode his dream.

My dream in 1984, and indeed for many years before that, was to pass an oceangoing craft right through Europe by way of the Rhine and Danube. I made ready in St. Katharine's Dock, London, in October 1984.

Most people who have never made a long river voyage imagine that it must be far easier and safer than making voyages across oceans. The reverse is generally true. On an ocean passage, for ninety percent of the time, on average, a boat, if she is properly navigated, is clear of hazards. On a river passage, under way, a boat is rarely, if ever, clear of hazards. The chances of an accident to the vessel and to the people in her are much, much more on a long river passage than out at sea. That might not seem so to the average landsman, but that is because inland on a river he is surrounded by familiar things; land and trees and people, towns and villages, and does not understand the hazards of shoals and fast currents. I have known some of the toughest voyagers dead and alive, and not one of them would not blanch at first sight of the upper river Danube in full spate.

I have voyaged all the oceans in the world. Only two months before I headed for the Rhine I had made a transatlantic passage in *Outward Leg*. I can truthfully say that the voyage across Europe was far more hazardous than any ocean leg, both to me and the boat. We crossed the Atlantic, both of us, with not a scratch; as you will see, by the time we emerged from the Danube into the Black Sea we were both battered and bruised, almost beyond bearing.

This only goes to prove what I've been saying for a long time about ocean passages; it's the unexpected, the unknown element, the dark side of ourselves, that frightens us. It's being away from the rest of humanity, in the dark spaces, alone, that's the real fear, not the prospect of death or disablement. These risks are far greater on a long river passage, yet we can accept them, or even dismiss them from our minds because we foolishly imagine that death might be easier in familiar surroundings or in company. That's an illusion, because everyone dies alone, wherever he is. Considering some of the company on the rivers we voyaged, and especially in the lower reaches of the Danube, I think it would be infinitely preferable to die alone in the clean open reaches of the ocean.

The very fact that my boat is twenty-six feet wide was enough to put off most of the "sensible" people. The depth of her they didn't even think of, although to me that was far more important. If she had been one inch deeper the voyage could not have been made— but I might have cut off the offending inch. Her height, even with the mast down, was crucial, too. As it was we lowered it by six inches and even then, in some places, she cleared bridges with only an inch to spare.

The looks I raised in London among some people when I told them where I was bound told the whole story. Not from everyone, mind, but from the vast majority. I have no doubt that, had I been younger and not made some of the voyages I have made in the past, most of the others would have had the same attitude too. Perhaps the false leg helped, and I *had* just arrived from investigating piracy in Colombia.

For passage-pioneers those attitudes, those looks, those scoffs, are familiar things. I had had them before my Arctic voyages, before the vertical voyage to the Dead Sea and Lake Titicaca; I get them now, when I propose a passage in an oceangoing craft to *Tibet*, but it's water off a duck's back to me. The test of my "sanity" (if there is such a thing) is whether or not I am aware of these attitudes. As long as I am, I'm all right. When I'm not, I'll still be all right.

In London I listened to all the objections, carefully. So far as anyone could tell, there was no water connection between the Rhine and the Danube. Yet the *Black Sea Pilot* (1969) said that there *was* one. It didn't say how wide the Ludwig Kanal was, but it still might be used, if it existed, to raise *Outward Leg* up on barges and float her through that way. There were rumors of a new canal being constructed, but even the German embassy in New York and Washington could give me no information as to the state of work there. Some said it was finished, some said it was not even started. So far as South Bavaria was concerned, it might as well have been on the upper reaches of the river Amazon, for all the information I could seize in short breaks between finishing my book and getting *Outward Leg* ready for the North Sea passage and the haul up the Rhine.

My good friend Peter Drew, of the London World Trade Centre, who had carved a beautiful place out of the old St. Katharine's Dock, offered to fly me out to Nürnberg to view for myself the obstacles. Could the boat be dragged over the existing canal bed? Would the authorities allow her to be hauled by road? Could she be flown over the gap by helicopter? These questions might be solved by going out there and talking to Germans and seeing the hazards and possibilities. But I knew enough about the potential problems by now to know that if I did fly out there, and if I viewed the prospects, I might quail at the sight of them, and abort the passage. As things turned out, I was right to turn down Peter's offer. If I had not had *Outward Leg*, and all she stands for, with me when I arrived at Nürnberg I would have scrapped the whole dream, returned to London and sailed for Biscay and Gibraltar. It would have been far easier to reach the eastern Mediterranean that way in a well-found craft like *Outward Leg*. But I knew that once at the headwaters of the Rhine with my boat, *nothing* would turn me back. It would be a fight to the finish. The Amazon had defeated me once, more than a thousand miles from the ocean. There was too much symbolism in the Rhine for me to let any kind of obstacle, geographical or human, prevent my passage in *Outward Leg*. It would be a case of shit or bust, and I didn't feel like busting in Germany.

I had always been fascinated by rivers. Indeed, for me my ocean voyages have often been merely passages to and from some river. Like Bill Tilman, whose long ocean voyages were mainly aimed at arriving at some remote mountain in order to climb, so many of my voyages have been some attempt to get to a river estuary. I doubt if I've ever passed by a river mouth and not ached to get inside it to see what it's all about. There may be, to the Freudians, God help them, something symbolic in this, and perhaps, God help us, they're right, but the plain fact is I like rivers. To me they are all mystery, all magic, no matter how cold and bleak, hot and swampy, dirty and despoiled. Rivers are rich. They tell more about a country than all the monuments, all cities, all the rail- and motorways. They are the story of all who live around them, as they flow on and on, darkening by humanity's wastes, rich, rank, often stinking and more often beautiful. Unending as is all life, alive, dark, wise and full of exotic knowledge and immortal time, the rivers flow on and on, as do we all, to the sea.

For years I had gazed at the atlas, at the map of Europe, and seen the possibilities: that Europe, in fact, could have an *east* coast, and that it might be possible to make a voyage direct from the North Sea to the Black Sea. For fewer years I had been aware that others had, long before I had discovered my dream, been working at it; in fact the mad King Ludwig of Bavaria had actually made the dream come true, in a small way, for almost a century. Some small monohulls had made the voyage, but they were not of the ocean. Now, other engineers had completed or were busy digging out the mountains of Bavaria to allow ships to pass. But they were aiming for river ships and coasters. The only ocean ships that would ever pass through, it seems, are yachts. *Outward Leg* must be the first ocean vessel to make this passage, to be the first of thousands of "wild geese" that one day will pass north and south through Europe on their seasonal migrations, like birds of passage.

*Outward Leg* is a trimaran. This means that she does not heel much and so, with my one leg, I can hop around her decks fairly easily. But it also means that she is wider than the average vessel. Indeed, at thirty-nine feet length, she is as wide as some ships five times her length. She is as wide as some modern naval frigates. At sea this does not matter much; in fact it is a blessing, for it gives her, to others, an envious turn of speed and makes for great stability. But in harbors or rivers it is a curse. She takes up much more room than my presence on earth should allow, and it makes maneuvering in close quarters a pain in the neck, especially if there is any kind of a stiff breeze. Because of her anti-capsize "cooltubes" *Outward Leg* has a keel which pokes down four-and-a-half feet. This means that she can only float in water just over four-and-a-half feet deep. Her height, with the mast down, from the waterline to the top of the boom gallows, is just over six feet. Now, with her width, or beam as we call it, of twenty-six feet, this means that *Outward Leg* occupies a space twenty-six feet wide by forty feet long by ten feet deep. That is quite a package to transport over dry land for over one hundred kilometers, even with the aid of modern transport equipment. It is the size of two large living rooms. Being a boat, she is full of equipment and fittings, all of which have to be maintained in good order. For land transport her only saving grace is her weight, which is a mere three tons, empty.

"Now," say many "sensible" people, "because trimarans are so wide, they cannot possibly go where monohulled boats can go."

Thus another reason for the Rhine-Danube expedition—to prove the "sensible" people wrong, and in fact not only that, but to take *Outward Leg* to some places where the average monohull of the same length cannot possibly go, and never will go, until either the rivers are deepened or monohulls are made drastically lighter. This I would do by reaching, for the first time in history, the upper waters of the Danube with an oceangoing vessel; and that a trimaran. I would make an incontrovertible statement, to end all argument about where, and where not, a multihull may go, and what she may, or may not, do. I would set a challenge that will take the monohullers years to meet. All for fun, you understand. I'd never take a thing like that seriously, of course.

Yet another reason: you only have to look at your atlas to see how much of a cultural kaleidoscope a passage across northern, central and eastern Europe is. But besides the political maps, look at the weather maps, the rainfall, the population diagrams, religions and languages.

In the north we have the flat lowlands of Holland, the West German moors and heaths, populated by the businesslike, lively Dutch and the dour Germans; then the highlands of Bavaria, with their surprisingly lively leavening of Celts, the mountains of Austria, the old plucked heart of an ancient empire, left dangling. Next the gloomy dreariness of the Slovakian Danube, then the great Magyar plain of Hungary with its beautiful peoples, then the mountains and the primitiveness of inland Yugoslavia, so utterly different from its Adriatic coast, and then some of the most dramatic gorges on earth, and finally the long and beautiful, but potentially still deadly dangerous traipse through contrasting Rumania and Bulgaria, down to the shores of the Black Sea at Constanta. There can be no small-craft itinerary in the world which is so full of cultural and artistic riches from the recent past. There can be no river passage so quaint and yet so modern. Nowhere can the paths of Roman soldiers and Celtic tribesmen, Attila's horsemen and Turkish generals, crisscross in such profusion under the feet of contemporary communist frontier guards. Nowhere else on earth can things seem so hopeless and yet so full of promise. Nowhere else can the collapse of rotten empires past and present be so closely observed, as it can on this European leg.

Apart from all these reasons for heading across Europe, there was another. There are millions of amputees in the countries to be visited; some older ones, survivors from a terrible war, some younger, the victims of defective birth, or illness. To these, by my own endeavors, I aimed to bring hope by example. I did not want to say "Look what I can do!" It was much more to say "Look what *we* can do!"

I wear a United States ensign on *Outward Leg* because she is an American vessel and because her ownership is American. I am British, and I could probably, had I insisted, have changed her nationality.

It might have been wise to change her to British registry, because the British diplomatic service is much more helpful to stranded sailors than is the American. Considering the political climate in Europe, and especially in eastern Europe, it would seem the sensible thing to do. But curiosity overcame common sense, as it so often does when dreams have to be changed to reality, and I decided against it. In plain words I wondered how the arrival of an American vessel would be met, on the reaches of the rivers of central and eastern Europe.

This leads up to the political side of the dream. The Iron Curtain slashes Europe in half. On the western side (for it is our curtain, too) the Americans garrison the land, supported more and more by their European allies, but not overwillingly it seems. On the eastern side the Red Army and Air Force maintain a grip over their satellites. From the Austrian–Czech border down to the Black Sea the Danube flows through communist-controlled countries. But it is an international waterway, and vessels of any nation can navigate it. On a tit-for-tat basis (which seems to be the bottom line of international politics) the free navigation of the Danube *must* be allowed under the terms of the Danube Treaty of 10 February 1947, on penalty of offending nations having their own ships restricted in western waters.

The Rhine–Main–Donau Kanal is to be opened in 1992. The eastern bloc countries, and especially the Soviet Union, are more than anxious to obtain navigation rights on the Rhine for their fleet of cargo vessels. Therefore the West has a powerful lever for insisting on the rights of small craft to navigate freely on the Danube. This means that the gaping hole in the Iron Curtain, which exists now but is little used, can be kept open and crammed with vessels of all shapes and sizes heading mainly south, but in theory both ways. The more the better. Events in this story will indicate why.

Eastern Europe looks to Paris and London, not to Moscow. The Danube river is a great highway right through the Soviet European empire. To take an oceangoing sailing vessel along it is to drift with a dream of freedom and true values through the heart of darkness. One small western boat on the Danube is like a leaf floating down a conduit. But a ton of leaves can jam or even break that conduit. It can certainly change its course. The first leaf has made its bobbing progress and has reached the sea. That is important to me and perhaps to you. What is much more important is that it has been *seen* to pass by *thousands*. And where one leaf can go, there can go many.

This I knew in St. Katharine's Dock. I did not set off for the passage across Europe merely to have an interesting trip. I did not, certainly, go for ease or comfort. I did not go simply for curiosity or for want of something better to do.

I grabbed a dream, stowed it below, laced up my boot and *went*.

# 2

# *Some Boot, Some Lace*

When I say "I laced up my boot" only dyed-in-the-wool voyagers would know what I mean, so for the sake of those of you who haven't marlin spikes for fingers and hair of spun yarn, here's a short account of what it means.

I had a crew on board: Terry Johansen, twenty-eight, culled out of the streets of New York, and Martin Shaw, twenty-eight, picked up in the Azores. Terry had been a waiter and student of Russian history. He had, among other things, two assets; he was a good cook and he didn't suffer from seasickness. I thought his knowledge of Russian methods might come in useful on the lower Danube.

Martin Shaw was hitchhiking his way home to England by sea from being shipwrecked in the Indian Ocean. He was an engineer and had built his own boat. I could not think of anyone better to help get *Outward Leg* across the gap between the Rhine and the Danube. They both seemed to have the sort of stamina needed for such an effort; they both had plenty of energy. Whether they had the two other vital requisites of pioneers, patience and compassion, only time would tell.

We had fetched up at St. Katharine's Dock on 29 August 1984. Only ten months before, I had set out from San Diego, California, and since then I had covered fourteen thousand miles. Much of that had been directly against wind and weather in the southern Caribbean, so as to gain easting for the transatlantic passage. I had encountered ten full-fledged storms between San Diego and London, and the boat was superficially shook up. There was work to do·in London before we pressed on.

21

With all the heavy windward work, the forward edges of the two wing decks which were cosmetic curves of fiberglass, had caved in and shattered. The lockers in the wing decks had never been painted, due to leaving San Diego in a hurry and having had little opportunity to dry them on passage. The ship's sides were scratched in a few places. This was work for Martin, besides finishing the construction of the bunks in the crew's cabin forward. As I said at the beginning, if you wait until the boat's a hundred percent ready, you'll never get to sea; we had sailed almost a quarter of the way around the world before we finished the berths. It gave Martin some work to do in between well-earned visits to his family.

Terry painted the galley white. The previous coat of dark blue had been too gloomy. He also toured London like any other tourist.

The mainsail was handed and sent off to Ratsey and Lapthorne on the Isle of Wight for a complete resew with three lines of stitching. A very fine job they made of it too and, bless them, they didn't charge one penny for the job. That helped me more than they know.

In Colombia my rubber dinghy, of some shoddy American make, together with its outboard motor, three horsepower, had been stolen from the deck while the previous crew had slept only inches away from them. In London I had very little money and was working day and night to finish writing *Outward Leg* as well as several magazine articles. Unlike doctors and lawyers and truck drivers and garbage collectors, writers do not receive pay as they work. They are paid when the publishers see fit to cough up, and so there is never very much money in the kitty when it's needed, while there might be a sudden little windfall at other, unexpected times. Work done in September might, or might not, be paid for during the next six months, if it's accepted.

There's not, in this life, an angel on every corner, but somehow they seem to turn up at the bleakest moments. This time it was my good friend Clare Francis who filled the role. She turned up one rainy morning bright and early, as perky as ever. I am never at my best before noon, and especially when I'm in the middle of struggling with some awkward chapter about events such as hobnobbing with murderous pirates in Colombia that have nothing in common with the serene surroundings of St. Katharine's Dock.

Clare is a real ocean sailor. She didn't bother much with niceties like "How are you?" or "When do you leave?" as do most landsmen.

She came right out with the most important question a voyager limbering up for another voyage can ever hear. "H'lo Tristan; what do you need?"

"A dinghy and an outboard, Clare."

"Is that all?"

"And a kerosene stove; I'm going to have a hell of a job finding adapters for this American butane gas system we have, and we can expect to find kerosene oil anywhere . . ."

Clare threw her hair to one side, as is her habit. "Well, I'll see what I can do about the dinghy and the stove. On the outboard engine I can't promise anything. What about Avon? Have you tried them?"

Wearily I shook my head. "Clare, they're the only company based in Wales that makes anything of any international repute for ocean yachts, but all they can offer me is a small discount, and I've hardly two beans to rub together. The Welsh Tourist Board, however, has sent me a bloody great Red Dragon flag to wear down the Danube . . ."

"Oh," Clare grinned, "well, that'll be very useful, anyway. Get you out of trouble in no time!" She thought for a minute, then said, "Tell you what I'll do. I'll phone Dunlop's in Liverpool for the dinghy and Taylor's in Southampton. Let's see what they can do for you, eh?"

So it was that two days later a huge box arrived on the jetty. In it was a brand-new Dunlop dinghy twelve feet long. It was the first new dinghy I'd had in thirty-two years in small craft. Few can imagine what a godsend it turned out to be on the Rhine and Danube. The voyage, without it, would have been almost impossible. On the same day a brand-new kerosene stove with two burners and spares arrived from Southampton. I hardly spoke at all with the people who provided these things, but they must have known that inside me I was awash with gratitude. Then, no sooner had the dinghy been inflated than Peter Drew of the World Trade Centre arranged an outboard motor for me; a brand-new Suzuki eight horsepower. With that buttoned on its transom, *Middle Leg* (our chosen name for the dinghy, because it sits in the middle of the boat when we're under way) can make all of ten knots.

Besides the gathering of gear there was the press to deal with: *The Times, Observer, Standard, Yachting World, Yachting Monthly, Sea Trade, Portsmouth News*, and sundry interviewers, real and self-deluding. This is an important part of the activities on board *Outward Leg* because I need to reach as many handicapped people as possible, to let them know what I am doing, and why. It isn't a matter of self-glorification by any means. Fame doesn't feed anyone, and many journalists are a pain in the ass. They turn up at the most awkward times and the vast majority want only to hear of danger, disaster and death. Only the best ones see what is really happening. As for press photographers, I can think of some very remote islets where they should, many of them, be sent to photograph sooty terns, penguins or something. How they can drag a one-legged man around the deck and ask for the most ridiculous poses beats me. Some of them even asked me to remove my working leg and don my wooden one!

London was busy with tourists. No one had much time for a crazy crock heading for an impossible journey, but Clare Francis invited us to dinner, and toward the end of September we spent a lovely Sunday at her family home in the Buckinghamshire countryside. It was the first time in years that I had been out in the British countryside, and I devoured the sights of trees and flowers, tidy lawns and hedgerows.

Toward sailing day, 14 October, a windfall came our way. "Operation Raleigh" had its headquarters in St. Katharine's Dock. Its schooner was fitting out nearby for a world voyage. A steamship company, now defunct, had contributed to it a full set of world charts. Operation Raleigh had many, many charts that they would not need, for areas of the oceans where their expedition would not be heading. Could they be of any use to us?

Within minutes I was climbing the steps of Operation Raleigh's plotting room and within an hour or two two hundred charts—up to date, in the main, to 1980—were sitting in the after cabin of *Outward Leg*. They were a treasure of maritime information on the Mediterranean, Red Sea, Indian Ocean, Strait of Malacca, South China Sea and the coasts of Japan. The cost of a new chart is on average about £10.00. The cost of the same charts, second hand, around £5.00. Thus we had £1,000 worth of charts on board, and apart from the Black Sea and a few areas of the Far East we were set up for the rest of the whole world voyage back to San Diego. It all happened so fast that I had hardly time to thank Operation Raleigh. They relieved me of a continuing and enormous expense which I would have had to meet for the whole voyage at various times.

By the beginning of October, that is five weeks after we reached London, I had finished writing *Outward Leg* and had negotiated a contract for the writing of this book you are reading now. The advance wasn't in my hands yet, but it should be before long, or at least the first third of it. That would be enough to keep the three of us and *Outward Leg* going for a couple of months. I had also sold the British rights to three articles to *Yachting World* and an account of our journey to *Nautical Quarterly* in the United States. All told I had now about two thousand dollars in the kitty and another fifteen hundred due within a few weeks. It was time to get moving; October was upon us, and with the autumn rains the Rhine current would soon be in full spate. By the end of the year the freeze of winter would descend on the highlands of Bavaria, and then there'd be no getting over the German Gap before the spring. If we pushed on now, I reckoned, we might make the upper reaches of the Danube by New Year's, and be in the middle reaches, perhaps, by the time of the great February freeze-up. Then, in Hungary perhaps, we could hole up where the living, I knew, was cheap, and await the thaw, and then, in March, push onto the Black Sea.

On 14 October, exactly a year since *Outward Leg* had departed from San Diego, all was ready for this new departure. All that had to be done was await the high tide and the opening of the Dock gate, and say good-bye to friends. The first two events I anticipated with relish; the last with apprehension. The passing years do not ease the pain of parting.

That's what I mean by "I laced up my boot."

# 3

# *More Haste—Less Speed*

There was a small group of friends on the Dock as *Outward Leg* turned in St. Katharine's basin to head out into the river Thames. There was also a large crowd of idle onlookers, tourists mainly, together with another mob of odds and sods who had been held up by the raised drawbridge. I don't like being "seen off" in this way. It's too emotional for me, and when it comes to maneuvering a boat out of harbor no emotions should be involved; only cold, steady concentration and calculation; and especially when your boat is twenty-six feet wide and the lock looks twenty-seven feet wide or so.

Clare Francis had sensed this, I think. Indeed she probably knew very well that the last thing anyone wants when leaving harbor is repartee with onlookers. She had come down to the boat a day or two before our departure. Many of the foremost names in present-day British seafaring and outlandish exploration had expressed doubts about the success of my effort. Many of the editors with whom I had proposed accounts of it had turned me down flat when the prospects had been explained to them. Even the ones who did accept my proposals stipulated that when (not if) I turned back and headed down-Channel for Biscay and Gibraltar they must have accounts of the retreat. Only Clare seemed to believe that *Outward Leg* would get through. "If anyone can do it, Tristan," she had told me, "it's you." Wally Herbert never doubted it at all.

I replied, "I wish I had your confidence. I'm full of doubts, but anyway I'll give it a whirl." Secretly I calculated that we had a five percent chance of getting *Outward Leg* into the Black Sea in one piece. But then I thought to myself as I started the engine, "Five percent

27

of something is better than a hundred percent of nothing."

My crew were excited at starting the voyage, or perhaps they were ruminating on what I had told them as the lock gate slowly opened and the gray waters of the Thames came into view; a holy sight after five weeks of being locked up in a basin. There was a flock of crows circling over the Tower. "Lads," I said, "I've tried to think of everything, but you can bet your bottom dollar there's some unknown quantity—probably more than one—that we just can't take into consideration. I was never on a voyage yet that didn't have some worms in the woodwork, somewhere. Don't worry, though, the bad unknown will be balanced by the good, in the long run. It always is." Terry nodded his head, wisely. Martin looked at me as though I should be led away to a funny farm, and got on with tending the mooring lines.

As the lock bridge swung up, slowly, I shoved the engine gear into "slow ahead" so as to move the boat forward a touch into position for entering the lock. I was trying to ignore the shouts of well-wishers on the dock, but I shoved just a mite too hard. The boat moved forward too quickly, so that the starboard upper shroud caught on the corner of the rising bridge. It was a moment before the young lady raising the bridge heard, over the crowd clamor, our shouts, and for a full minute there was a tangle of wire straining not to snap as the bridge, inexorably it seemed, rose higher and higher. It was as if London was catching me by the coat sleeves and holding me back, telling me not to be a damned fool.

But things turned out well; the young bridgetender eventually realized what was happening and slightly lowered her charge, as my crew freed the shrouds from the bridge's clutch, and the rigging wires snapped back into position with a loud twang. I thanked my stars that *Outward Leg* has no mast spreaders. If she had, the starboard spreader would have fractured off the mast and we would have had to return into the basin to make repairs. That's one advantage of a wide trimaran; you can lead the upper rigging to the outside of the amas direct. Most builders of multihulls don't do that, although I can't figure out why not. I think it's a case of "Well, Dad had spreaders, so must I." As it is, *Outward Leg* is the only vessel of her size that I have seen without spreaders.

Soon we were free and out in the Thames. The first thing we had to do was refuel the engine diesel oil tanks. We had been directed to a fuel barge lying just downstream from St. Katharine's Dock entrance, so I headed there and we tied up alongside. It was about three-thirty P.M. The fuel-barge attendant, after about ten minutes of our shouting, eventually emerged from his cabin, freshly washed and carrying a small case. If ever there was a walking case of what foreigners call the "British disease," he was it. The first words he muttered as he shook his head at me were "I'm not serving you. We shut at three. I'm on my way 'ome."

Patiently I explained that we had not been able to leave St. Katharine's Dock until three-thirty because of the wait for high tide. "And we're bound for Holland, and I've only a gallon fuel left in the tank," I pleaded.

"Can't 'elp that, mate. There's a good show on the telly . . ."

Eventually, after we had promised to tip him well, the "attendant," grudging and surly the while, donned gloves and passed the hose to us, grumbling all the time about "bloody yachtsmen" as we quickly and humbly filled our tank. Terry, a native New Yorker, was all for grabbing the bloke and heaving him over the side of his barge when we had done, but I silently passed our TV fan our last remaining five-pound note and some coins as a tip. He stared at it contemptuously for a moment in his clean, open palm, then, without a word of thanks, pocketed it and turned away to clamber down into the bargetender and shove off home.

On the ebb tide, once clear of the *Welcome* fuel barge, as we named it, we motored down the Thames. There was little wind. Evening was hovering, and light rain drifting in from the east, a sniveling drizzle, cold and sticky, such as I had known so often in my youth, when I was the nipper in *Second Apprentice*, which regularly had plied these waters so long ago. But in those days the London Docks had been busy, crammed with shipping from all parts of the Empire, and sailing barges in flotillas working the tides. Now the Docks were a scene of empty desolation, destroyed by the trade unions. We drifted past miles and miles of still, silent wharves with rusting cranes and broken-windowed sheds.

By eight o'clock the night was down around us. By that time we were off Shellhaven, where the river widens into the Thames Estuary proper, and the channels between the mudbanks become intricate and the currents and tides puzzling. The whole Thames Estuary is well buoyed; perhaps too well; at night the number of winking buoys in their dozens makes navigation a continual confusion. The tide was now against us. The best thing to do was to find some berth and head into it for the night. This we did, at Hole Haven, which is exactly what its name says: a hole in the mud, on the flat, dreary, bleak, misty shore of Essex. It is hidden in a gap between monstrous oil refineries, with their eerie glows of fire from the tops of strange, delicate-looking chimneys that gleam silver under the flame, as if detached from the ground below them.

At two-thirty A.M., on a cold, rainy October night in the Thames Estuary there was no heroism, no intrepidity, no determination. Until the teakettle was boiling and six rashers of bacon were sizzling in the galley there was only a silent shuffle as oilies were donned, hatches opened, and the anchor line shortened up. There might have been a muffled curse from the foredeck as someone stubbed a toe, but there was no witty repartee. It was a dead, serious, necessary ritual, carried out with all the gravity of a funeral service. No words were used that did not need to be used, and those were mainly gruff monosyllables. From the cockpit, as the skipper peered through the flickering rain searching for a dim buoy flash out in the blackness beyond the eerie light-shadows, a moving wall of reflections from the gas flares, pretty nearly every second word was a curse. Then Tommy Lipton's tea, hot and steaming, worked its magic and we had before us a whole day, an ebb tide, and a fair westerly breeze for Holland. So we said farewell to Britain.

Soon we were out in the estuarial channels, and the ghostly glows on the shrouds and stays softened to silver, then blue, then black, and we were away, dodging the coastal shipping making for Greenwich Reach against the rising flow of the sea-bound tide. Up went the mainsail, as soon as we passed the North Tongue buoy, then the roller headsail on its pole, and off we bowled on a dead run and headed straight for the Lowlands, bounding along at a good seven knots.

That didn't last long. Breakfast time showed us wolfing soggy sandwiches in misty rain with the sails drooping like the old red flannel drawers that Maggie wore. The breeze had got tired and gone somewhere else to warm himself up. The air was cold and clammy, as only the North Sea air can be. It was as if the rain was reaching into our very bone marrows and the cold to the pits of our stomachs.

Midmorning showed a snot-nosed, driveling day which couldn't make up its mind whether to cry or die. It sat there on a fence, gray and cold, not knowing which way to fall, all the while taunting us with pale silver sunbeams peeping through the dark puce clouds all around our horizon. It was a day for sea burials. All it needed was a few wreaths floating around on the gray slop.

*Outward Leg*, her Yanmar engine purring below, slid from one arguing chop-swell to the next, demanding her passage between the dozens of big cargo ships moving by in intent procession along the busiest sea road in the world. About midday a fogbank, as white and diaphanous as a lace curtain, threatened to form up on the northern horizon. But this day was one born of irresolution and soon the fog gave up and disappeared, so as not to hide the misery of the whole scene from us.

On a day like this there are only three things you can do: keep on trucking with the engine, whistle for a wind, or tempt the gods. As I detest motoring at sea, and as I lost my whistle when my jaw broke in an aircraft crash some years ago, I decided to do the latter. "Lads," said I, "it looks like we're going to have to motor all the bloody way to Rumania! We have to lower the mast in Amsterdam because of the bridges on the canal system in Holland . . ."

No sooner had I made this observation, in a resigned tone, than this sniveling, whingeing, dripping, drizzling autumn orphan of a day fell off its stool with a bang and whoosh! the wind swooped down on us with a sturdy promise, again from the west. Up went the mainsail, out came the headsail, off went the engine, and we were away, goose-winging at six or seven knots, soon increasing until we were flying like shit off a shovel, straight for the Noord Hinder lightship. I wanted to sight the lightship before darkness fell, so that I could work up our exact position in the seven-dimensional moving southern North Sea, in among the myriad shoals off the Dutch coast.

We have a sat-nav (Satelitte Navigation Unit), but I never trust anything man-made at sea; not even Dutch lightships' lights. I suppose it must come from years of knocking about off the beaten tracks of the sea world. A few voyages off Third-World shores would convince anyone of what I've always said: "There's four kinds of voyagers in small craft—Novices, Retired, Dead and Pessimists."

This time my pessimism was ill-founded; the Noord Hinder lightship was on station and its light, as we soon observed when night descended like a horse blanket, was working. It takes some effort to accept the dependability of the navigational aids of the coasts of advanced countries. It's all so incredible to anyone who has ever voyaged in the back of beyond.

The sat-nav is another matter. I know that it has enabled a lot of people, who otherwise could not have navigated their way across the English Channel, to make some longish sea and even ocean voyages. But I also know that it has piled an increasing number of yachts on reefs in recent years. I look upon mine as a nice, silent, helpful crewman, who unfortunately has been adjudged by the headshrinkers as a potential schizophrenic psychopath, who could, in a moment of aberration, stab his skipper and crewmates in the back. I talk to it, I humor it, I encourage it, I like it, but I *never* trust it. Anyone who does, and who does not back up his dependence on a sat-nav with celestial knowledge and equipment is a fool and, unless he's lucky, will one day be a dead fool or, at the least, a boatless fool.

That night, coasting in the Lowland Sea, our sat-nav behaved perfectly and put us off the Ijmuiden lighthouse at dawn. It was three hundred yards or so in error, by my dead reckoning and observations by bearings, but I allowed that that wasn't bad for a crewman who doesn't grumble, nor eat or drink anything but a bit of electric juice through the day and night. Either the sat-nav was in error, or the chart is wrong. But the most important thing was for the boat to be in the right place according to the chart; not according to the whims of man-made bits and pieces. We headed in for the Ijmuiden seawall and the great locks of the Noordzee Canal. As *Outward Leg* approached, still under sail but with her Yanmar ticking over (just in case), the gates loomed big enough, but innocent somehow. These gates gave no visible sign that they were for us, the entrance to a wonderful waterway system which laces Europe from the Baltic and Berlin, from Poland even to the Mediterranean, to the English Channel, to Switzerland; and perhaps even, dared we hope? to the Black Sea and Aegean and beyond.

As we approached, a voice called out over the loudspeaker on the control tower by the seawall, in good English of course, for these were Dutchmen, "Good morning, America, how are you?"

"Good morning" replied Martin, on the foredeck, while he and

Terry, after a quick glance and grin at each other, took up the words of the song:

> *Good morning, America, how are you?*
> *Don't you know that I'm your native son?*
> *I'm a train they call the City of New Orleans;*
> *I'll be gone five hundred miles 'fore the day is done!*

*Outward Leg* had arrived at the continent of Europe. All we had to do now was conquer it.

We entered the Noordzee lock at seven-thirty A.M., had breakfast inside the lock, and by ten-thirty A.M., after a swift passage along the Noordzee Canal, we had entered the twenty-eight-feet-wide, twelve-feet-deep, passage into Sixhaven, the Amsterdam Municipal Yacht Haven. By twelve o'clock we had emerged again, out into the river Y. The Y might not be the shortest river in the world, but it does have the shortest name.

Berthing, for a handicapped person as I am, unable to clamber easily or walk far without pain, is a complex matter. I have to look for a berth as near to transport or shops or harbor offices as I can get. Otherwise all the chores ashore are thrust upon the crew, which is unfair to them. Sixhaven is on the far side of the river Y from the city of Amsterdam. If we stayed there we would have to take a ferry to reach anywhere in the city. The ferry jetty is a few hundred, for me painful, yards from the yacht marina. After some inquiries from the Dutch Customs who board yachts in Sixhaven, I found that there was a public small-craft dock on the Amsterdam side, near to the railway station, on the river Y side itself. This dock is known by the original name of *Jachthaven*. With an eight-foot depth alongside, we could move over there. The only problem was that, being public and near the Central Station, it was liable to attention from drunks, druggies, thieves, and other flotsam and jetsam who hang around the Central Station area.

I telephoned my good friends at the Amsterdam Maritime Museum, and they advised me that the best and safest berth in the city was in the Oosterdock, very close to the museum. I would have to wait for the city rail and road bridges to open at around two A.M. (which they do every night), then enter the big basin, which was a minimum depth of twelve feet. The entrance to the basins, under the railway bridge, is about thirty feet wide.

At two A.M., for sailors are not minions of the daylight, we slowly chugged in through the Oosterdock entrance. Light rain made the decks slippy. After my crew had tied up I clambered down to go below, slipped and fell six feet straight down the after companionway. My false leg hit the deck with a thump that knocked me senseless with pain, and I collapsed.

Next morning found me still in intense pain and hardly able to move. I thought I had merely broken a rib. I decided to await events for the next two days. I needed all my time and resources to beat the Rhine and the German Gap before winter set in. There was nothing to waste on unnecessary medical treatment. "The way to treat a broken rib is to strap it up with a bandage and wait for it to heal," I gasped. I was wrong.

On the third day of bitter pain Terry sent for an ambulance. Hardly able to stand or breathe I was carried to the Onze Lieve Vrouwen Gasthuis (Our Blessed Lady Hospice). After a wait in pain a doctor told me that the X rays showed I had three broken ribs and my right lung had collapsed entirely. Try walking with a missing left leg, three busted ribs and collapsed right lung.

"But I've got to get up the Rhine, Doctor," I gasped.

"But you've got to go to bed, Captain," she replied, and that was that.

"And November is approaching, and the Rhine is rising," I groaned to myself as someone stuck a tube into my right chest. I felt it burrow into my lung cavity, just as I should have been burrowing up the Rhine, into the heart of Europe. Then, as pain shot through me yet again, I lost consciousness and everything was all right.

# 4

# *The Pause That Refreshed*

For the next two or three days I went through the hoop. The weekend staff had connected me to a lung pump that was defunct. At first they didn't realize this and thought it was the lung-suction tube that was wrongly inserted. This was extracted again, then reinserted, twice. Each time it was like the start of a disemboweling session, I imagine, only from the soft spot just below the collarbone. By the time I'd been skewered three times I was wondering if the gods of the sea were trying to tell me something about this voyage. So far, ever since getting hung up on St. Katharine's Dock bridge, it had been one bad omen after the other. Then I realized that they were probably only playing with me, delaying me until the Rhine flooded, to test my will, and in between bouts of severe pain, swallowing tablets, being injected and willing myself well again, I started to organize things according to the new situation. Language was no problem; almost everyone in Holland speaks at least some English.

Terry was to keep the boat shipshape, bring me newspapers and help Martin, who was to insulate the deckheads in the cabins, fore and aft, against the coming cold. This Martin did very well, with one-inch-thick fiberglass held in place with ceiling board. That's not a small job. In my hospital bed I comforted myself that it would be better done with me ashore and the boat not moving.

Onze Lieve Vrouwen Gasthuis treated me very well. It was a thousand times more sedate a place than St. Vincent's Hospital, New York, and several interesting old men were brought in, but they died soon after they caught my interest. When I realized that this was a croaking-shop I asked for the bill. That was about ten days after I had entered the place. I was still in pain, often, but I thought I could manage, as long as I could get back on board *Outward Leg*. The bill came to £1,620.00 (almost $2000.00). No sooner had the hospice bursar told me the charge than I was out of bed and crawling about, discharging myself.

World Trade Centre, London, lent me the hospital charge for a month. By that time I would have the advance due on this book, from England and America. But the hospital payment would take a mighty big bite out of it. However, one of the rules of pioneering is not to look too far ahead for your welfare, but to reach for immediate objectives. The most important priority for me was to chunder off up the Rhine before the river was in raging flood from the expected November rains, and before the Alps and Jura Mountains froze, when the river would be too low for safe navigation with our four-and-a-half-foot craft. As I hobbled out of the hospice, with my lung hurting in the cold air, and actually feeling the halves of my loose ribs scraping one against the other, in pouring rain, and with 440 miles of river to plug against, things looked gloomy. If I had been well, I would have coughed, blown my nose and taken the short-term view of things. But I could neither cough nor blow my nose; it was far too painful. The only thing remaining was to take the short-term view.

By the time I reached the boat it was obvious that I would have to delay sailing by a few days, to recover a little more and let my ribs heal better. Besides, I'd promised *Nautical Quarterly* some pictures of *Outward Leg* cruising inside the city of Amsterdam. There was another reason to linger a short while, too. The Central Station Square was where my leg had given way in the first place, two and a half years before. I'd made a vow that one day I'd stick an oceangoing sailing boat only yards from the place. We had sailed almost within sight of it when we entered the Oosterdock, but that wasn't good enough. Nothing is good enough when you are challenging and conquering yourself. I determined to make for the Central Station wharf as soon as the mast was down and we could navigate under the canal bridges.

We had to wait a couple of days to get alongside the Nieuwe Vaart crane dock to lower the mast, I recruited Terry to help me explore the canals in the Dunlop dinghy, and take photographs. From where we were moored in the Oosterdock, we could drive the dinghy right into, through and out of the heart of the city of Amsterdam. It was as convenient as having a car, and far more pleasant, because there

was very little traffic on the narrow city canals. We had to take care
where we left the dinghy while we shopped or rambled ashore, and
especially when I went alone. On one leg with three broken ribs it
would not be easy to catch a dinghy thief.

The charge for lowering the mast at Nieuwe Vaart boatyard was
twenty-five guilders. This seemed a mite expensive to me at the
time, but on hindsight it was cheap, and the staff did an excellent
job. Soon *Outward Leg* was looking almost naked, with her mast and
spars laid along the wing deck. Apart from one of the crew letting a
turnbuckle slip over the side, we lost nothing.

The satisfaction I felt when the boat at last touched alongside the
long, low, passenger boat pontoon beside the Stationsplein wharf was
almost enough to make me fit and well again. We were a mere ten
yards from the spot where I had fallen between the streetcar lines in
February 1982. The lads must have thought I'd gone off my rocker
when I hauled myself up to the cockpit side deck and waved my stick
at the esplanade wall and the streetcar stop beyond. "How's that,
you bastard?" I cried.

I've always liked Amsterdam, ever since I went there soon after
the city was liberated at the end of World War Two. Like any really
great metropolis it lets you get on doing your thing and interferes
hardly at all. We were never once challenged at any place we chose
to moor the boat, never told "You can't stay there." There were no
jetty-defenders. God bless Holland.

But in the center of Amsterdam in *Outward Leg* we were always
warned to watch the boat and our gear. It seems that some of the
Third World's return for western beneficence is channeled through
the city, and so there are many drug addicts, who are inclined to steal
to support their habit. I suppose I must be one of the last of the
Victorians, and while we may have hidden a few things under the
carpet we always called a spade a spade. I saw quite a few wily-
looking gentlemen pass by eyeing the boat and us. They were obviously not Hollanders, they sure as hell weren't tourists or students,
and it was almost certain they'd never lifted a finger to any kind of
work in their whole lives.

On 5 November we set off for the Amstel river. "Fireworks Day,"
as I observed to Martin. I wondered if this was another omen, but if
it was, it turned out to be a damp squib. It rained and rained and
rained. Under the bridges of the Amstel river, which leads to the

Neder Rijn, we had exactly one inch clearance in height, and about five feet in width, while the depths were just under five feet.

I had been concerned about setting out too early while I was yet in pain, for this was quite severe at times if I made any effort to reach or bend. I determined not to be any more of a burden to my crew than could be helped. I would steer the boat, stick on the helm, so that they, who were both agile and fit, could be free to hop around when that was needed. This I did all the way to Nürnberg. I doubt if I was relieved at the wheel for more than ten minutes during the whole way. This isn't a case of "hogging the wheel." We were not out for a joyride. River navigation with heavy traffic, swift currents and doubtful depths is a risky business. Even if he leaves the wheel, a good skipper, unless he has a good pilot on board, must stand by to give directions when they are needed by the helmsman. It is unfair to expect crewmen, relatively inexperienced at river work, to have the responsibility of dealing with these risks. The skipper should steer, I believe, so that if disaster occurs under way he has only himself to blame. As for autopilots, the best thing to do with them on any river is wrap them up carefully, well greased, and stow them below in a nice, safe place and forget them until you are back at sea. If steering the boat means long hours in rain and cold, so be it.

Generally speaking, people with ocean-sailing experience or with only coastal-cruising background don't make good riverhands. At least not at first. Rivers and canals are one emergency after another, and there is not much letup while the boat is under way. Vigilance must be kept at all times. Most seafarers are not accustomed to that, not to navigation in confined waters, with heavy traffic. The best hands for rivers and canals would be people who are fast, but inexperienced, or with previous river-canal trips under their belts. The novices can be taught to handle locks and moorings in short order. They take the risks and hustle and bustle for granted if they haven't known how relaxed things can be at sea. Sea sailors can become discontented and even critical and grumpy in rivers and canals unless they are kept busy, and they should try to do as much maintenance work as is practicable while they are under way, in between tending lines. If they don't gravitate toward such activity the skipper should lead them to it. Or push them.

The first day's run, because it started late in the day, took *Outward Leg* to Noordensluis which, as the name tells us, is the north end of a lock off the Amsterdam-Rhine Canal. The river dikes are about ten feet high, monotonously tidy, and hide the houses, farms and villages on the lower, land side. Apart from the ducks there's not much to look at except for the water, the sky and huge barges at every turn, making ten to twelve knots and slowing for no one.

By the tenth day we were back on the Neder Rijn river and pushing away for the real Rhine itself, although in Holland it is called the Waal. Once we hit the Rhine (that Americanism expressed very well what occurs) we were shoved downstream, with half speed on the Yanmar at fifteen knots, so that the river current must have been running at about eleven knots midstream.

Nijmegen town is refreshingly different from the rest of Holland. After miles and miles of flat countryside behind high dikes it is a pleasure to sight the high ground on which the town sits. That is, it's a pleasure until the hill has to be tackled on one leg and with three busted ribs. There are two havens in Nijmegen, off the river Waal. The downstream one, Waalhaven, is a big, very safe basin, with deep water, but it is used heavily by river barges loading all kinds of dusty and dirty cargoes, like cement, oil and coal. Also, it is on the far side of the railway tracks from the town center, and a good ten minutes' walk, even for able-bodied people. For me, in my state, it might just as well have been on the far side of the moon.

The small-craft port at Nijmegen is close by the Vluchthaven, where passenger craft, in season, land their charges. There were no passenger craft around in November, of course, nor would there be all the way up the Rhine, but I observed that their landing pontoons were still there. This cheered me up immensely. It meant that we would have possibilities of mooring up to them farther upstream.

Nijmegen small-craft port has about six feet of water in its middle, shelving to two feet and less near the shore and the river wall. I used a Mediterranean-style mooring, with the anchor over the bow and the stern poked in toward the shore. That was the first time we had used the anchor to hold us since Hole Haven, almost a month before. The next time would be far more outlandish, as we shall see.

Getting ashore in Nijmegen was a pain in the ass. The shore is littered with old iron junk and broken-down jetties. I was forced to clamber into the dinghy, scramble over a barge being used as a greenhouse for growing plants, scrabble over a locked gate and then navigate a six-inch plank, very wobbly, onto a muddy shore. With my disability

I felt a bit like Blondin tightrope-walking over Niagara. Somehow I made it, and Terry and I took off to explore the town.

Soon after I had negotiated the obstacle course to get ashore in Nijmegen the gods relented, or perhaps submitted to my determined obstinacy; the rain stopped at last, and the sun shone. It was a pale, northern winter sun, anemic and wan, but to me, as we reached the cobblestoned hill that leads to the main square, it felt like a full tropical blast in Tahiti. I was winning. I hesitated, glanced back at the Rhine waters far below, and muttered to myself, "I'll getcha, you Teutonic sonovabitch!"

On the way back to the boat I bought some thick socks which were to be a godsend to me. Later on as the winter clamped down I discovered a curious thing. When the weather is freezing, not only does my real foot get cold, but also my false one. So I have to wear *two* socks. It's a good job I bought three pairs in Nijmegen and not just three socks, as I had asked for, and as the stout lady in charge had refused to sell. She had more sense than I thought.

The thirteenth of November fell on a Monday, and not on a Friday. I thought that was a good enough omen to take off from Nijmegen and start to tackle the Rhine. There are 238 miles from Nijmegen to the confluence with the river Main. The crew slipped the lines and weighed the anchor. It was seven o'clock in the morning, with the promise of a fine, dry day ahead. *Outward Leg* moved out of the haven and into the swift-running current of the river. There was no going back now. She was bound for the heart of Europe and we'd get her to it even if we had to drag her there. She knew that, and bent to with a will, to fight the Rhine, to beat it before the whole land, and the waters of the land, iced over. I tightened the bandage strapped over my ribs, gritted my teeth and tried not to breathe too hard.

In the immortal words of Sherlock Holmes, and not to press a point too far: the game was afoot! There were eighteen hundred miles to go to the Black Sea. "Easy," I commented to the crew. "Christ, I could do it on one leg!"

# 5

# *Deutschland über Alles*

With the clear plastic screens bought in Rheden, Martin made wind-shields for the dodger. These proved a blessing; the wind was cold and the rain persistent for much of the haul to Frankfurt. The original windshields of canvas and clear plastic, fitted to the dodger top in San Diego for sea use, were useless for work on rivers. There were too many blind spots caused by the canvas structure, and any blind spot, with about ten ships passing in as many minutes, is a hazard. With the large, clear screens in place I was comparatively shielded from both wind and rain. They weren't perfect; there were gaps between them and there was no windshield wiper, but they were a thousand percent better than nothing.

The heater in my cabin gave nothing but trouble from the time it was first lit in Amsterdam. For one thing the air capacity in the pressure tank was too little, so that the burner extinguished itself at awkward times during the night, and for another thing it leaked. If it didn't leak at one place it leaked at another. It was made for California, and behaved exactly as a heater made for that sunny state would be expected to. It was beautifully made, but of copper and stainless steel, two metals with an expansion compatibility about as genial as that between me and the Moonies. It either had to leak or explode.

The extra air pressure tank for the heater was installed on the after engine room bulkhead, and a pipe to the heater tank was led through the bulkhead to the heater pressure tank. As I write, the pipe and the extra tank are still there but the heater has gone, consigned to the oblivion of a watery Danubian grave, which it fully deserved.

41

For two months we struggled, Martin and I, with that heater. Finally, as we shall see, it almost killed me. It slowly and steadily blackened everything in the after cabin, including, most likely, my aching lungs.

In the forward cabin the lads were lucky; they had a small, old-fashioned but efficient kerosene stove and the new super stove arranged for us by Clare.

On departing from Nijmegen we found out several things about the river Rhine. First, there are rarely, day or night, fewer than twenty big river ships in sight, astern and ahead. Second, the river is well buoyed and lit. Third, if *Outward Leg*, with a low twenty-two-horsepower engine, followed the Rule of the Road and passed ships coming downstream on their starboard sides, she made very slow headway indeed, and was in danger of being swept downstream in some places by the stiff current.

The only way to make decent speed over the ground was to stick as close to the shore as we dared, always bearing in mind the groins that protrude from the banks, often underwater, for much of the way.

These groins, or river-retaining walls, are on average about 350 feet apart and are there to direct the current away from the banks and so save land erosion. Between them the current was less, so the trick was to navigate around the ends of the groins and then steam up to the next one in a lesser current. It was a matter of dodging in and out all the long, weary day. There was bound to be a collision with a low groin sooner or later and we hit one sometimes ten or a dozen times a day. Where the current ran strong there wasn't much damage as the vessel was making slow speed over the ground, but sometimes eddies whirled round inside the groin bays, and then the boat hit at quite a speed. With our four-and-a-half-foot draft we managed to pass over most of the groin ends, but we ruined the cooltube structures, projecting sideways from the keel. These were not important for the crossing of Europe, and they were but superficial additions, so I accepted their destruction for the sake of making enough speed to reach Nürnberg before the freeze.

In most of the Rhine we found fairly low water, caused by the comparatively dry European summer that year. The average depth was about fourteen feet. Certainly big ocean yachts drawing nine feet could navigate the Rhine at low water, but they would have to keep to the middle of the stream, well away from the groins. Most big river barges draw nine feet.

The Rhine is probably the busiest river waterway in the world. We sighted many Dutch, German, Swiss, French and Belgian ships, with a few East German, Norwegian and Danish ensigns among them. On one occasion we saw even a Luxembourg flag. Later we sighted a Swedish river-sea coaster, with her masts down and her bridge lowered.

Many of the river ships carried a motorcar on deck. This was because all the cargo-carrying deals were fixed in certain ports; Amsterdam and Hamburg were the main ones. The owner-skippers, as soon as they off-loaded one cargo, hared off by roads to the shipping bourse to get another cargo arranged. Most of the river ships on the Rhine are owned by their skippers, usually on a mortgage, and they spend their lives either motoring up and down rivers, day and night, in all weathers, all visibilities, or rushing to the bourse for their next job. Anyone who thinks European barge skippers have a romantic life just doesn't know the facts. They are engaged in one of the most frantic rat races imaginable. Usually there is just the skipper and his wife, and they take turns steering the big wheel day and night. Sometimes, if they can afford it, there is also a deckhand, but the working money margins are so narrow that few can afford the extra help. In between steering the boat and helping moor up, the wives do the cooking and shopping. They very rarely moor up anywhere other than at a dreary commercial port among other barges and dredgers, and often they are at coal or cement wharves. It seemed to me that the only saving grace about the way of life of a family on a Rhine river ship was the countryside scenery between the big industrial centers, but on the lower Rhine there isn't even much of that. To the bargees, it might be a bit better than a dreary existence in some industrial suburb, but to me it seemed as far removed from real freedom as the life of a railroad or truck driver: all go, go, and never being able to stop when they feel like it. It is true that we in *Outward Leg* were more or less in the same situation, but that was because we had purposely put ourselves into it, and could get out whenever we might feel like doing so. Besides, for us there was no terminus, no railhead. We aimed to keep right on trucking, past all barriers, and there was no bourse, we knew very well, to fix our deals; not on this earth, at any rate. For our bourse we wouldn't need a car, but a pair of wings between our shoulderblades.

Heading upstream we plugged away from dawn to dusk. Navigation at night on the Rhine would have been possible, but very risky in the rain and fog, with big ships speeding downstream all the time at anything up to sixteen knots. In any case, by the time I had done twelve or fourteen hours on the wheel, most of the time in pain with my ribs, lung and leg, I'd had enough. At sea, with plenty of leeway we could have hove to; on a river it is best to tie up to some berth.

So it went on, for nine days, from Nijmegen to Frankfurt, where, hopefully, there would be mail to collect. Even inside Europe, *Outward Leg* was still a little world of her own, self-contained, with all the land moving slowly past her as she plugged away, and out of touch completely with everything ashore except what we could see. Heading upstream there simply was no time to stop and explore; it was push on, push on, as long as there was a glimmer of daylight in the sky, to beat the current, so as to make as much distance as possible before rains swelled the river and made its obduracy stronger. On the Rhine it didn't take long to realize that we were fighting against every drop of water running down from the Northern Alps, the Schwabischer Jura Mountains, the Fränkischer Jura, the Bohemian Range and the Erzgebirge, besides the water that fell onto the great north European plain. For a geography lesson there's nothing like staring over the side at a mighty river's rush and then finding out where it all comes from.

Our first day's push up the Rhine (its name changes from Waal at the Dutch-German frontier) led us first to Emmerich, where the German frontier post is, on the left bank. The day turned out, for a change, to be fine and sunny. I was continually reminded of the voyages I had made as deckboy in *Second Apprentice* up this stretch of the Rhine in 1938 and early 1939. She had been a big, bluff-bowed, boomy ketch and we had had no engine, yet our skipper, Tansy Lee, had sailed her against this same current, along with dozens of other sailing craft, also engineless. Certainly, sailing gear then was not as good as it is now, yet they had made it under sail, slow but sure. I couldn't imagine many modern-day sailors making it. The only conclusion I could come to about this was that it's not the gear so much as the men. I reckoned that if our mast was up, with the wind at fifteen knots blowing downstream, *Outward Leg* would be hard pushed to make a knot and a half over the ground against the current, which was running at around two and a half knots to three. Yet Tansy had pushed up, I remembered clearly, all his three hundred tons in a hundred-foot-long hull, at an average one knot. That was until we reached Homburg; then a small steam tug had taken over until we finally fetched Remagen, where we were bound.

At Emmerich the customs post is on a barge marked *Zoll*. It is backed by tidy lawns and manicured trees winding up over a hill which hides everything else. The customs entry of *Outward Leg* into Germany was a mere formality. The crew hiked up to the office with the ship's papers and passports, paid the pittance for a six months' entry permit, and were back on the boat within an hour or so. Soon after noon we were slipped and under way again. We plugged at the Rhine all day in monotonous surroundings, until about six o'clock, when the light began to fade. The town of Wesel was in sight on the left bank, when a German River Police (*Flusspolizei*) launch came tearing up at high speed.

"Right lads, clear the deck, man the bloody torpedoes!" I was not yet reconciled with Germany. But the policemen, three of them, were too young for my resentment, very well outfitted, and friendly. They insisted on escorting *Outward Leg* into the basin of the canal, where we moored up alongside a barge, after first making sure she wasn't going to depart during the night.

In *Outward Leg* we depend on the Yanmar for lighting and power as well as propulsion; there is no auxiliary generator, so if Yannie were to conk out we would be light- and power-less. This is not so much a case of not wanting an auxiliary generator. It's because in a trimaran every ounce of weight must be regulated carefully so as not to impede her sailing ability. Besides, I couldn't afford one.

Next morning, as on all the mornings following, we were up at first light. Most times it was either drizzling or foggy. Sometimes the fog was so thick that we were delayed from sailing for an hour or so, but on those occasions it usually cleared away enough by the time the sun was fifteen degrees in altitude to allow me to see a hundred yards or so. Then it was time to start up Yannie and cast off, having first donned winterjackets and gloves to protect ourselves from the freezing fog, a daily reminder of the reason for our haste.

All day now we ran the engine at full speed, 3,200 revolutions to the minute. This, in calm water with no current, on a windless day, would have given *Outward Leg* a speed over the ground of seven knots. As it was, in the Rhine the speed over the ground varied between four knots and one third of a knot. By simple calculation this means

that the current in the Rhine varies between three knots and six and
a half between Nijmegen and Mainz, but more on the Lorelei stretch.

The next port of call was to be Düsseldorf, forty miles upstream
from Wesel. Here we chugged on all day through an industrial waste-
land, dirty, smoky and ugly, like a scene from the ninth circle of
Dante's *Inferno*. It was obviously the result of Mammon gone mad.
I tried to keep my thoughts away from the horror of what had happened in Europe when all this stark power had fallen into the hands
of madmen, and observed that, after all, the wild ducks somehow
still made their home here. Not many of them, but enough to reinforce
a growing belief that life is indomitable.

On this run the dinghy, *Middle Leg*, came into its own. We launched
it, still under way at five knots through the water, in the narrow river
channel off Homburg. Martin clambered into the dinghy, started the
outboard, and took off to shop, while Terry and I continued plugging
away against the mighty current. An hour later, when *Outward Leg*
was four miles farther away from Homburg, *Middle Leg* came scooting
back with our food for the next two days. Then the crew hauled it
on board again. Our wide wing decks allowed this, of course. I would
not leave the dinghy trailing, because of the drag astern. I wouldn't
give the bloody Rhine one ounce, one foot-pound, of encouragement
to hold us back. These dinghy launches on the run became an almost
daily feature of the river voyage, and saved much time when we were
heading upstream or later, when we were in some stretch of the river
remote from any civilization. It was a blessing and a godsend and I
silently thanked Dunlop over and over again for their generosity, and
Clare Francis for bringing it about.

For the purposes of launches on the run on the Rhine–Danube
route, the minimum size of dinghy needed is eight feet, and the
smallest outboard engine six horsepower. Anything less than that will
not deal with the currents in many stretches. Oars for the dinghy are
a must, because otherwise there is a risk of it being swept downstream
for many miles if the engine fails, especially on the Lorelei or Danube.
For winter passages inflatable dinghies are mandatory, for reasons we
shall see later.

The current through Homburg (from where I presume the hats
come) was very strong. On the Rhine, as on most rivers, it is strongest
where the riverbed narrows. At Homburg the river is no more than a
hundred yards wide at a well-educated guess, and very deep as rivers

go—seventy feet. The town seems to be surprisingly quiet after the roar and bustle of the riverside lower down. It all looks very Victorian, like a scene out of *Hard Times* by Dickens, and I fully expected to see small chimney sweeps lurching along the piers, but they were deserted.

That night at seven o'clock we tied up in Düsseldorf, at the most godawful place I have seen for a marina. It is tucked away in the corner of a big industrial cargo basin, right below the huge chimneys of the city power-generating plant. The noise from the machinery is deafening. "Jesus Christ," I shouted to Terry when we had tied up to a pontoon (fresh water and electricity available). "No wonder Rhinelanders have loud voices!"

False dawn in the morning showed a scene from some lunatic's idea of a weekend retreat. There was the marina, dwarfed by the power plant, and on the concrete headland of the port a full-blown yacht club, with all its burgees drooping in the drizzle and smoke. It had a senior members' veranda, which looked out over a vista of railroad sidings and a great dump of compressed scrapped automobiles, and beyond, the Rhine, with a dozen barges rushing past in as many minutes. I stared amazed at the whole forlorn scene for a minute or two. Then I couldn't help but admire the spirit of a people who could pursue a hobby like yachting in such miserable surroundings. It just goes to show, We Are Everywhere.

That day was overcast and cold. It looked more fit for an undertaker's picnic than a jaunt up a river. More industrial slums and yet more lined the river all the way to Cologne, where we sighted the spires of the cathedral just before dusk, and tied up in the tight small-craft basin hard by the city center. The place was packed with wintering yachts, sail and power, and there was a fuel dock with a water tap and hose.

We pushed on upstream next day, on a cold, bright morning, away from the spires and chimneys of Cologne, against an ever-strengthening current. In places now, where the river was narrow, it was five knots against us. On and on, hour after hour, dodging the fast shipping, weaving in and out of groin bays, to Remagen, twenty-seven miles above Cologne. It took *Outward Leg* thirteen hours to cover this distance, an average speed of just over two knots, with the Yanmar flat out. Twice we hit hidden groins on this run. The last time was so hard that I was thrown forward over the wheel, bruising yet again my still-not-healed ribs. Martin shouted something as we recovered from the shock, and pointed astern. There I caught a glimpse of white and yellow particles floating away astern. That's the cooltubes buggered! Nothing could be done about it. If we moved farther out from the shore we would be in stronger currents and would lose all forward way. The cooltubes, unnecessary for rivers, would have to be sacrificed to the gods of the river. My own votive offering.

In the morning, by the dawn's early light we sighted the United States flag drooping over the broken bridge upstream from Remagen. This was where the American troops had flung themselves over the Rhine in 1945. We would not, as it happened, see another American flag from on board, apart from *Outward Leg*'s own ensign, until the Aegean Sea, nine months later.

# 6

# *The Lilt of the Lorelei*

From Bonn, halfway upstream between Cologne and Remagen, the scenery along the banks of the river Rhine is much more pleasant than farther north. Victorian and Edwardian houses and hotels line the banks at Bonn, affording visions of placid, relaxed summer holidays long ago. There are even rowing-clubhouses on the water's edge, with low pontoons fronting them. Probably, in the season, we could have tied up to one of these, but it would have been risky, as the river traffic is heavy and sets up an almost Mediterranean-like quarrel of a sea all the time, day and night, winter and summer. The hilly east bank is mostly backed by vineyards.

Remagen brought to me memories of myself at fourteen being towed in *Second Apprentice* up the little river Ahr by barge horses to the mineral-water factory a few miles from the Rhine. It was forty years later, in the New York Public Library of all places, that I discovered that the factory had been the personal property of Sturmbannführer Heinrich Himmler. He had been onto a good thing, it seems; the SS recruits were allowed to drink only mineral water.

Koblenz was our next stop. From the river it is an attractive old town fronted by ancient fortifications. Here we headed into the debouchment of the river Mosel, which ascends from Koblenz all the way to Metz and Nancy in France. It is canalized, and narrower craft than *Outward Leg* can pass from here to Paris, the English Channel and the Mediterranean by way of the Seine and the Rhône. The Koblenz end of the river Mosel is shallow, with mudbanks cluttering the fairway, but we managed to reach as far as the first road bridge. Wearily we tied up against a high wall at the bottom of a steep ladder

49

in seven feet of water. We were told here that we were close to shops and post office; the town center was a mere block and a half away. In fine weather then it would have been an ideal place to linger; we were overlooked by fine, high, medieval-looking houses and surrounded by a cleaner river and green parkland. At Koblenz the people seemed a lot friendlier than farther downstream. From the Dutch border all the way upstream they had appeared to be dour and gloomy, miserable bastards. It was a great relief to me to reach the Middle Rhine, simply because of this. For the same reason, apart from being bone weary and in continual pain from my recent injuries, I didn't go ashore at all in Germany until we arrived here. There is simply no point in going ashore where people are unfriendly, offhand and bloody glum.

A few miles above Koblenz, between Boppard and Kaub, is the Lorelei, famous and beautiful if you are a tourist, infamous and downright dangerous if you are a river voyager. The river passes through a cliffy defile, narrows to a matter of a dozen yards or so, and at the same time makes an almost 180-degree turn. This rush around a tight corner causes very strong eddies and whirlpools. It also puts the living fear of Christ into any sailorman because sitting in the middle of it all is a bloody great rock only inches below the surface. Going upstream the danger of hitting the rock wasn't too bad because the current was about six and a half knots against us. That is as long as the engine doesn't fail. I ordered the crew over the side in the dinghy so as to lessen the weight carried on board. That made a total of around 225 kilos less for the Yanmar to shove. Then, on board alone, I tackled the Lorelei while the crew followed close astern, at the same speed as *Outward Leg*, with a long line between her and *Middle Leg*, in case the outboard engine should fail and they be swept downstream onto the rocks, or in case Yannie packed in and *Outward Leg* hurled to destruction.

There is a watchtower at each end of the Lorelei maelstrom, with big looking glasses poking out, so that the watchkeepers can see around the corners. They signal to craft downstream if a ship is heading their way. If there is one coming, then the upstream-headed craft must stop to one side and wait; the craft coming downstream simply cannot stop once she's in the Lorelei, and the fairway is as tight as a linnet's throat. Between the Lorelei rock and the shores the passages are a matter of mere yards, no wider than some of the river ships are long. As I said to the lads when we'd passed through, "If they would open one of those in Disneyworld, they'd make a bloody fortune."

Closer and closer to the first, downstream bend *Outward Leg* crept against the mighty current. At times she was barely moving against the rocky shores. Sometimes she stopped altogether, with the engine screaming at full power; then I grabbed her sideways toward the shore as much as I dared, to find a weaker current. All the while I glanced astern, to check the dinghy and her crew. They had their outboard running so as to give it the same speed as *Outward Leg*. They were getting wet now, as the wind-over current set up quite a slop. After two hours plugging away, inch by inch, creeping along the cliff bottom or rocky shore, keeping well out of the way of passing ships, plodding upstream or rushing downstream, *Outward Leg* reached the second, upstream watchtower which hangs perilously, it seems, on a vertical cliff above the roaring river waters. Here the current was the strongest of all we had encountered on the Rhine. It must have been over seven knots most of the time, because it stopped me completely, and that was even though I had a twenty-knot wind astern helping the engine. At a guess, the current's fastest rate was eight knots. I thanked my lucky stars for the stern wind and that I knew it blows upstream in the afternoon nine days out of ten, and I thanked them for the dependability of Yannie. If the engine had failed at any moment going through the Lorelei it would have caused sure and certain disaster; very probably the destruction of *Outward Leg* and my death by drowning, or other injury. With three broken ribs and a missing leg and hardly able to breathe with the recovering lung, there was no way I could have possibly survived. Against that current, on a rocky bottom, no anchor would have held. Without the steerageway given by the engine, and with no line ashore, there would have been absolutely nothing to stop the boat being swept downstream onto the rocks of the Lorelei. That is, unless the crew could have kept their wits and swiftly come over and taken me off *Outward Leg* before she hit. That was one of my reasons for having them in the dinghy. I had said it was to save weight, but there was an unspoken understanding between us of the other reason. Silently, as *Outward Leg* crept by, slowly, inch by bloody inch, past the rocks and menaces of the Lorelei, I thanked the Japanese engineers who had made Yannie so well, so gutsy, and prayed that their workmanship would hold out.

Then, not suddenly but gradually, little by little, the current eased

until it was down to a mere five knots and the river widened. By the
time we had reached five miles above the Lorelei it was down to four
knots and we, panting with relief, took the dinghy aboard, wordlessly.
But I think we all knew what we had done, and what risks we had
taken to do it. We had overcome the third of the major obstacles to
the European Leg. The first had been gathering the will and resources
to tackle it in the beginning. The second had been my willed "re-
covery" from my injuries in Amsterdam.

The place where I finally clambered ashore in Germany rejoices
in the name of Assmannshausen. Don't ask me what it means; I leave
that to your own imagination. It is almost two hundred miles beyond
the Dutch-German border, a summer riverside resort, overlooked by
vineyards, miles and miles of them. Its banks are lined with fine
hotels and shops, but they are beyond an autobahn and a railroad,
which in turn are beyond an iron fence beyond a gangway with a
high, locked gate leading from a big pontoon. Try that for size with
a missing left leg and your right side, the one that is supported by
your walking stick, in ruins and pain.

With all the traffic rushing by on the autobahn I thought the town
was busy. I fancied sitting down to a cup of coffee. I headed for the
gangway gate, clambered over it somehow, climbed over the iron
fence, hobbled as fast as I could over the autobahn, dodged an express
railway train by yards, and scrambled into town triumphantly, only
to find that everything was shut and locked tight. I had only wanted
to sit and drink a coffee. Pissed off to the limit, I returned to the
pontoon. As I was lifting myself over the locked gate Terry showed
up to tell me that there was underpass below the autobahn and the
rail line, but it was three hundred yards away. I glared at the river
and the concrete all around. "That's an anti-invasion device," I told
him. I slithered down the gate onto the gangway and sighted a duck
on the pontoon. I bent to pick up a pebble to chuck at it, I was so
pissed off. Then I noticed that it had part of one wing missing and
was hobbling along. I stared at it for a few minutes, and felt sorry for
it. Then, as I realized that the duck and I were kindred souls I burst
out laughing. The duck scrabbled along the pontoon, tried to fly off
it, and dropped into the Rhine. It squawked and struggled, until
eventually it reached the shore downstream, and hobbled ashore.

Later a barge pulled alongside the next pontoon upstream. Its
skipper clambered over to talk to me. He seemed a decent man, and

would have been interesting, I think, if my German, or his English, had been better. As it was we conversed in a sort of bastard Eurolingo, in German, French, Dutch, English, and with even some Spanish, Italian and Portuguese words thrown in by me for good measure.

He gave me to understand that the river was being sounded to check the depths. These are continuously changing on this part of the Rhine, with shifting sandbanks sometimes covering, sometimes revealing, dangerous rocks. He also indicated that the current, very strong hereabouts, lessened above Bingen, a few miles upstream. Then he told me the Rhine–Main–Donau Kanal was almost completed.

Above Bingen, sure enough, the current eased off to a mere three and a half knots, and we made fine time to Mainz, where we left the Rhine and entered the first lock on this passage since Holland, at the confluences of the Rhine and the Main. We had covered 250 miles or so from the North Sea. Now we were truly entering the heart of Europe.

The Main–Rhine junction lock is some miles from the city of Wiesbaden, in rural surroundings. The lock itself, we found, is not as well provided with mooring rings as the Dutch locks are. They are few and far between—about twenty yards apart. This was the case at all the other sixty locks between Wiesbaden and Bamberg. Our solution to this was simple. Instead of tying up to the rings, we tied up one line only, led from forward, to the ladder on the side of the dock, and then led it aft, where it was again secured. At the ladder a round turn and two half hitches were tied in the line, and this held the boat steady against the lock wall while she rose. Of course we put all our fenders over the wall-side, too. As the boat rose with the water, we held onto the ladder tightly with a boathook to untie the line from time to time, and shift it up the ladder a few rings. This system worked very well, and we never had any mishaps using it.

The lockkeepers expressed what we presumed was surprise at our passage through their charge, and even more surprise when Terry, the linguist among us, replied 'Schwartzes Meer'' to an evident inquiry as to where the hell we were going. Wisely, they nodded their heads and shouted "Jetzt offen!" ("Now it's open!"). That cheered me immensely; those canal diggers must be working like blazes to have it "almost completed" in the morning, as I had been informed at Assmannshausen, and "now open" as they told us now in Wiesbaden.

A few miles above the Rhine–Main confluence is Rüsselsheim. The traffic on the river Main is much less than on the Rhine and the current is a great deal less. We reached there in an hour, just as dusk was falling. In the lowering gloaming I sighted a small pontoon tied up between trees. We moored up alongside it and ate our supper below. It was far too cold, now, to eat topside in the cockpit. Between us and the brightly lit restaurants beyond a parking lot, there were trees, so no one seemed to be aware of our presence, and we slept undisturbed. When we tied to the pontoon, as we were to do at all small pontoons, we made fast lines ashore to trees fore and aft. If there were no trees we set small anchors on the shore.

There were factories and even an oil refinery nearby, but little else to show that we were only a few miles from Frankfurt, one of the biggest urban sprawls in Europe.

Before turning in at Rüsselsheim I surveyed the scene from the after hatch. Loud music blared from the bar closest to us. Shouting revelers made their way to their cars, entered them, fumbled with ignitions and roared off. It amused me to imagine what their reactions would have been if they had realized that only yards from them they were being observed from an oceangoing sailing vessel, almost three hundred miles from the sea. But they obviously had no idea that *Outward Leg* almost shared the parking lot with them, and I didn't want them to know, anyway. Booze and boats don't go together, not even this far inland.

Early next morning, in thin fog, we set off for Frankfurt. There were two locks to negotiate. This delayed us for two hours, as the lockkeepers waited until they had passed a downstream-heading ship through, before letting *Outward Leg* enter their ponderous gates. We finally arrived at Frankfurt just after lunch, slowing down the boat to accommodate the mealtime. I had no idea where to moor the boat, and keeping in mind Nelson's maxim "A good captain can do no wrong if he lays himself alongside the enemy," I laid her alongside the quay right in the city center, just underneath the footbridge which crosses from Frankfurt to Sachsenhausen.

# 7

# *Bounding on the Main and Rebounding*

In the five, mostly rainy and cold, days we spent at Frankfurt waiting for mail, we did maintenance work on the engine and steering system. Dealing with incoming mail was simple: there was none.

One day a lady called out excitedly from the jetty. I stuck my head up through the companionway to see her waving a book at me. This turned out to be a copy of *Ice* in German which she wanted me to sign for her. At first I must have looked at her as though she were crazy. Then I took the book from her and stared at it for some time. She must have thought I was a bit short in the head, too. She spoke very little English, so I could hardly explain to her that I'd never seen the book before in German and in fact I had no idea that it existed.

From Frankfurt to Nürnberg by river is 218 miles. It is much less by road. This is because the river makes two enormous bends; twice we pushed sixty and more miles to make a mere thirty or so in the direction of Nürnberg. The Main winds through picturesque country, first between the Odenwald and the Spessart range of hills, then through a gap in the Steigerwald hills, and so along a plain skirting the foothills of Fränkische Jura Mountains, which separate the Rhine and Danube watersheds in Bavaria. There are sixty-two locks on the river. The current is much less strong than on the Rhine, most of the time. On the river where it is held up by the locks, there is mostly no current at all, but the rate increases to about a knot and a half on the lower side of the locks.

There are few groins on the Main, but there are many shallows, often unmarked, on either side of the channel, but mostly on the

55

inside of the bends. We could take no shortcuts. We had to follow the longest way and follow the channel around all its tortuous windings. The average depth of water we found in the Main was nine feet, but in parts, especially just above the lock at Schweinfurt, this dropped enough for us to touch the soft bottom a few times, and we drew four feet three.

I suppose because of the shallowness of the Main in parts, there was little traffic and most of that was in smaller river vessels lugging light cargo such as timber for pit props and oil.

Navigation on the Main is fairly straightforward except through Aschaffenburg, when the course is very tortuous and the current strong.

Pushing hard all day, from dawn until dusk, it took *Outward Leg* one week to navigate from Frankfurt to Nürnberg, an average of thirty-one miles a day. We were negotiating seven locks a day; sometimes waiting for ships to pass downstream through the locks before we could enter. These delays were because the summer had been comparatively dry; there was not enough water in the river system to afford to empty a lock especially to allow the passage of one small craft.

On the Main the locks are immense by British standards; about three hundred feet long, about forty feet wide and sixty or more feet high. In locks farther upstream the released water is channeled into holding tanks, from whence it is pumped back into the upstream side of the locks. Many of the locks are beside wide electricity-generating hydro-power plants. Over these in normal times, the river pours in a mad torrent but now the low metal dams were raised, and the waterfalls at each lock were a mere trickle.

As Frankfurt dropped astern, so the scenery along the Main improved, from a dreary industrial and urban desert to neat villages, tree-clad hills and fairy-tale castles perched on craggy hilltops covered in vineyards on their smoother slopes. Usually we tied up on the upper side of a lock, where there are long jetties conveniently provided with fresh-water taps, sometimes telephones and often garbage bins. The locks work from dawn until dusk. Navigation is not allowed at night; the river channel is too tortuous for safe navigation then. Berthing on the upper side of the last lock of the day allowed us to set off before dawn on the following morning so as to get as early a start as we could and reach the next lock just after it opened. As the river was comparatively low, and there had been no rain to wash tree trunks or other obstacles into it, we could take this risk of a few miles of night navigation.

At Obernau, we moored at the lock, half a mile from the town. This is the first place above Frankfurt where the scenery is rural. It is set among rolling hills covered with larch plantations. There is good fishing from the lock jetty for those with local fishing licenses. The whole stretch of the Main is good fishing. Above Obernau the view is of hills on either side of the river becoming bigger and bigger, with large palaces and castles, manor houses and hamlets and vineyards set among them, especially in the valleys and on the river bends. At Gemünden again, we tied up, on a beautiful winter's evening, surrounded by teeming wildlife; herons, moorhen and wild geese.

All the way along the river, now that we were far into the countryside of northern Bavaria, people ashore greeted us. They looked surprised at our appearance, as well they might have been; *Outward Leg* wore all her flags as well as our ensign. This was not an affectation on our part. Flags, burgees and ensigns are an aid to visibility by other craft, and the more we wore, and the bigger they were, and the more they flew in the wind, the sooner we were sighted by other craft when they emerged from a bend in the river. But the reason the people stared and waved was not, I am sure, because of the number of our flags, but because of what they represented; the American Old Glory ensign, for the boat, on the stern staff, the British Red Ensign, for Martin and me, on the starboard side, and the Welsh Red Dragon on the port side, for the Wales that I once knew.

As we pushed up the Main, so the lockkeepers became more friendly and accommodating and, although the messages we could exchange were very rudimentary, they understood what we were trying to do, and shouted encouragement. Some evidently thought that the Rhine–Main–Donau Kanal might be finished; others looked as though they had never heard of it.

At Schweinfurt lock we again tied up just above the gates. Ever since some vandals in Frankfurt had let go of our after lines we had set the Bruce anchor over the bow, so that if it happened again we would not be pushed far downstream. As it turned out, there was never again another case like the Frankfurt effort all the way across Europe. We had learned our lesson; that it takes only one fly to spoil the ointment and so we always dropped the pick when we tied up on a public wharf.

Although we didn't know it at the time, this next stretch of the Main was to become all too familiar to us. *Outward Leg* was to navigate it three times in the next two months.

Above Schweinfurt the next stop for us was at Hassfurt. There there is a public jetty, but with a "no parking" sign on it. We couldn't imagine any river officials being out in the cold weather to supervise the "no parking," so we moored up. It is an attractive berth, on a little square and only half a mile from the town center. Here we tried to find a new burner for my cabin heater, which had again packed up in a cloud of filthy black smoke. There were no kerosene stove spares that we could find, in the town. Everything was geared to electricity, except for some wood stoves, but they were too big and heavy for the boat; besides, at 300 deutschmarks I couldn't afford one. I had to save every penny for the coming effort to reach the Danube, so I hobbled back to my cold cabin.

Twenty-one miles above Hassfurt, between wooded hills beside the river, lies the prettiest town in all Germany: Bamberg. There we stopped for the night, at a public wharf under the Kettenbrücke, one of the two town bridges, and took a short ramble ashore. It was a cold, dry evening; all the shops were decorated for the coming Christmas, now only three weeks away. Many homes, too, had their gaily lit Christmas trees, Santa Clauses, gnomes, elves and other reminders of a dark Teutonic past, now all tarted up and lit, courtesy of Thomas Edison.

The crew and I walked over the bridge and to the main square. There, almost five hundred miles by water from the sea in any direction, is an unbelievable statue of Poseidon. I stared at it, disbelieving my eyes, but there was no doubt about it, the god of the sea was there in all his glory, cast in bronze and holding his trident, naked as the day he was born and looking about as out of place as I would feel at a soap-manufacturer's board meeting. "It just goes to show," said I to Terry, whose nose was glowing with the cold, "We Are Everywhere!"

Secretly, though, I wondered if this statue, so far from the ocean, was some kind of omen, and if it was, was it a good or a bad one? Eventually I decided that old King Neptune was telling me not to feel too much like a fish out of water here in the middle of a continent. In any case, I told myself, his trident had been pointing more or less south, in the direction of the Danube. I convinced myself that the old bugger was showing me the way back home, back to the sea. He wasn't pointing north, the way we had come. Then we found a McDonald's in all its International Glory, and forgot about Poseidon and the sea while we munched our first meal ashore in Germany on this voyage.

The following morning the fog was as thick as a Ganges blanket. We were held up by three hours until it cleared enough for me to feel my way through a swirling mist to the first lock above Bamberg. Some few miles upstream we left the Main and entered, according to a sign, the Rhine–Main–Donau (RMD) Kanal. We were cheered by this evidence that the canal to the Danube did exist, after all, and as there was little current in the canal, a wide and easy waterway, we pressed on joyfully toward Nürnberg.

After the locks on the Main, which are big enough by any standard, those on the RMD Kanal are almost overwhelming. The sight of the first lock, at Erlangen, was staggering. It was all of eighty feet wide, 600 feet long, and the rise inside the lock was sixty feet. It brought to mind memories of the monster-locks on the Panama Canal.

Compared to the winding and picturesque Main, the RMD Kanal is boringly straight. The depths in it are comfortingly level at twelve feet from side to side. It is bordered, mostly, by a concrete retaining wall and grassy dikes which hide the countryside and urban sprawls thereabouts. Sometimes the canal, which is about two hundred feet wide, crosses over the old riverbed on bridges, and in one place as it does this it is itself crossed over by an autobahn bridge.

On we chugged, now at a good six knots with the engine at full working revs, and passed the Nürnberg Yacht Club at Gebersdorf. There we saw the first lone sailing craft in many, many miles, laid up on the bank for the winter, along with a dozen or so power craft.

We were in too anxious a mood to inspect Gebersdorf properly, though. I wanted to see how far this canal was completed, and if, in fact, it was possible for *Outward Leg* to reach the Danube by this easy means. I soon found out.

Forty-seven miles above the confluence of the Main and the RMD Kanal, just past the great, silent, empty docks of Nürnberg, the canal is blocked by a huge lock gate, brand-new in appearance and very, very heavy and immovable. It overlooks a great ash dump on one side, and a huge automobile-wrecking yard on the other. The air was full of ash fly from the dump. The wrecking yard looked like a prairie of broken dreams. Overhead the sky was black with heavy cloud, angry with the threat of snow.

On the great black lock gate of km 73 was fixed a sign: *Eintracht Verboten*—Entry Forbidden! No further passage!

I slowed the engine and hove *Outward Leg* to off the gate. I stared at it for a full minute. Then I said to myself, *'We'll bloody well see about that!'* My ribs were still clicking whenever I moved my upper body.

We moored the boat up below the lock gate, silently. I clambered ashore, with Terry to help me slither up the thick mud, and climbed to the top of the rampart. There, as the snow started to flitter down I gazed on the canal bed under construction. It was cluttered with machinery, both mobile and stationary. The concrete canal bottom was half-finished, almost as far as my eyes could see, but beyond that there was only a sea of mud, with mud-shifting caterpillars crawling through it noisily.

"What do we do now?" asked Terry.

I thought for a minute. I'd little idea what to do. All I could reply was "Trust in God and keep our powder dry."

Then we slithered back down the mud bank to recover my walking stick, which I had thrown, in disgust, in the direction of Poseidon, north in Bamberg.

# 8

## 'Mid Pleasures and Palaces

I learned long ago that when forward movement is impossible, then I must make myself as comfortable as possible and hang on. At sea we call it "heaving to." Then, when the weather abates, we can sail on.

Silently, *Outward Leg* slid back down the Rhine–Main–Donau Kanal. I had explored around the Nürnberg Docks with the idea of perhaps staying and working out our advance from there. But the docks are miles outside Nürnberg or any other inhabited place and are about as attractive an abode as Hole Haven, Essex, or the Smith's Knoll Lightship on a mad March day. At least the Nürnberg Yacht Basin was near houses, and where there are houses there is usually a shop nearby, and in the West a telephone, and some means of transport. It all boils down to food and communication.

In December the scene each side of the Kanal was bleak. On one side was an autobahn noisy with rushing trucks and cars, on the other fields and factories stretching into the distance. Far away, to the south and east, the city of Nürnberg sprawled out, gray across the horizon. There were no hills or rises to break the rush of the wind, and it swept across the plain cold and damp, pushing before it lumpy black clouds, full of snow. I named the plain "Little Siberia." It was an unfair soubriquet, but its not easy to be fair when you're cold, tired and frustrated.

The Nürnberg Basin lies just off the Kanal. It is square in shape and has an entrance about thirty feet wide. The depths inside are twelve feet in the middle, diminishing to seven feet alongside wooden floating pontoons on the southern side. There is a brick clubhouse and a public telephone box on the hard, also a water tap and a *hot shower* inside the clubhouse lobby, as we found within minutes of tying up. These were treasures indeed.

The Basin is about three miles from Nürnberg city center, and a bus runs about every twenty minutes from the bridge nearby. The Basin is cared for by Herr and Frau Beigler, who came to the jetty to welcome us. It was 4 December. I had, I estimated, about three weeks in which to get the boat across to the Danube, which ran about sixty-two miles to the south of Nürnberg. Then the winter freeze would start, and last until about February. There would be no chance of moving *Outward Leg* between Christmas and the end of February.

Once the boat was settled in I made my way into Nürnberg on the bus to seek out the Ludwig Kanal. After long, cold walks in the rain I found it all right—buried ten feet under a busy autobahn and as dead as a doornail. It had been bombed and destroyed by the RAF in 1944. It seems that the Nazis had used it to transport war materials, including prefabricated sections of U-boats, from southern Bavaria to the northern German plain. As I told Terry, "The silly buggers never realized that *Outward Leg* would be coming through one day." I was half-joking, and yet not.

Now the Ludwig Kanal was part of the foundations of a highway. But even if it had survived the war, we could not have navigated on it. I learned later, when I finally found one of the old locks still intact, farther south of the city, that the canal could take vessels only up to ten feet wide, and the last of the surviving bridges showed that the governing height was only ten feet or so; we could not have even floated her through on her side.

I also learned that it took three thousand men only three years, in the mid-nineteenth century, to dig out and construct a canal seventy-four miles long, with one hundred locks and bridges, without any machinery except horsecarts and primitive cranes. Now, with all the advantages of modern technology, the RMD Kanal, about the same length, had been in the process of construction for two decades and more, and would not be completed for another *eight* years.

After making sure that English newspapers and good tea were available at Nürnberg Central Railway Station, we returned to Gebersdorf to tackle the job of planning the haul from Nürnberg to Regensburg. I had seen the autobahn along which we must travel.

Like a crippled spy, I had hobbled over it and along a section, measuring with my walking stick, in between the roaring traffic in light snow, the distance across the road, from one set of telephone poles and traffic signals, to the other. On the approach roads, where the lanes are narrowest, the distance was thirty feet. *Outward Leg* is twenty-six feet one inch wide. This meant, of course, that a road haul *was* possible.

Peter Brunner, the Commodore of the Nürnberg Yacht Club, called on us that evening. He was a well-setup man in his sixties, with an interesting past, it turned out, especially during World War Two, when fortunately for the Allied cause he had been captured in Greece by the British Army. After weighing him up for a while I decided that it was probably fortunate for the Greeks, too. There was no love lost between us. We respected each other's presence and I stuck to the problem of hauling *Outward Leg*.

With Martin's help I had drawn a plan of the boat and roughly calculated the stresses she could stand while being lifted by cranes and sitting on a bouncing road truck. A road contractor was brought in; he merely scoffed at our efforts. For the autobahn authority, the Autobahn Amt, a piece of paper with a diagram of some figures scrawled on it was not good enough. Only a complete, detailed account of the whole of the boat's construction, together with specifications of all the materials used, and exact measurements of all dimensions, would do, and those to be in quadruplicate. All weights of all items removable from the boat had also to be reckoned and listed, every block, every line, every can of food, each one separately. In an oceangoing sailing craft, the number of removable items is around two thousand, so it took most of that night to make the list. When it was finished, as reasonably accurate as we could make it, I wanted to add my grandmother's name to the specifications, but the crew dissuaded me. Instead I added my three false legs to the list of removable gear, and signed it.

Next day the contractor called for the specifications and took them away. He was back the following day. In my exasperation I'd only signed the top copy of them, and all four copies needed my signature. So the process went on, for three weeks. When something had to be added or subtracted on the lists the whole thing had to be done again. It was very soon obvious that there was a malignancy at work somewhere ashore; by 9 December it was obvious that its source lay at the

Autobahn Amt. They asked for the equivalent in deutschmarks of a thousand pounds to remove road signs along the route, over and above the haulage costs and fee for a police escort. I knew that we could haul without touching a road sign, but agreed to it anyway. I didn't have the money, but first I wanted their agreement to the haul. Then I'd find the cash, somehow, or fight the demand.

On 10 December back came the loud reply of the Autobahn Amt in the form of a message from a certain Herr Rittmeyer there. It was *Nein!*

Rittmeyer, it seemed from what the contractor told me, was obdurate. He had fumed in his warm office and laid down categorically that *Outward Leg* was too wide for the autobahn haul. He'd also made some very personal remarks about me.

I kept my counsel and changed my tack. I approached the U.S. Army public relations office for help. As it turned out I might just as well have appealed to Colonel Qadaffi. Sure, I was made welcome, sure they listened to me, sure they passed me from one office to another, but General Salikoskvila was out of town . . . Before I hobbled out of his office Mr. Maloney did promise me a new U.S. flag to replace my old one. I wasn't cadging it; I'd offered to pay for it. But it never arrived.

By 15 December the cold was biting. My stove was still leaking, and the Autobahn Amt, just a centimeter below God to anyone who drives a car in West Germany, was obdurate in its refusal to allow me passage. The word was *Nein, nein, nein.* Now the Teuton and the Celt were eyeball to eyeball.

By 20 December the first ice was forming in the Nürnberg Basin. It was only an inch thick, and had disappeared by midmorning, but the threat was there, sure enough.

Unlike any other form of solid, water, as ice, expands when it freezes, and keeps expanding as it gets colder. That is a law of nature. It also sends the shivering shits through any mariner whose vessel is in danger of being trapped in ice. The *anomalous expansion of ice*, sideways against the hull, can crush the ship's sides. It's as simple, and as deadly, as that. That is why, wherever there is a threat of ice forming, mariners haul out their boats, if they possibly can, or escape the threat.

"What about hauling out here, in Gebersdorf?" asked Martin. Like any honest sailor his first thought was for the safety of the boat.

"No. If we haul out here, we become yet one more boat waiting out the winter like good little boys. We have to remain afloat so that we are ready to advance, if the Amt changes its bloody mind. We also have to be ready, if necessary, to retreat before the ice threat." This was a new one on the crew. They'd never, I think, heard me use the word "retreat" before.

"It's like this," I told them as they huddled round the smoking stove for warmth, "I learned long ago some of the Lore of the Jungle."

They looked puzzled.

"If you meet a wild animal, say in the bush, you don't turn round and flee. No, you stare it straight in the eye, and you walk slowly backward, beating the ground with your stick and making as much noise as you can manage!"

"What's that to do with the mess we're in?" asked Terry.

"Stupid, unthinking bureaucracy behaves just like a wild animal. First it growls and warns you off, then it roars and glares, and then it attacks, if you persist in crossing its prowl-path. What we're going to do is retreat slowly before the ice, and raise as much of a row as we can."

"There's no way they'll let us haul to Regensburg," muttered Martin.

"The hell with Regensburg," I replied. "It's the Danube I'm reaching for, and there's more than one way from here to the Danube."

"?" They both looked perplexed.

I smoothed out our now-tattered map of south Bavaria and pointed a sooty finger at the road from Nürnberg to Ingolstadt. "That's it," I said, hopefully. "That's not only our way out of this mess, it's also *theirs*."

"How do you mean?"

"The animal won't move from the path he's guarding, but if you make enough noise he'll let you walk round him, and leave you alone."

"And?"

"That way he'll salve his pride."

"What about your pride?" asked Martin.

"There's no room for pride when it's a matter of reaching for your passage. Make the passage first—then be proud, if that's your inclination."

So we waited in the ever-deepening cold, but not idly. There are always jobs to do in a boat, as well as the day-to-day work of keeping fed and maintaining the ship's routine. All the while I hobbled to and from the telephone in Herr Beigler's house in the thickening snow. On it I spoke to people in a dozen countries. I pleaded with them for the wherewithal to fly the boat over the Gap by helicopter, at the same time contacting German, British and American officials in high places to persuade the Amt to let us through by road. Now, I would have pawned my soul to beat Rittmeyer.

I looked closely, in the cold confines of my cabin, into the matter of flying a wide, flat shape like a trimaran under a helicopter. The U.S. Army engineers said it couldn't be done; the trimaran would continually, even at low speed, keep trying to fly itself upward, and so risk collision with the helicopter. Besides, they said, the downdraft from the chopper blades would blast down on the deck and strain the lifting wires unacceptably. "What," I asked them finally, "if we *hung her bows upward*?" This flummoxed them, and their only reply was that private helicopter hauls by U.S. military helicopters were now forbidden; they'd dropped a civilian electric transformer in someone's backyard recently . . .

The first public blast at the Autobalm Amt was published in the Nürnberg *Mittwoche*. They reported what I was doing and, more importantly, why. It was the first broadside in my campaign to bring to our cause nothing less than the whole of West German public opinion. I had two big advantages; I was not a car driver, and the German public mostly were. Being human, they subconsciously hated the road authority. I would raise to the banner of *Outward Leg* all their frustrations, all their resentments at blocked roads, crowded rest areas and choked traffic; I'd make Rittmeyer's seat so hot he'd hum.

The third week in December was foggy and colder. It was also Christmas week. We didn't suffer too much. German friends made life easier by their hospitality, and Frau Beigler took us all to see the children's candlelight procession up to the old royal castle in Nürnberg. As we sipped *Glühwein* in the shadow of the Kaiserburg, and watched all the young faces so serious in the candlelight, I dreamed of flying the boat over them and the Kaiserburg and Herr Rittmeyer's office, and imagined how the kids' eyes would light up.

Karl Svoboda, the harbormaster at Nürnberg Yacht Basin, showed up with an electric fire and a long cable. This made a Christmas gift so warm that it will never be forgotten. Several members of the Nürnberg Yacht Club called on us, bringing cakes and other comforts, along with bottles of good wine. One of them, well under the weather, blurted out what a nuisance I was to Germany, and what a pity it was that I hadn't been sunk four times by the Kriegsmarine instead of three. That was daisies in a bull's mouth to me, for I realized that my campaign was beginning to succeed, but only beginning. To him I maintained a frigid silence.

"When right-wing fascists say you're a nuisance, then you know you're doing *all right*," I commented to the crew, afterward.

But there were dozens of other Germans who made us as welcome as they could, and helped us to survive in every way. There is no doubt that the Bavarians whom we met were, on the whole, generous, sympathetic and kind; without their help *Outward Leg*'s passage would have been a thousand times more difficult, if not impossible. We found the older Germans to be extremely reticent about the Third Reich, while the young ones were quite open about that tyranny. This makes a generation gap in Germany far deeper than any I have observed in any other country, including, amazingly enough to me, the United States. In Germany, dealing with the young and the old is like dealing with two separate nations.

I found the Germans of any age to be very trustworthy. There, a man's word—or a woman's—is a bond which will be kept through hell or high water. But with it comes a certain inflexibility of view, of mental process or intention, which for a Celt, accustomed to happily hopping from one psychical foot to the other, made dealing with them difficult, to say the least.

But the German intractability of mind and intention, although it was sometimes infuriatingly obdurate, was one of the qualities in them that, most of the time, I admired. I decided that as it would never be changed or shifted, it would have to be employed in our cause, to defeat the intractability and obduracy of the Bavarian Autobahn Amt. All I had to do was gather the reins of it into my hands and give it a gentle twitch. Its own volition would carry it forward into a head-long collision with the authorities, and we, hanging on its coattails, would be carried along, forward to the Danube or we would be destroyed in the attempt. Manfred Peter, a journalist, and one of the most human beings I have ever met, handed me the reins I was blindly groping for.

To write of all Manfred's troubles and efforts on behalf of *Outward Leg* would need a book in itself. He doused to ashes in me the old burning hatred of anything and anyone that hailed from the German land. He opened many doors for me, but the most important one of all shed the light of reason on my Celtic soul's view of Germany. For that I can never thank him enough. Manfred Peter unbound me from the ulcerous chains of a real and, I had once thought, undying hatred. He and his wife did me the greatest favor anyone can do for another; they proved to me that love was stronger than hatred.

On 31 December the thickness of the ice in the Nürnberg Basin was one inch. We were running the engine at odd hours and moving the boat gently fore and aft to keep ourselves free.

1 January saw the start of our slow, painful retreat, as the coldest winter that Europe has known for over two generations clamped down with arctic viciousness, and the ice crept on us, inch by murderous inch.

The next ten weeks I spent in fighting my way through a web of bureaucracy which made anything I had previously experienced, anywhere in the world, seem like child's play. Time inevitably revealed this bureaucracy and the people who run it for what they were: pedantic, blinkered little men of stilted imagination confined to a limited view of life from behind their office desks, and their prospects of a pension at the end of it all.

It was a time of almost hopeless confusion, of bitterness at the intransigence of Herr Tubbsinger's minions, themselves bitter at being brought out into the limelight and exposed for what they were: small-visioned people with the lives and imaginations of cart horses, and the meanness of challenged and cornered rats, and the viciousness of outwitted wolves.

To the very end they snapped at the heels of *Outward Leg* and even then, in despair, maneuvered her into what they thought was an impossible situation and hazarded her very life, as we shall see. But Herr Tubbsinger never once revealed himself. He stayed, he thought, hidden throughout.

As we pushed off from Gebersdorf in the bitterly cold morning light on 30 December, Frau Beigler was waiting to wave us off. I blessed her, waved "Au revoir" and grudgingly shoved our tape of Tchaikovsky's "1812 Overture" into the player, to remind us of another hopeless retreat. *Only, we were coming back.*

"I'll take her over if I have to chop her into pieces and lug her in suitcases," I told myself.

# 9

## *Blocked and Beset*

Between Frankfurt and Nürnberg the difference in altitude at river level is several hundred feet. My plan was to retreat slowly down the Main, thus by stages reducing *Outward Leg*'s altitude, and the risk of being beset in ice. My first stage was to Bamberg, where I recalled there was a jetty in the town center. There, if we were delayed long, communications and shopping would be conveniently close to the boat.

All day long we descended the river in cold wind and rain. Close to the six locks between Gebersdorf and Bamberg, in each case, pack ice, one inch thick, had blocked the entrance gates, sometimes for as much as a mile before we reached them. With the engine running "slow ahead" and the crew shoving the worst of the ice packs aside with long poles, *Outward Leg* moved forward into the locks, one after the other. From the lockkeepers we had only pitying glances as they worked behind wide windows in their warm control towers.

Finally, after a hard day's work for the boat, the crew and for me, we arrived beside the Kettenbrücke and the town jetty in Bamberg. It was around six o'clock and already getting darker. Horst Besler, recommended to us by Karl Svoboda, the harbormaster at Nürnberg Basin, was there to meet us. A train driver by profession, he is a big, obviously strong man with a merry red face, clean-shaven, aged about forty.

In reply to Horst's cries of welcome, I clambered up onto the jetty, and shook his hand. Then I tried to climb over the chest-high iron fence that runs between the edge of the jetty and the path, where

Horst was standing. This is never easy for me, and I hesitated in pain, as my ribs were still loose. Suddenly Horst leaned over and grabbed me under the armpits in a bear hug and I saw stars. He lifted me, cursing like a trooper (which he couldn't understand as his English then was nil), clear over the iron fence. He set me back down on my feet, real and false. As he had lifted me I distinctly felt and heard my ribs snap back in place, end to end, and now there was no pain when I breathed. It was the first time that I could breathe easily since I had left the hospital in Amsterdam, two months before. When, by sign language and basic German, I explained this to Horst he laughed his head off. So my rib therapy was completed.

Horst insisted that next day, as soon as it was light, and as soon as the thin ice would allow us, we should move a mile or so downstream to the river Regnitz confluence with the RMD Kanal, where the Bamberg chapter of the Deutsche Lebensrettungsgesellschaft (DLRG) or German Lifesaving Association is placed. This has branches all over Germany and, besides running a rescue service, encourages water sports activities among people of all ages. The day after, New Year's Eve, they were holding a party, and we were invited.

Martin had gone to Nürnberg with a friend for New Year's Eve. Terry and I stayed on board for the night, and next day moved the boat a mile downstream to the river Regnitz. This took some time, as we had to break ice two and a half inches thick to reach the Regnitz. There we found that the river was not frozen, due to a warm-water discharge from a cotton mill some few hundred yards upstream from the DLRG clubhouse pontoon.

In the evening Terry and I attended the party. Besides the two of us, there were six other adults, one of whom was a young Bundeswehr Panzer Grenadier on leave, who insisted on playing, at odd times, a huge portable radio. None of the adults spoke any English. Besides adults there were six youngsters, boys and girls, who all spoke some English. This more or less forced Terry and me into the company of the kids most of the time.

To drink, there was Coca-Cola and beer. Buckets and buckets of beer. The adults danced, men and wives, jitterbugs and Strauss waltzes mainly. At midnight, all around the clubhouse, from across the Rhine–Main–Donau Kanal, frozen stiff, and across the Regnitz, ice free, the glare of rockets and other fireworks blossomed in the sky. Terry dashed down the slippery, snow slope of the river bank to *Outward Leg*, and extracted the flare gun and two flares. We fired them up in the sky for the DLRG. Only one of our white flares worked. The other fell like a lamb's tail straight from the barrel of the pistol. I wondered if this was an omen for the New Year, but decided that what it really indicated was that we needed new rockets.

Horst's mother, eighty-one years of age, was at the party, and looked interesting. What tales she could have told me of the changes she had seen in her lifetime, if my German had been up to understanding her. I made up my mind to learn as much of the language as I could, and as fast as I could.

I do not want to bore readers with the ins and outs of the complex negotiations over the next few weeks. Let extracts from the ship's diary speak for themselves.

*1 January*

MS[1] returned from Nürnberg at 9 A.M. Thick snow all around on the trees and on the shores of the Regnitz, but the river itself is ice free. I had intended to return to our favorite berth by the Kettenbrücke, but a small horde of visitors in the afternoon delayed shoving off until darkness was falling at 4:30 and it was too late to move in safely. We decided to wait until morning. While the visitors were on board (the survivors of last night's party) I presented Horst Besler with our Welsh flag, the one we had worn from San Diego to London, which thrilled him. He said it was the best souvenir his club had ever had. The evening was spent reading and listening to the radio, while outside the snow fell steadily but lightly. Temp. outside at midnight: $-50°C$. My stove needs pumping up every half hour or so, but it keeps the cabin warm. I turn it off at midnight, and it is lit again at 8 A.M. This saves expensive kerosene. Temp. at 8 A.M. in cabin: $-45°C$.

*2 January*

Horst brought milk and bread in the early morning and he is to see the Bürgermeister with our case today. We shifted to the Ketten-

---

[1]Martin Shaw.

brücke at 10 A.M. in a mild snowstorm. There was a barge passing upstream, which broke up the inch-thick ice for us nicely. The ice seems to pack below the Löwenbrücke and the start of the river Main. We set up the after cockpit screen. Sat-nav antenna not working; had some corrosion. This is a nuisance and means $350 for a new antenna as they are not under guarantee. Martin phoned Mike von Tülff[1] at 10:30. No news. He came to see us from Nürnberg yesterday, but of course we were not here at this berth and no one knew where we were. We shall probably not see him again soon, as he is off to Holland this week, on business. (That means that our line of communication from U.S.A. and U.K. will be broken, since Mike was taking and delivering all messages for us while we were on the move.)

### 3 January

Last night dinner at Horst Besler's place. Roast pork, sauerkraut and potato dumplings. Guinness and white beer for Martin and Terry, white wine (a little), for me. Crew had a sauna and shower. Lit heater on return to boat. Temp. at − 40°C. Heated to 60°C, then turned off for night. Also at Horst's met Herr Kempf, who is in charge of roads in Bamberg. He is trying to persuade Rittmeyer to let us use the hard shoulder on the Regensburg autobahn, but no one has much hope that he'll succeed. As for me I pretend, even to myself, I am getting weary of the whole thing, and accepting the retreat easier now. There is very little pleasure in winter cruising. A spending of effort and money is all. Just keeping warm is a chore in itself. This heater is a pain in the ass. In the morning it smokes from fuel leaked into bottom tray, and keeps smoking for three hours, filling the cabin with vile fumes, dirtying everything again. TJo[2] shopping. Meanwhile we wait forlornly for news of a change of heart of bloody Rittmeyer. In evening to Matthias' Mum's and Dad's for supper—cold meats and beer, radishes, etc. Not feeling good. The temp. in cabin on return was − 40°C. Heated up to 60°C.

---

[1]Michael von Tülff, a good friend of Manfred Peter, q.v., p.68. Mike was an experienced yachtsman and a leading light in the Erlangen University Yacht Club.
[2]Terry Johansen.

## 4 January

Horst brought aluminum and five gallons of kerosene.[1] I wrote to EC,[2] AS,[3] RC[4] and Peter Drew[5] re move to Frankfurt. It's got to be a bit warmer there, and there is supposed to be electricity at the West Dock. Felt very sick in A.M. and took it real easy. Maybe stove fumes getting to me? Forgot—Mike von Tülff and Manfred were on board yesterday. Press campaign going well. Radio man on board again today. Also Doktor Schmidt. Also Alexander. Also fat boy from club. Also Angie, etc. In evening party at Hildegard Hoffman. The usual crowd. Left at 12:30 after drinking glass of champagne for Hildegard's birthday. Very cold indeed. Canal frozen over. Heater on all night.

## 5 January

Up to a raging headache. Must be fumes and beer. Only two bottles though. After had been in fresh cold air for five minutes went away. Horst and Hildegard and usual crowd there along with Dr. Schmidt who brought *Guardian* and *Express*. Took off into inch-thick ice for a very cold run of 31 miles to Schweinfurt. Ice thick just above locks for half a mile or so. Luckily barge passed us at first lock, and we followed it all the way. Very cold; river smoking. Low visibility. Trees all gleaming white, like ice-coral. Moorhens and ducks; swans having thin time of it. Arrived Schweinfurt just after dark at 5:15 P.M. Berthed tired above lock, opposite town. Here to await events. Frau Beigler had phone call from U.S.A. but doesn't know who it was . . . so will try to phone Groesbeek,[6] from here A.M. Also Adidas showing interest. I too tired to think properly. Nerve-racking crunch of ice on hulls. Hitting propeller at times . . . But we are 150 feet lower than at Bamberg.

[1] Kerosene costs $10.00 per gallon in W. Germany.
[2] Euan Cameron, editor at the Bodley Head.
[3] Abner Stein, agent in London.
[4] Richard Curtis, agent in New York.
[5] Peter Drew, Chairman of the World Trade Centre, London.
[6] Charles Groesbeek, an arctic-explorer friend in Colorado, who was trying to interest film companies in funding a helicopter haul in return for filming rights. The attempts came to nothing.

*6 January*

A very cold night. I leave the aft cabin door, the engine room door and the after cabin window ajar for entry of oxygen. A slightly better night. In the A.M. comes the local paper. I give them all info. on the Rittmeyer case. Should come out tomorrow. Later Manfred comes with his wife and a friend, so I invite them all to the local Brauhaus for lunch. A delightful afternoon. When return, boat iced in half inch. Run engine to clear ice. Forecast is for − 25°C, tonight, then warming up. As we retreat, so we make noise. The local consensus is that the bureaucrats are to change their mind. I am as yet not fully convinced. I told Manfred I would do deal with Adidas for the help in getting to Regensburg. In return I could publicize their excellent sailing shoes free for next two years. We await results. I to phone Groesbeek tomorrow. Very, very cold evening. Canal completely frozen over. Coldest winter in Italy and Yugoslavia since 1939. Coldest spell here for five years. Tomorrow should bring local contacts in Schweinfurt. We'll see. No papers. Quiet evening ahead. Shakespeare?

*7 January*

The night was hellish, having to get up every thirty minutes to pump heater. Maintained heat at 60°C. Opened door leaves no head-ache though. Still cold. TV crew from Nürnberg turned up at 10:00 A.M. and made my half of the Rittmeyer v. me dialogue. They are very pro us. They took us to lunch at the same Brauhaus where we went yesterday. I had mutton, very good. Horst came, very excited, and had lunch with us. Newspaper tale out tomorrow. TV thing out Wednesday, so I will wait here until Wednesday in case Rittmeyer has change of heart. Then we slowly go back to Bamberg when ice diminishes. If not, retreat onto Kitzingen and Würzburg for further media blasts. Photographer from local paper gave us pix of me and crew. I signed one for chief of police (!). May get solid-fuel stove.

*8 January*

We are running the engine every four hours or so, astern and ahead, to keep the ice from forming fore and aft. The temp. goes down to

− 20°C at night. News reports in the local press, many spectators around the bridge[1] and jetty. All day trying to keep warm and dry. Set up Weatherfax and received weak signal from Paris which shows we are in a stopped low, held firm by highs over the Atlantic, Scandinavia and Russia. We can only hope that it moves in the next few days. The ice is one inch thick. In the afternoon dropped the braking line[2] around the boat. The idea is to haul it up tomorrow noon, to break a line of ice around boat. Spent 100 DM on food. A miserable day, knowing we are trapped, but a bright light is the possibility that the autobahn people will give way under public pressure sometime this week.

*9 January*

A rough night as slept with leg on to wake and run engine, but stuck fast by 3 A.M. with thermometer at − 25°C. Jerry came to help Martin get kerosene. We start to break ice up at 10 A.M. Method: bust hole through ice astern first and run engine ahead and then bust around the sides with spike. Actually, as have no spike we using my old crutch, which just about works. Fairly sleepless night working out the worst possibilities. U.S. Army nearby may help to crane her onto shore. I am awaiting news of permit before sending off change of address. But will try inform London today of situation. A confusion of people on board, from local YC, canal authority, police, etc. I sent copies of local press pictures and news articles to Abner Stein, express. Told him to hold off Frankfurt address for now. Local paper to publish our story. I asked Manfred to contact *Die Yacht*. Also to contact *Bild* through Martin Gasper and through journalist here. Hoping for support from *Bild* or Adidas. Meanwhile just struggling to keep boat free. Later a box of clothes comes from Adidas, but message of no money support for haul. I wrote letter thanking them and saying would wear next year in Japan and it's a pity we can't wear them at TV show in Mainz. Hint at (nonexistent) competition, and for 10,000 DM for the haul.

---

[1] I had moored the boat right under the Maxbrücke to avoid the worst of the snowfalls.

[2] A line of man-made fiber rope floated around the boat so that ice pressure would attack it and not the boat. It only works in thin-ice conditions.

## 10 January

Ice thickness three inches about two feet away from boat to starboard. About fifteen feet fore and aft. Breaking up with poles. Arranging gas heaters. *Die Yacht* sent along Mr. Bart who interviewed me. I asked him to chase up stuff already with them. Hoping for decision shortly. I wrote to Clare Francis yesterday explaining situation and asking her to pass pictures onto the press in U.K., copy to Peter Drew. Again local press photographer here to photograph ice breaking, for tomorrow's edition. Manfred sent copy of letter from autobahn authority. Looks like it's good. He is sending press release on our situation all over Germany. I am hoping British press picks it up. Meeting on board arranged for tomorrow re safety precautions for when ice breaks up.[1] Think best bet is to get boat into lock so gates protect.

## 11 January

Saturday brings hordes of people to boat and a crowd of helpers, who extend our thin ice perimeter out to about ten feet and pack bales of straw alongside to act as fender when the ice breaks up. Gas fires on board make life human again. Electric light. Martin ill later with stomach flu. Doctor sees him and nurses him. Lots of public interest. A tiring day. But we are safer. River authority says we must haul out of water (perhaps) when ice breaks up. Arrangements being made with U.S. Army at Kitzingen for this; re cranes etc. I wrote long letter Abner Stein, copy to P. Drew which will send Monday.

## 13 January

Another busy day breaking ice. Crowds of people came to *walk on* the canal, which is frozen solid for the first time since 1971. Just our luck. A crowd of Americans from the German-American Friendship Society came to help us and many well-wishers showed up. I stayed in my cabin quite a bit, as I am very tired with all the goings-on. In the evening we all went to Missie's for soup and I had a bath. Missie is the German–American wife of a German, Edwin, who is quiet.

---

[1]When a river is full of thawing ice, any vessel downstream of it is in jeopardy from thousands of tons of moving solids aiming straight at her.

She is vivacious and full of funny mistakes in her English, but has some amusing stories. Very feminine. Kind and generous, even though they have little. Back on board at 10:30 to break the ice again. Timmie, an American ex-GI from Minnesota, brought an electric heater, about five feet long, which at least solves the heating problem, and for the first time this winter the cabin is warm and drying out properly.

## 14 January

Television crew came for the icebreaking shots at 8 A.M. and Jerry arranged with slaughterhouse for more straw for the port side. It will be delivered this afternoon. No, it arrived while I was writing. We have a lot of help, for which I am quietly very grateful. I find some consolation that we are almost halfway through the month of January but so far there is no sign of a letup in the cold. All of Europe, it seems, is under deep freeze. It seems to be something to do with sunspots; the cycle seems to be every 21 or 22 years. In the afternoon Martin finds that the Sail Drive flexible mounting is ruptured. Sent cable through Dieter[1] for a new one from Yanmar. We think of the alternatives; to patch old one, or dismount and take to Bosch factory for repair. Evening on board (rare). Chicken for supper. Bed at 10:30.

## 15 January

Up at 8:30 to break ice. Inch thickness during night. Broken with dinghy engine mainly. Boat good and warm with electric heaters. Waiting for Dieter to come with news. TJo went shopping for new kettle as old one's handle broke off. Lots of things brittle and breaking. An old man brought us some tea and a brochure on Schweinfurt and wished us a happy voyage. Some retarded kids came, but we were very busy on ice[2]. At noon temp. up to −1½°C. Hope we are in for a slow thaw. No hurry. Less danger. There was no news from Charles Groesbeek. I'm afraid we might be up the wrong tree, but the phone calls cost nothing. I left him Manfred's phone number so he can chase me if aught turns up. Two people ashore wished us good luck. This is morale boosting.

[1]Dieter Landgraf, a journalist on the Schweinfurt newspaper.
[2]I later took the retarded kids for a boat ride through the ice.

*16 January*

Broke ice. Then to Mainz with Dieter, Jerry (driving) and TJo. Jerry has only 10% vision in one eye. Ten-minute show on television. It seems as a result they got calls offering accommodation and a helicopter, and the producer goes to Bonn tomorrow, where the German National Police want to volunteer their helicopter, too. Lunch in a small, boozy bar decorated with old TV lamps. Back in the evening hurtling along the autobahn to Schweinfurt to a Chinese meal. Back to boat to turn in and see what the morrow brings. The ice is a little slushy on top, an indication of, we hope, a slow thaw.

*17 January*

Broke the ice with dinghy in A.M. We are held here in any case awaiting the new engine mounting on the gearbox. Schoolteacher wants to do a "show," but I'd already talked to Dieter yesterday about doing a slide show for all the schools in town if he can get it organized. Lots of idlers on jetty and bridge, from 8 A.M. onward. −5°C. I wrote to Richard Curtis and Abner Stein telling them about TV show. Surely they can sell at least a couple of my books to the German publishers? Concerned about mail arriving at PO now. Have heard naught for a month. MS had cleared the cause of the sharp words the other day. That was not necessary. I would much rather have done it myself. Nothing said. Tension easier. I must start to write my treatise on being ice-threatened shortly. Puerto Rican soldiers at boat in A.M. promising all the equipment the U.S. army has. It's not equipment we are short of—it's permissions. By the way, the TV paid me 500 DM. That was the first TV interview I have ever done in Europe, but I hope not the last, on those terms. So made profit of 400 DM on the whole trip. I paid Chinese meal. Message from Manfred says that they are to open a helicopter-haul fund in Nürnberg and any surplus to go to screen actor Karlheinz Böhm's Ethiopian relief fund. I reply that I strongly object; surplus should go to poor handicapped kids in Germany. I think to myself I was feeding starving kids in Ethiopia before Mr. Karlheinz even knew such a place existed and I will not jump onto a fashionable show business bandwagon. An exercise in professional publicity for show business types. Manfred says that the autobahn authority spokesman on TV yesterday kept referring to me as "poor" Mr. Jones, etc. We'll see about that. I wrote a brief account to Ray Kennedy,[1] New York.

## 18 January

Broke ice. Colder— − 10°C. In early P.M. went to main post office—no more than a brick shed for a town of this size—but no mail. TJo got one letter, so right address. Phoned Stein—not in. Phoned EC at BH—not in. Back to boat. ABC wants to "film the helicopter haul." I told Dieter if they want to film it they can help bring it about. For supper to Ernst. He is artist who paints here and in Nürnberg. Good bits and pieces. His apartment reminds me of the village. Chicken and rice, but I had tea and not wine. Back at 10:30 in case of vandals. ABC Germany man's name is Jumberg and he's in Frankfurt. My leg's feet started to slide about because the glue has come unstuck. Must put a securing screw in tomorrow. Two boys came on board to interview me for local school newspaper. One of the questions was, "What are your hobbies?" I replied, "Dancing." Not a glimmer of a smile. They stood and bowed before leaving. The younger one was expressionless but handsome. The older one was awkward, shouted, and disproportionate.

## 19 January

Broke ice. Still − 3°C at noon. Plenty of people on board—Horst from Bamberg, Mike Tüllf and Manfred. Busy all day.

## 20 January

A guy from Nürnberg brought us seven gallons of diesel. A lady gave us 70 DM. Some kid gave us 1 DM as it's all she had, but I don't really want to get into that. Lunch with local sailing association—like the Erlangen crowd they charter boats in groups. At the Wild Man, very good cordon bleu steak and a small salad with coffee. Back on board Karl Svoboda came with his Frau. Their English is nil, but somehow we made conversation. He invites us to his home when we return to Nürnberg. Big attraction through TV programs, of course. But all this public adulation does not move the boat. I wrote to Peter

---

[1]Freelance reporter for *Sports Illustrated*, U.S.A.

Drew saying I'd pay his loan back at end of month. Also wrote stiff letter to ?? saying let me know what's going on and what's with the articles???

*21 January*

A real thaw is setting in. Temp. up to +5°C. Lows coming in from Atlantic bringing warmer air. No messages from Manfred. No mail. I cleaned slides ready for show, Wed. To Missie's in evening for bath and supper, cold ham and tea. Bed at 10:30.

*22 January*

Thaw still on. Temp. +7°C. All set. Misty, damp. Ernst is to mix up touch-up paint for us. Handy. Jürgen is ordering boathook heads. We will arrange poles. No news from Nürnberg but Brit. newspapers sent by Mike. That's a blessing if they come each day. In evening to Missie's mother where grannie 72 years old diabetic strong as ox. Missie loquacious as ever. Meat, beef, pork, potstew, very good, sustaining food, and tea for me. Wine and beer for the lads. Father who is to interpret for me was three years in Australia. Mother in U.S.A. thirty years back speaks with strong Carolinian accent. Back to boat at 10:30. Raining. Strong thaw. Slight current.

*23 January*

Thaw continues. But still ice solid sheet. No mail. New mounting for gearbox arrived and MS fitted. Also worked on sat-nav connection, but can't test it until we move from bridge. In evening to church hall for slide show. Went well and even made Germans laugh. Slight snow on emerging. After the crowd went to rather dreary Gasthaus where I ate pork medallions on toast with tea. On getting back to boat found the ice broken over far half of river and the flow fast as sluices open. Set alarm clock to wake at 4 and 7 as TJo and MS both sleepy and tired after hard day. But the ice around boat held all night.

*24 January*

Little changed except ice melting rapidly now. Temp. now about plus one degree. But warm front due Fri. night/Sat. Party of schoolkids came on board in A.M. and brought food and goodies. Most spoke some English and some of the boys had pendants in ears. I invited them to come to first sluice on Sat., when we should be clear to head for Bamberg. I don't suppose that will sit well with crew, but can't be helped. Boat will be crowded. Little news from Manfred Peter in Nürnberg except that they are trying for another road hauler. I decide to let them go ahead their own way. Every little helps. 260 DM in local hauling donation account. That grew from only 10 DM yesterday. Ernst brought touch-up paint for 15 DM. Boathooks arrived and MS went for them with Jürgen.

### 25 January

Finally the icebreaker arrived and broke up the little field 'twixt us and the lock. We came out of this icing with luck and very little damage—just a bit of waterline paint here and there. Prepared boat for sailing tomorrow. Straw loosed. Stowed towing line. Then to department store, where management laid on lunch and gave us 1,000 CV's with our North Atlantic chart background. Lots of people. In P.M. back to boat and parties of schoolkids on board. Then usual hangers-on and would-be camp followers. Sent message to Manfred that we go. Cook from department store is arranging for newsman to meet us. Evidently, from a canal official, the locks on the Danube 'twixt Ingolstadt and Regensburg are 13 yards wide, so only one cranage—from the truck—required. No news. No mail from U.S. or U.K. I fix hopes on haul-donation fund. We need minimum of DM 4,000 more so that I can preserve 500 for down-Danube trip to Hungary. Then cost of living should shield us for two months. To a party in a Greek restaurant in Missie's village. I had pork and some sweet red wine, which knocked me out. Back on board at about midnight. About twelve people there.

### 26 January

Up at 9 with a bad head. To Hassfurt, where local newspaper came on board. People crowded boat until well after dusk.

### 27 January

Up at 7 to Verieth Lock, where waited for Horst Besler, first in gray cloud and snow, then brilliant sunshine. All lockkeepers know us, and people come to windows to wave. Thick ice at lower entrance to locks, but no damage. Horst showed up at 2 P.M., excited. I let him steer most of the way to Gaustadt. At Gaustadt the chief of DLRG (Deutsche Lebensrettungsgesellschaft)—ex-German Navy—was there with family, femme-fatale daughter. Went on about *Kameradschaft* of sailors etc. Then to clubhouse to drink beer, then to Horst's home for sauna (crew) and tea (for me). I tired, but lasted until 10:30. Back to boat. Very cold again, with frost. Gas heater turned off to sleep, and woke cold despite sleeping bag and two blankets and tank hat. Turned on gas again at 7 A.M. Then HB brought water from his house. We steered to town and went for lunch; lots of U.S. soldiers in fatigues.

### 28 January

To post office. Tried phone AS. First engaged, then no reply. No movement at bank yet. Very cold in wind. Good to be back in Bamberg as at the bridge it's relatively interesting and convenient.

### 29 January

Early to Schweinfurt with Horst and crew by road. Reception by Oberbürgermeister in Rathaus—medieval bldg in town square. I had fish-and-chips in Ratskeller with fine old vaulted ceilings of stone. Jerry and Dieter there, also, of course Horst. Some white wine from locale sent me sleepy. To Horst's on return, for cold meats and cheese. Coffee for me. Sat around until 10:30, then home to cold boat. Temp. in night −5°C.

### 30 January

Boat to Kettenbrücke. I sent check to Pete Drew along with nice thank-you note. Toothache last night.

### 31 January

Foregoing was the onset of a sickness—bronchial cough but with loss of appetite, severe headache, etc. It cut me out sweating. That was soon after I phoned Abner. I stayed on board all day. Wrote to four magazines to try to catch up contacts.

*1 February*

Up at 2 P.M. feeling weak but marginally better. Managed eat some bread, butter, drink tea. Much trouble getting sleep. Extremely depressed. Don't know how long can go on.

*2 February*

Up at noon, marginally better but still aching all over. Managed to eat omelet. Weather warmer. Willy's house like a ship with four decks, all decked out with rope banisters on the ladder stairs, and pictures and certificates from his two years as a German Navy stoker. Paper model of battleship *Bismarck* on dresser. These people really stuff themselves with food—usually cold in the evening, and knock back the beer. It coarsens them greatly, and even some young women show signs of it at sixteen or so. Even their holiday films feature much eating and drinking, usually wine. The crew don't seem to be aware of how ill I become. Maybe it's because I try not to show it too much. When I was young it was sissy to be ill. Last night they both took off to disco with girls and left me, half alive, at Willy's. MS went off somewhere and TJo was at boat when I returned with Horst.

*3–6 February*

Very sick with bronchitis. In bed most of time. On 6 to post office with Horst. Phoned Abner, but he not in. Horst has permission (unofficial) of Wasserschutzpolizei for us to go to Ketten bridge if we want to. So at least we are not tied up here all the time.

*7 February*

Better sleep, but still coughing much. Yellow phlegm. Boat to Kettenbrücke at 10 A.M. TJo and I to post office: no mail. I forgot. Yesterday the World Trade Centre sent me contact in Bulgaria. Visit to bridge will ease tension by having others around.

*8 February*

Thick headache. Rested. Newspapers came in A.M. No mail. MS to Nürnberg to chase steel beams. Thick snow. Very cold. Water-police captain friendly.

*9 February*

Thick snow in A.M. We stay at Ketten bri. MS has located steel beams, at last. Later to DLRG for *Fasching* party, where all paint faces and wear funny hats. I wasn't up to it. Talked to the boys and girls as too much game-playing going on with women here.

*10 February*

At Gaustadt until early P.M. Mr. Neckerman of Würzburg, boss of DLRG, came on board in A.M. I could barely meet him and his wife. My cold is still bad. In P.M. Ivan and ? came to help to Ketten bridge and stayed on board. Quiet night. Thick, heavy snow.

*11 February*

Canal iced over one inch. Broke it up in P.M. after barge passed. Pissed off, just doing nothing. Waiting, waiting.

*12 February*

Iced in with one inch. Clearing with motor. Very pissed off as this will mean probably more delay getting to the Danube. No news from Manfred. The lads went to dinner last night, but I want no more fuss, so stayed on board. Kerosene heater working okay for a change.

*13 February*

First—we moved back to DLRG at Gaustadt yesterday afternoon. Now I am truly in prison, as the snow is so thick I cannot walk ashore. I am absolutely dependent on other people—mostly Horst. That goes against the grain. Temps very low, − 20°C. Kerosene heater gave up and has to be pumped every half hour. Local repair useless. In P.M. feeling rotten. Went to Horst's for bath. A bit better. Then to local hall in Bamberg to give slide show. About 120 people turned up some from Schweinfurt—and about 60 paid—so we earned a total of 220 DM for the evening. Show was lackadaisical and audience quiet and bored. I still suffer greatly with chest cough. Tempted to sleep in Horst's house but Krystal's mother, 84, fell, and so I slept on board. Very cold.

*14 February*

Wrote circular letter to all at Bodley Head, AS, RC, re lack of support, but put it very uncomplainingly. I am resigned to about another ten days in Bamberg. Hope it's not all at Gaustadt. At the Ketten bridge at least I can get ashore and to shops, etc. MS ashore to Horst's house to work . . . and Terry getting supplies in. MS is making a bookshelf for the forward cabin and doors for the crew's clothes' lockers. It keeps him off the boat and busy, so I say nothing about priorities.

On 21 February I flew to London, to appear on the Terry Wogan show, in an attempt to raise interest in my efforts in Britain. At first Terry Wogan treated the whole affair as some kind of outlandish joke, but I soon put him right on that score.

I stayed in St. Katharine's Dock for ten days in an apartment kindly provided by the World Trade Centre, and there recovered from my winter illness. I flew back to Bamberg on 3 March. The day after I arrived, Martin told me he'd had a job offered to him as skipper of a charter boat in the West Indies, and that he could give me only a few day's notice before leaving *Outward Leg*. I have never been one to stand in the way of anyone else's advancement, social, economic or moral, so I replied that he could feel free to leave anytime he wished. Three days later he left the boat. The same day I received the message that I had to, if *Outward Leg* was going to be hauled to the Danube, do it on 20 March. We would have to haul out of water on 16 March. Not a day sooner, not a day later. Terry, Horst and a couple of other friends helped to get the boat ready. We put on board wooden beams in case the metal beams were not suitable, and we braced ourselves for the coming test. The cold now was slightly less; the ice on the Main and in the Rhine–Main–Donau Kanal was very slowly thinning. It was now 10 March. All I could do was pray that it would melt by 15 March.

But it didn't, and there was no sign that it would do so soon. We had just eight days to get everything ready and break seventy-nine cm of ice for forty miles, or I would be forced to give up and sail to the Mediterranean via Gibraltar, and carry on the eight thousand miles through the Black Sea and up the Danube, so I could *hobble* the autobahn from Regensburg to Rittmeyer's office, as I had sworn I would if this attempt failed.

# Part Two
## *Through*

The minimum depth [of the river Danube] between Passau and Vienna is four feet, when the river is low, excepting at Fischermeat rapids, where it is three feet . . .

The Iron Gates, six miles below Orsova, are nearly one mile in length, and are so named, not from the surrounding heights, which here slope gradually to the river, but from the number of submerged rocks in the waterway . . .

The general width of River Danube between Vienna and the Iron Gates is from 2,000 feet to 6,000 feet when the river is low, and from seven miles to thirty miles when the river is high . . .

The mean velocity of the current from Vienna to the Iron Gates is from two to three knots, but in the narrow defiles it attains a rate of eight knots at high flood . . .

*The Black Sea Pilot, 1969*
British Hydrographic Department,
Ministry of Defence.

*Her Britannic Majesty's Principal Secretary of State for Foreign and Commonwealth Affairs requests and requires in the Name of Her Majesty all those whom it may concern to allow the bearer to pass freely without let or hindrance, and to afford the bearer such assistance and protection as may be necessary.*

Note on the inside of the front cover of
British Passport No. C 158972D, issued at
the British Consulate, Vienna, 15 April 1985

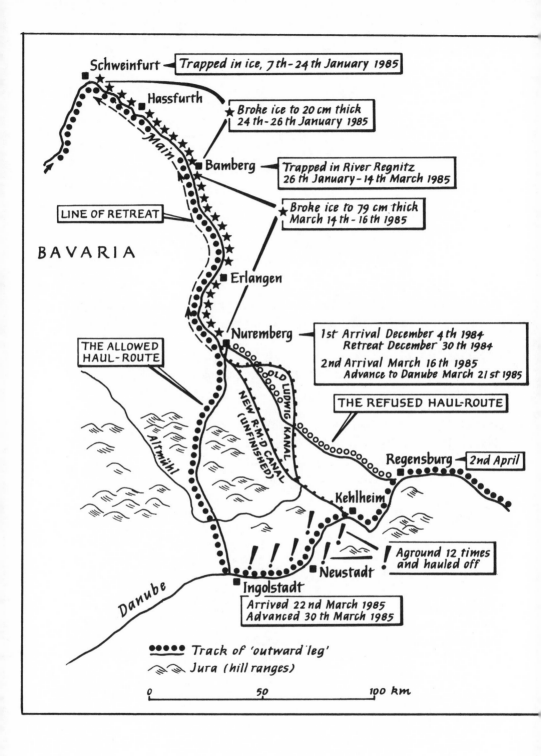

Schweinfurt ← Trapped in ice, 7th – 24th January 1985

Hassfurth

Broke ice to 20 cm thick
24th – 26th January 1985

Main

Bamberg ← Trapped in River Regnitz
26th January – 14th March 1985

LINE OF RETREAT

Broke ice to 79 cm thick
March 14th – 16th 1985

BAVARIA

Erlangen

Nuremberg ← 1st Arrival December 4th 1984
Retreat December 30th 1984

2nd Arrival March 16th 1985
Advance to Danube March 21st 1985

THE ALLOWED
HAUL-ROUTE

OLD LUDWIG KANAL

NEW R·M·D CANAL
(UNFINISHED)

THE REFUSED HAUL-ROUTE

Altmühl

Regensburg ← 2nd April

Kehlheim

Aground 12 times
and hauled off

Neustadt

Danube

Ingolstadt

Arrived 22nd March 1985
Advanced 30th March 1985

●●●●● Track of 'outward leg'

Jura (hill ranges)

0          50          100 km

# 10

# Out of the Trap and Over the Gap

In the three days that followed, I trained a scratch crew in methods of icebreaking and mooring the boat properly. Now the only remaining member of the original crew, Terry, wanted to go home to New York. I couldn't blame him, but asked him to see *Outward Leg* at least to Nürnberg Docks, if we could reach them. As his air passage home to New York was contingent on that, he stayed with us.

It looked to the world that the main reason for Terry's disheartenment was the rumor, half true, that the Danube was now freezing too, and icing up. But I put it down to spring fever, when a young man's heart quite rightly turns to pastures new. But I'll give it to Terry; while he was still with us he did his best to aid the cause of *Outward Leg*. Perhaps the real reason he lost heart was that Martin had left the boat, and Martin was the reputed "expert," the "technical" man of the expedition and this had been true to a degree. After having lived in the close confines of a sailboat with one of those paragons of "know-how," who would not be shaken when he disappeared? I told Terry that there were probably a million yachts afloat in the world right at that moment that were managing, somehow, to get along without engineering experts on board, and if they could do it, so could we.

"Yes, but they're not stuck on one side of a mountain range with iced rivers on both sides of it for six hundred miles, no certainty that the boat can be supported properly on the truck, and with a hell of a risk that the truck might slither on the icy roads anyway . . ."

"And," I finished for him, "an obstinate old bastard who won't take no for an answer . . ."

91

"Oh, you'll manage, Tristan, but without me from Nürnberg. I just don't want to be associated with a failure, and the risks of it are too great."

So that was that, and in that lay his failure, understandable enough, to see that the only real failures are those that occur inside us, like the failure of faith in oneself, or hope in one's dream.

By 14 January it was obvious that the cold was not going to relent during the next two days. We had to be at Nürnberg by the sixteenth. With Horst and a couple of other, younger acquaintances, whose names escape me, on board, we set off for Erlangen. My four-person crew broke ice with long, iron-tipped poles before each bow, with one man standing by as relief, making hot drinks in the galley, all the way to Erlangen, twenty-eight miles. On the face of the bald words, that seems a tame thing, a normal thing, an everyday activity. The reality was that as we rose in altitude with each lock we passed through, so the ice thickened, until by the time we reached Forch-heim, halfway from Bamberg to Nürnberg, it was thirty-one inches thick, a solid mass from one side of the RMD Kanal to the other, with big ships frozen solid in it, all the way.

Our method was for the three men on deck, one on each of the three bows, to run aft as far as they could on the icy decks, thus bringing up the bows an inch or so and making them rise slightly over the splintered ice ahead; then the men would run forward while I shoved the engine into top revs and we smashed the ice with the rocking boat's hull, from Forchheim to Erlangen. There the steel beams for lifting the boat were loaded on board by a very surprised crane driver alongside an electric power station.

All the time, as we passed slowly, yard by frozen yard, toward Nürnberg Docks, people *walked and skated and slid onto the ice* to cheer encouragement as *Outward Leg* smashed her way through for fourteen of the hardest miles I ever saw an ocean craft make, anywhere.

All day long we progressed, and as news of *Outward Leg*'s temerity was reported on the local radio stations, so long lines of cars made their way through the snow to the canal banks; the people in them waved and cheered us through their car windows. Some even alighted from their cars to wave gloved hands at us. We fell into our bunks at Erlangen and slept, cold. Next day we were up before false dawn glimmered in the frozen silver morn.

By the time we reached Gebersdorf Yacht Basin we had fought

eight hours to bash our way from Erlangen Power Station, a matter of six miles. It was almost dusk. Frau Beigler, faithful as ever to *Outward Leg*, waved us on. The ice ahead was thick. Frozen barges lay all along the banks, their idle crews waving us on and cheering. We had tried being towed by cars sent by the DLRG, but had failed. The tow ropes, of two-inch nylon, snapped like cotton threads and endangered the heads of anyone standing within a hundred yards of the break. I recalled my old rule for craft under way with her own powers in any dangerous circumstances—"When in Danger or in Doubt, Nothing Outside the Boat If You Can Possibly Avoid It."

The last mile to Nürnberg Docks was the slowest of all. Progress was down to about one hundred yards to the hour, and as quickly as we broke the steaming ice ahead of our smashed bows, so it froze up again astern of us. From the shore, it must have looked as though we had been frozen in the river for weeks. All night long, in the eerie yellow glare from the dock floodlights, we labored away, and for twenty-nine hours I stayed glued to the engine controls, breathing frost and shoving Yannie ahead and stern, I guess, more than a hundred times an hour. The scratch crew, by now ice veterans, took turns off every fifteen minutes, to go below into the warmer galley, to thaw out their fingers and feet. So it went on, all night, and the air temperature dropped to − 30°C. All night long, despite the killing cold, cars wound their dangerous ways to the canal banks, and shone their headlights on us. Their occupants cheered us on in thin voices skinned by the freezing fog. Horst broke off at 2 A.M. to drive a train to Frankfurt!

We tied up at nine o'clock in the morning of 16 January, just two hours before *Outward Leg* was due to be hauled out and sat on the snowy ground, to conform with the icy-hard decree of the Bavarian autobahn authority. They thought they had issued a greater challenge to me than I had to them, but they were wrong.

By now *Outward Leg* was a legendary heroine in southern Bavaria, and indeed throughout the rest of West Germany. The Germans, with plenty of bitter experience, know a fighter when they see one and knew that *Outward Leg* was such. They crowded over our tired heads, as we helped the dock riggers to fix the steel beams in place under each wing deck—the beams weighed about two tons apiece; as heavy as the boat herself, but somehow we fixed them in place.

As the crane took the weight of the beams, and the boat with them, and as she started to rise just an inch out of the icy water, so

I clambered onto the vertical ladder up the dock wall, and up to the top. A dozen hands reached out to help me, but I waved them away. They stood back while I somehow scrambled up from the icy edge of the dock, onto the support of my walking stick. I heard the crane motor growl, and knew that behind me *Outward Leg* was at last going to be out of danger, if she didn't topple over, for the next four days and nights anyway.

The Germans around were standing back, fascinated as *Outward Leg* rose higher and higher behind me. Their attention was, it seemed, torn between her and me. I expressed what I believed *Outward Leg* was saying to herself as she was being lugged up, up, out of the ice — *"Fuck the Rhine!"* Then I looked round at *Outward Leg*'s battered bows and shattered cooltubes, at her three hulls, scraped and abraded by the cruel daggers of broken ice for thirty-three and a third bloody miles, and knew I'd spoken for her in truth.

The Nürnberg Docks' port captain was introduced to me as the boat swung, now free of the water and ice. "Captain Jones," says he, "that is the toughest ship I have ever seen in thirty-five years working on the rivers of Germany. What you have done, no river ship, of the best German steel, could have done." He spoke good English and he said that, clearly.

I could understand his point. *Outward Leg*, on the surface, looks frail and delicate, but in her heart and in her guts and in her body she is far, far tougher than any man alive. She'd proved it, too.

Back in Schweinfurt, while my attentions had been almost wholly bent on outwitting a seemingly obdurate and omnipotent bureaucracy, others had investigated the problem of supporting *Outward Leg* on the ground and later, on the truck transporter. They had even gone as far as putting the problem to a university computer. It (and they) had come to the calculated conclusion that the matter could be (*a*) very complicated, (*b*) very risky and (*c*) almost impossible without the attendance of certified structural engineers. In other words, the problem, while my attention was elsewhere, had been maneuvered into the never-never fantasy world of the button pushers with their fancy jargon and self-importance-inflating esoterica. Now, as the boat swung on the crane in the ten minutes to spare to find a real-world solution to the problem, I hobbled and slithered fast around the docks and railway sidings close by. No sooner had I clapped eyes on a nearby warehouse and what was sitting just inside its doors than the real-world solution resolved itself. There were about three hundred wooden pallets, the small platforms used for loading shipping containers with cargo by fork-lifts. I commandeered thirty-two of them for six days.

My German had improved by now. Besides half a dozen swear-words I knew about thirty brief terms for shifting gear and securing lines. I used them all. Within a matter of minutes there were four piles of pallets, each eight pallets high, sitting under the crane. In another minute the boat was swung over, lowered so that the wing decks sat on the pallet piles, and there she was, as safe and steady as the Palace of Westminster.

Later, I took great delight in returning, with thanks, a two-inch file of calculations on the stresses and strains involved in lifting and setting down *Outward Leg*, to the university. I had been going to save it for toilet paper, but in trimarans we have to watch weights carried, and this was far too heavy for its usefulness. *Lean and Mean* was our slogan, now.

As soon as the boat was safely sitting on the ground, at 1,650 feet above sea level, in what must be practically the exact center of the European continent (if we calculate distances from all surrounding seas), Terry took his leave. I was sorry to see him go. For a newcomer to voyaging he had shown much promise, and in the dreary weeks of waiting, frozen in the ice, his quiet good cheer and patience had brightened an otherwise gloomy prospect.

In the four days and nights, at all times by electric light, I worked at repairing, as much as I could, the damage to the hulls. The gel coat on all three hulls was abraded all along the six waterlines, and in places the ice daggers and splinters had penetrated the polyester outside membrane and water had penetrated into the polystyrene foam between the two membranes.

For the innocent among us, that means that the sandwich slice on one side was holed, the meat paste was watery, and that made some bits of the sandwich filling soggy and heavy.

The only material I could find to repair the damage was plastic filler for damaged car bodies. The Germans call it *Spackel*, and this I whopped on liberally, after trying to dry out the foam with an electric air blower, under a plastic sheet, with the freezing wind and snow blowing every which way around my frozen ears. The drying out took up two precious days and nights, and the *Spackel*-whopping the rest of the four-day wait for the haul.

As Sam Johnson wrote, "If you are idle, be not solitary; if you are solitary, be not idle." I was alone again, but I was too busy to be lonely or to even think much about it, except when I inspected the forward crew's quarters. Then I knew that the new crew's first important job, whoever he was going to be, would be to have a damned good cleanup. All the effects of the three months' wait by two men in close confinement showed forward.

On the second day in Nürnberg Docks a German yachtsman appeared. He was a local businessman with much cruising experience in the Mediterranean and North seas. His name was Peter Steinhausen and he was another of those angels that God keeps in special reserve, to come to the aid of stranded voyagers. Peter took me and *Outward Leg* under his capacious wing and set to, helping us in his time off from business.

On the third day he telephoned his friend, a well-known single hander, Wolfgang Quix. "I know just the chap for you," Peter told me. "He's been helping Wolfgang build his new boat. I'll tell Wolfgang to send him along as soon as he can spare him."

"Wolfgang can spare him now, Peter. We're hauling tomorrow night," I told him.

The prospective new hand turned up at mid-forenoon next day, Friday the twenty-first. I was busy knocking odd jagged pieces off the ruined cooltubes on the keel. Suddenly, through the howling wind, I heard a voice. It was a young voice, very German, very solemn, very formal, very polite, very steady.

*"Guten Tag,"* it said. *"Mein Name ist Thomas Ettenhuber."*

"Morning," I replied flatly. I'm never at my friendliest before noon and there had been dozens of idle curiosity seekers hanging about.

"I have been senden by Volfgank Kviux," it stated.

I crawled out from under the hull and into the gently falling snow. At first, as I stared at the apparition before me, I thought that some kind of joke was being played on me. He was small, slight, obviously very young, and wore huge spectacles. But what surprised me most was his hair. It sprang out of his head like a hedgehog's quills, and was deep *red*. But when necessity is the first consideration, you don't look at the way people appear, you listen to their words.

*"Volfgank* said you vant me to vork for you."

"Yes, I need a hand," I replied, doubtfully.

"Vot can I do?" He looked flustered and nervous.

That was it. I had a crewman, and *Outward Leg* had a new Man Friday. I had not heard those words on *Outward Leg* for weeks. They might have been spoken, but if they were I had not heard them.

"Go up and clean the galley—*der kuchen.*" I made a rubbing gesture with my hands. "*Und machen der tee* while you're at it." I made as if I were drinking a cup of tea.

The apparition bent his slight frame stiffly and picked up his haversack and bedroll. He turned to do as he was bid, staring round for the ladder as he did so, confused.

"*Und* get your bloody hair cut as soon as you can!"

He turned round and at first frowned. I made cutting signs with my fingers and ran my grubby hands over my frozen head. Then he understood and burst out laughing. It was the first laughter I had heard from a crew near *Outward Leg* in weeks, and I knew that with it we would beat river Danube and anything else that stood in our way to the sea. I was also aware, but only half aware at that time, that I now had an asset almost priceless to the Danube voyager. Now I could, through Thomas, speak the language most readily understood on all parts of the river where any foreign languages were known. Now I was no longer half dumb before non–English-speaking strangers. Now the mental age of our communication could be much older than in the recent past. Now, perhaps, I could know how the vast majority of people we met might think, or at least might speak with us. Now, through Thomas, I could speak and understand the language of the Danube for, make no mistake, that language is German, despite all the superficial contrary evidence from the Austro-Czech frontier onward. As he clambered lightly up the ladder I noticed Thomas's litheness of movement, and *Outward Leg* seemed to purr as his footsteps above sounded below the wing decks. Later I found that Thomas was not only a good dinghy sailor, but also an expert skier, very strong for his size, and loyal to the last corpuscle in his German bloodstream. Thomas Ettenhuber was an ocean sailor before he even stepped foot on board any ocean yacht.

After the fight up the Rhine waters and through the ice, the actual haul of *Outward Leg* from Nürnberg Docks to the Bundeswehr base three miles downstream from Ingolstadt on the Danube, was anticlimactic. It was as straightforward and simple as I had always claimed it would be in the three months that I had been battering down the gates of the German autobahn authority. It was as safe for other traffic, too, as I had always said it could be. The only real hazard was to *Outward Leg* in case, in the icy road conditions, the truck should slither and she be thrown off onto the concrete road. But with a good, careful driver from VRS Haulage Company, there was no untoward incident. Put simply, we laid the two big timber balks from Bamberg across the low-loader bed, piled the wooden pallets from Nürnberg Docks atop them, and lowered our boat on top of the lot. Then, supported by her keel and under four points below her wing decks, close to the main hull, she sat very well and bounced not at all, thanks to careful, smooth truck driving. She traveled as light and as smooth as a feather.

The Nürnberg police escorted us, for free, from their city to Hallenburg, halfway to Ingolstadt. There fog descended thick and heavy, and made driving with our load impossible, so we lay by until the fog cleared, which it did at freezing dawn on the twenty-first. The Ingolstadt police escort was late in arriving: in fact they did not arrive at all. They informed our driver by radio that the fog was too thick still. So we pushed on with, I thought, un-Germanic but very Bavarian *élan*, without a police escort, and arrived at the Bundeswehr base at midmorning.

The complete staff of officers at the base, it seemed, were waiting to greet us. They were under the charge of a large and courteous colonel, looking stern but very smart in his gray uniform greatcoat. I alighted from Manfred Peter's car, in which I had followed *Outward Leg*, anxiously watching her every sway for ninety-four miles. The colonel saluted and shook my hand. Then he stared up at *Outward Leg*. I thanked God mentally that Thomas's head was now shorn.

Then I stared down at the Danube waters twenty feet below my feet. In the Bundeswehr basin the waters were still. I could see mudbanks peeping above the surface across much of the haven. Then my eyes wandered over past the basin exit. There was a seething mass of moving water, relentlessly flowing past into the distance. Much of its surface was frothing white. I must have turned even paler than I already was.

The colonel looked down from his inspection of *Outward Leg* high and dry on her truck. "You say your draft is four feet three and your maximum speed is seven knots?" he asked peremptorily.

I nodded my head. He spoke the best English I'd heard from a German.

The colonel smiled. Then he said, "Turn round and go home, my friend. Forget about heading down the Danube. Look . . ." He pointed his chin in the direction of the gleaming white, sinister, linear maelstrom beyond the basin.

I gestured up at our boat, battered and bedraggled above us. The colonel turned to look at her with me. *Outward Leg*, to me, was listening very carefully.

"Colonel, she is our home," I told him, "and *her* home is the sea." I turned around again to point my walking stick at the raging river before us in the distance, "And the sea's *down there*."

The colonel laughed and clapped my shoulder. "We'll do our best," he murmured to me. "But we can't promise she'll get through."

I looked up again at *Outward Leg*. Her ensign and flags, American, British and Welsh, hung stiff as boards from their staffs; they were frozen solid to the wefts. Over all her life rails and spars, rigging wires and halyards, tied shipshape on her decks, hoarfrost gleamed and glistened. Suddenly she looked as if she had fallen off some gigantic Christmas tree, yet she looked as proud and expectant as a world champion boxer between rounds of some hellish slogging match.

Minutes later *Outward Leg* was hauled up off the truck on her steel beams, and steadily lowered down into the waters of the Danube. I had suspected the result; she promptly sat down on a mud shelf with an inch less water over it than she needed. There was nowhere else to lower her—all the rest was sloping banks and roughage by the river's edge. Everyone around, all the officers, all the soldiers, the truck driver, the press cortege, even Thomas, stared down as if surprised, as if fascinated that a vessel with a four-foot-three-inch draft would not float in four foot two inches of muddy water. There was complete silence.

I turned to the colonel alongside me. I said to him "Well, your bloody Kriegsmarine sank me three times, but I'm buggered if I thought your Army would ever put me aground!"

The colonel jerked around as if he couldn't believe his ears. Then he burst out laughing so much that his buttons almost burst off his greatcoat. The tension broke; the frozen bubble of morbid silence burst, and soon everyone in the Bundeswehr base was laughing and was now on *Outward Leg*'s side—it seemed, to the bitter end.

Let audacity be the voyager's watchword.

# 11

# *Docks, Rocks, Stocks, Old Jocks and Shocks*

We soon realized why *Outward Leg* was sitting on the basin bottom; she was over two tons overweight with the steel girders still strapped underneath her wing decks. In the excitement of lowering the first oceangoing craft ever into the upper Danube, everyone's attention had been on the strangeness of the sight, which was understandable enough. In minutes I had scrambled down the steep dockside ladder and swung myself over onto our vessel. Now that the waters of the Danube were bubbling around her I seemed to have the strength of ten men and the agility of a capuchin monkey. Down after me descended a gang of big, heavy, beer-and-sausage-fed Bavarians, and Thomas. Before I could say *Schweinsbraten mit gedunsteten Waldpilzen* (one of my favorite Bavarian dishes) the two girders had been released. Even then our boat still did not float. She sat there, like a child who's had its fingers rapped, sulkily. Thomas stared at me through his spectacles. His face and clothes were covered in grease and dirt from the lugging gear. His expression said, "What do we do now, Captain?" Only a German seems to use a title of respect when he looks at you wordlessly.

"The sooner this gang of fat buggers gets topside again," I told him, "the sooner she'll float. They weigh as much as the girders." Not understanding my words, but my gesture up the ladder, the Nürnberg heavy mob clambered ponderously, one after the other, in their enormous hobnailed boots, off the boat and up the ladder. No sooner had the last one eased his weight over the side than *Outward Leg*, like the proverbial cork, bobbed up suddenly and floated. Only just: I could feel her keel now and again touch the rocky bottom, but she floated enough to move.

I went below and showed Thomas how to prime the engine's cooling water system. It was done in a minute. Then I pushed the starter button and faithful little Yannie burst into life. That was after not running for five days in freezing temperatures.

I shoved the engine astern, ordered Thomas to let go of the lines drooping from the troops' fists, and slowly backed *Outward Leg* out (made a stern board, sailors say) of the basin. Little by little she pushed, stern first, through the calm, placid still waters of the basin, toward the exit. I told Thomas to ready the anchors—both of them. No sooner had we reached the exit from the basin than some monstrous *thing* grabbed *Outward Leg*, as if she were a child's toy boat, and flung her, beam on, downstream onto the nearest gravel bank, which she hit with with a shock. We knew this was the upper Danube all right, and that his current was a vicious, violent, unforgiving torrent. He had grabbed our boat all around, on every part of her three hulls, like some titanic octopus embracing her fiercely—I had physically felt it, with all his strong, slimy tendrils—and simply shied her at the nearest thing that could harm her, or stop her progress. It all happened so quickly that there was not enough time for Thomas to drop one anchor, let alone two. We were knocked sideways and grounded in less than five seconds.

Recovering from the shock of the first encounter with the Danube (it brought to mind being bodily flung into a cold bath), I tried every way we could manage to work *Outward Leg* off the gravel bank with the engine and the anchors set out into the raging torrent. Here Thomas first showed his utter disdain for danger, and demonstrated again how very deceptive anyone's appearance can be. He was, he showed, one gutsy little bugger. In the plunging dinghy, amid the white waters, he heaved the heavy anchors down and *up again* three times, both of them, before the German Army launch roared out to pass us some three-inch towing lines. The soldiers wanted to tow us off bows first, but I knew this would be useless, and persuaded them, eventually, yelling into the wind, to tow our port quarter upstream. We had hit the bank starboard bow on, and so we must get off in the diametrically opposite direction.

Once *Outward Leg* was free of the gravel bank, it was obvious that not even gallant little Yannie could deal with this torrent. Even flat out we could not move forward an inch against the current. Ingolstadt was three miles upstream. We had to reach there so as to plan the awful struggle downstream forty and more miles to Regensburg, from whence the river was supposedly comparatively tamed, all the way to Vienna and farther.

The German Army heavy launch with its three-hundred-horse-power engine, after the tow lines had been maneuvered laboriously to our bows, heaved *Outward Leg* all the way to Ingolstadt, with her engine at full power, in *three hours*. That was a total average speed over the ground of 0.9 knots.

As we followed meekly astern the German launch, with the three-inch hawsers straining and creaking, I wished we had been able to lower *Outward Leg* into the Danube at Ingolstadt itself, so that I would not have had to see the difficulties we would in time have to overcome. Later I was to thank God I had seen them. The unmarked channel was narrow—narrower in some parts than the boat was wide; at times the outrigger hull bottoms scraped on gravel either side of the main hull. The current, in these narrow stretches, was a swift-moving flow of smooth brown water, looking like an immense gleaming airport people-mover, only it was pushing against us at more than seventeen knots at times, and even in the wider channels it never dropped to below ten knots. I don't think I spoke one word to Thomas in all the three hours it took to reach Ingolstadt. I was too busy countering the vicious current eddies on the rudder, and on intently registering, and recording in my mind, every mark, every *remarkable* thing that would aid us to stay in the channels when we later headed downstream. I didn't merely record them in my memory; I engraved them as in acid in the deepest lockers of my head, one by one, hundreds of them, and glanced astern time after time after time, so that I would recall the angles of view on the way downstream. Each bush, each tree, each fence, each angle of each house, each telephone pole, was etched in my memory, and still is. When your life depends on what you must remember, your memory soon sharpens. I was so intent on our course and on its reverse consequences, that I completely forgot the cold, and reached Ingolstadt with dead fingers and foot. I managed to prevent frostbite by a matter of minutes; my fingers were already medium blue when I doffed my fingerless mittens.

The last stretch of channel downstream from Ingolstadt passes under a rail bridge. There the river narrows to about one hundred feet, and the channel to around twenty-eight feet. Deep chocolate-brown water cascades through the channel under the bridge supports at no less than twenty knots. Even with the German Army three-hundred-horsepower engine as well as our own Yannie heaving *Outward Leg*, she was for several moments brought to a complete halt under the bridge. It was only by crabbing sideways, so that the port ama scraped over a (fortunately) smooth rock, that we found slower water, running at a mere eighteen knots, and inched our way forward.

Then, soldiers being what they are, the German Army waved us a cheery *au revoir* and ordered us to cast off their hawsers. The current swept us back downstream for about a third of a mile from the town landing, stern first, in a matter of a minute or so. I only just managed to crab *Outward Leg* stern first, at engine full revs ahead, into a soft mud stretch of the bank. Immediately we touched, Thomas jumped ashore with a bowline and wrapped it several times around a stout tree on the bank. Then our boat was safe for the time being and I could look around us.

The first thing that struck my eye was a kilometer signpost on the bank just by our mooring tree. It read, laconically I thought, "2457." I did a quick mental calculation: "2457 divided by 1.8 equals 1365." There were one thousand three hundred and sixty-five miles of river Danube ahead of *Outward Leg* between Ingolstadt and the Black Sea. I looked at the hurrying river waters beside our boat. It was starting to snow again. Through the flurries I could see that the river hereabouts was only a hundred feet wide. I knew, from what I had read in the *Pilot Book* for the Black Sea (including the Danube) that at parts, much lower down, it was up to *thirty miles* wide at flood. I tried to imagine where all the water to fill the thirty-mile-wide stretch comes from, and my mind boggled. I turned to more mundane things. "Now we'll clean up our boat," I said quietly to Thomas, who had been staring at the river too, thinking his own thoughts.

As I said before, *Lean and Mean* was now our motto in *Outward Leg*. The first thing to be hauled out of her and dumped were the cabin carpets. They stank to high heaven with the reek of muck from the passing of hundreds of winter shoes worn by visitors over the past three months. Next out were the new library shelves in the forward cabin. If we had shelves for them we'd collect books, and books are weight. All the useful books on board, Shakespeare, the *Oxford Book of English Verse*, the *Admiralty Pilot* books for the Black Sea, Eastern

Mediterranean, Red Sea, Indian Ocean and Malacca Strait, already had their stowages in the after cabin, where they belonged. So did the Yanmar instructions book for engine maintenance, along with a dozen other instruction and specifications books. Anyone forward could borrow them at anytime. Bookshelves forward, high in the boat, in a multihull, were, to me, signs of incorrect priorities. Besides, to fit them, the previous crew had dismounted all my favorite pictures, which were now despoiled by damp. The pictures were cleaned and put back into place. Then the new doors on the clothes cupboards forward were dismounted and cast aside, before the meager clothes in them too were despoiled by airless damp.

In place of the carpets, Thomas fitted some very hard-wearing blue plastic "lino," the kind used in heavy-foot-traffic areas in airports and shopping malls ashore. It was a tenth the weight of the carpets and ten times as easy to keep clean.

We found in Nürnberg that the main bilge-pump diaphragm had been wrecked by ice expanding in it all winter. Getting a replacement American bilge-pump diaphragm in this part of Europe was hopeless. It would take weeks to be delivered, via customs, from the States. Instead, it was cheaper to buy a whole new pump. This was installed, in a position where I could pump it from the bottom of the after cabin companionway ladder. It was placed under a locker lid, so that if the pump went wrong, or had to be maintained, the whole thing could be removed lock, stock and barrel, and worked on easily, instead of being poked away in a cramped corner, as it was before. Bilge pumps in a boat, to me, are far more important than library shelves or cupboard doors.

All the while, in the week of waiting in Ingolstadt, Thomas, besides cleaning and drying out every corner, every niche, in our boat, familiarized himself with every pipe, every wire, every rope line, every block, and every rigging turnbuckle; the latter were lying, seized up and unpreserved, in a watery bilge in the engine compartment. It was, in the circumstances, a spring-cleaning to make up what seemed like a century of neglect. Mostly, that had been caused by my fault; over the three months in the ice trap I had kept my sights on things far away from the engine-room bilge and the turnbuckles. That's where a good first mate on any such expedition was a must. He can keep his eye on the vessel while the skipper's are on the cloud tops. To try to do both at the same time would dilute the single-

mindedness, the clarity of vision of the whole scene, and the imag-
inatory sparks, which are necessary if a skipper is to overcome almost
unassailable obstacles. But for both the skipper and the first mate to
ignore the ground or the vessel under their feet is dangerous. It will
mean, sooner or later, that there will be no vessel under the feet of
anyone, and the voyage will fail.

As our boat was gradually becoming her old self again, leaner and
meaner with each and every hour, so I took stock of our situation.
All the bills for the hauling over the Nürnberg Gap had now been
paid. They came to a matter of $4000.00 total. This included the hire
of two large cranes, the truck, the provision of timber and the labor
of a dozen workmen in Nürnberg Docks and en route. It did not
include the coat of maintaining the boat warm and dry, and feeding
myself and two crewmen for three months in the trap, nor did it take
into account all the money spent on expensive telephone calls and
transport where it had been vital. Fortunately we had been greatly
aided by friends known and unknown in the towns we had visited,
but the total cost to me personally had been well over $5000.00. A
small fund had been raised from local contributions in Germany. This
had amounted to $300.00 or so, and helped our food bill a great deal.
For the rest, I worked my ass off, as the saying goes, day in and day
out, even in the throes of a severe attack of bronchitis, to earn our
way and lay aside enough to cover the cost of the haul. I had appealed
in several directions for help (for the first time in my life, money-
wise) and had been answered from only two sources. One was a short-
term loan from the World Trade Centre, to get us over the severest
stretch of the winter, while I waited for income due to be paid, and
the other was an outright donation of $2000.00 from a source, which,
as agreed by them, shall be nameless. Suffice it to say that the source
was not British, American or German.

Most of the work I had slaved at during a hard time was wasted.
Someone else in London, who shall also be nameless, had agreed to
handle a magazine-article syndication for me. For one reason or another, he failed to do that without telling me until it was too late to
swiftly repair the loss of income. Now, in Ingolstadt, with three hundred
miles of Danube ahead of me, and another fifty thousand miles beyond
that to complete *Outward Leg*'s circumnavigation of the world east-
about, I had exactly $420.00 in hand, and a debt of over $1000 to

repay the loan to the World Trade Centre for medical treatment in Amsterdam.

The obvious aim for me was to get somewhere, and fast, where the cost of living would be lower than in West Germany. That somewhere was, I knew full well, Hungary. Once in that country I could take my time descending the Danube, and let my future income steadily catch up with me, enough at least to help me reach the Mediterranean, and perhaps even Singapore.

Besides resources, the next item on any voyager's mind must be weather patterns, especially if he's in a sailing craft. What had happened to *Outward Leg*'s intended itinerary is a prime example of how one unforeseen delay can cause much longer delays farther down the track. Because I'd been hospitalized in Amsterdam we had reached the headwaters of the Rhine two weeks late. Otherwise, even taking into account Rittmeyer's obduracy, we might just have made it over the Nürnberg Gap in time to descend the Danube before deep winter overtook us, at least as far as Hungary. There we could have waited out the deep-freeze in a comparatively inexpensive land, and left as soon as the worst of the Hungarian winter was over, usually in mid-February, so as to reach the Mediterranean in March. My original plan, then, had been to head for Suez and so to the southern end of the Red Sea by the end of April 1985.

As no doubt you all know, the monsoon winds in the Indian Ocean change from northeast (contrary for *Outward Leg*) in April. Then they blow from the southwest, a fair, though often strong, wind for Singapore, which I had hoped to reach by June 1985.

Now, with an ice-damaged hull and wrecked cooltubes I would have to refit somewhere before I tackled the Red Sea. That meant money for the refit, besides time. That meant, with $420.00 in hand and a debt of $1000.00, that before I could even think of refitting I would have to first earn our own way ahead, in fuel and food, then repay the debt, then prepare for the refit. That, in turn, meant that any hope of reaching the Indian Ocean in 1985 was futile. The two-week delay in Amsterdam had now multiplied itself into a one-year delay.

It had to do with the "Markov chain," which is about events. All we voyagers know the chain, I'm sure, but for nonvoyagers I'll give the definition: "A usually discrete stochastic process in which the probabilities of occurrence of various future states depend only on the present state of the system or on the immediate preceding state and not on the path by which the present state was achieved."

*We* were now in another trap. It was up to us to get ourselves out of it. We couldn't go back; we couldn't stay put, either. We could go forward only with great hazard. It was Hobson's choice. So forward it had to be.

But there's always a bright side to any set of circumstances, if we look closely enough for it. Our circumstances, time, money and weather-wise, told us that now we could take our time descending the Danube. To any voyager with an exploratory instinct, this was pure gold. The only way to beat delay is to lie back and enjoy it.

In the midst of all our hard work cleaning up *Outward Leg* the Deutsche Marine Kameradschaftsbund, the Ingolstadt German Naval Old Comrades Association, invited me, alone, to visit their clubhouse. They quite obviously did not want Thomas along. He was a young German, and they would, it seemed, have had nothing in common with him. They even told me so. But I insisted that Thomas accompany me; I would need an interpreter. Fortunately, they had no one who could speak English, even as well as Thomas, and so he was grudging-ly allowed along. The clubhouse was in a smart, modern building miles away from any water that I could see. The membership were all ex-Kriegsmarine men, mainly, they claimed, veterans from U-boats in the Second World War. They were mostly thick-set, heavy-jowled old men in their sixties and seventies. Most of them ostentatiously wore their wartime medals, kept brightly and lovingly polished, on their best suits. I wore my New York leg, old corduroys and my hat, with its badge, sixteen years old with all weathers showing.

For the first part of the meal the talk was innocuous. We discussed mainly the differences in everyday life, ashore and afloat "below decks" in the Royal Navy and in the Kriegsmarine. It was, at first, interesting, and, to some degree, even funny. But then, as these old men swigged their beer a few of them became boastful and arrogant. They named names and dates of ships which their skulking craft had sunk in their days of easy pickings. To Thomas, as he interpreted every one of the old men's hurtful words to me, it was evidently only a list of names, and dates, all faraway, but to me it brought back memories, in a rush, of young men's screams in freezing water, and many of them my friends, some my enemies, then. By the time the meal was finished I'd had enough.

There was a momentary silence as the old men's eyes inspected mine. I tried to display in my own eyes not one glimmer of emotion as I told them, through Thomas, who later assured me he had interpreted every word of mine faithfully; "I think that old men who clank around wearing medals and glorifying past wars are really only glorifying their own youths. It's an excuse to boast of the prowess they felt when they were young. The real way to glorify youth is to teach it how bloody futile and wrong war is, and how stupid we were ever to have been involved in it, and while we cannot apologize to the youngsters for having been concerned in war, we should beg their forgiveness for ever having let it happen."

That did it; as soon as Thomas, deadpan, had enunciated my words in German, there was a sudden shock in the air around the table. Then a downcasting of old, hard, cold-blue eyes for a moment or two, then frosty glitters from them, one pair to the other, all around the table. As one man they stood, and silently showed me to their door, gravely polite. I rammed my hat on, presented their secretary with our erstwhile library shelf, as memento of *Outward Leg*'s passage through their town, where they had probably imagined themselves so fondly and for so many years remote from the conscience of the sea, and marched out, with my head held high. For once my leg stump didn't twinge with pain at each step.

"Zey bin angry," murmured Thomas as we lugged ourselves back to the boat. He was having problems with the good old English plural of good old Saxon "be."

"Serve 'em right," said I. Thomas didn't understand me. I clarified what I meant, and he nodded his head, at last comprehending. "They can show their copies of *Mein Kampf* on the bookshelf." Thomas laughed at that.

In the lexicon of voyagers, the rule is "Never shoot the crocodile's mother until you've crossed the river." In Nürnberg, at Christmas, I had been silent before the diatribe of the Gauleiter of Gebersdorf, when he'd said before my crew "It was a pity the Kriegsmarine had not sunk you four times." I had not crossed my Rubicon then. Now, in Ingolstadt, I had, and there was no way of retreat, and so nothing to lose; nothing they could deprive me of, except the possible help of the present-day German Army, and that, along with much of the rest of young Germany, was already on my side. So I had let these ancient fanfarondos have it, with both barrels, in true Royal Navy Lower-Deck style, and felt much the better for it. Swiftly, *Outward Leg* and I were casting over the side the burdensome memories of the past three gloomy months, and girding our loins for the coming fray with Old Father Danube.

When we got back on board we hoisted up the Bavarian standard, a burgee of blue and white, for Thomas, to be worn along with the Old Glory ensign, the Red Duster for the British Merchant Navy and the Red Dragon for the Celts. Then we were ready for the river Danube, and for anything it might hurl at us.

# 12

# *Death Trap*

Perhaps because of my fulminating with the Deutsche Marine Kameradschaftsbund the Bürgermeister of Ingolstadt's reception of the
captain and crew of the first ever ocean vessel to visit his fair city
took place, not, as previously arranged, at his parlor in the great city
Rathaus, but outside a *Wurst*-and-coffee kiosk in the main square in
the pouring rain.

Neither Thomas nor I minded in the least. For one thing we were
grubby from days of dirty work on board our boat and our oilskin coats
covered with muck; for another, rain meant that the river height would
rise enough to ease our forthcoming dash out of the Ingolstadt trap.
Myself, I was content enough: to have told those old buggers what
I thought of their bragging of the killing of my comrades, I would
have eaten shit in a sewer.

As we munched on soggy *Wurst* sandwiches with the Bürgermeister, an inoffensive little chap who acted his role admirably, I
kept one eye on the sky, and on the water dripping from the Rathaus
roof nearly. I must have had a silly grin on my mug as more and yet
more black clouds rolled into the Danube valley from the south.

Thomas was, and still is, in German an assiduously accurate and
prompt interpreter. As we all, the Bürgermeister, his henchmen,
Thomas and I, sat in silence, I piped up, muttering "I hope this
bloody lot holds out, I like it." Thomas repeated this small-weather
talk to the officials, word for word. The Bürgermeister looked surprised, then said, through Thomas: "You like *Wurst*, Captain Jones?"
Formal lot, the Jerries.

I perked up. "Love it." I replied. Actually I couldn't stand the

111

stuff, but it was one of the few German food-words I could remember.

"Have one more," offered the Bürgermeister. "The stall is closing in five minutes. Have a *Blutwurst* sandwich."

"No, thanks. We've just eaten before we came ashore." It was untrue, but I just didn't want to accept his offer in these circumstances.

"But the sausage you are eating is not *Blutwurst*," he insisted.

"I didn't think it was," I replied.

"But Thomas said you like blood—a lot of blood."

"Oh Christ," I thought. "Oh suffering Jesus." I smiled my decline and made up my mind to teach Thomas not to be so goddam Teutonic as soon as I could.

The Deutsche Marine Kameradschaftsbund are not all like the braggarts of Ingolstadt by any means. Most of them were friendly but cool, while one or two were very helpful indeed. They had arranged a ladder for me to climb the icy riverbank, provided by the local fire brigade. They also called on *Outward Leg* each morning, rain or snow, to shop for daily supplies for us in their cars. They gave me a sticker from their club to set on my cabin bulkhead. It's still there in our boat as I write, but only for them, in gratitude.

During the week we had been preparing *Outward Leg* for the coming hazards, Manfred Peter had been organizing help for us, mainly from the DLRG at Bamberg on the Main, and had arranged the attendance at our departure of various assorted media representatives. I tried to stop him, on the telephone. I protested that our departure, hazardous in the extreme, would be in danger of becoming a circus. The last thing any skipper wants when he's heading out into a fifteen-knot current, contrary or fair, is a gang of amateurs, no matter how well disposed and willing, to clutter up the proceedings. Besides, there was a world of difference between the calm, placid river Main and the raging upper Danube.

But as Manfred told me (and to a degree he was right), I had been helped by many Germans and I owed the German public the right to know how we made out. And so I acceded to his plans. As I turned away from speaking to him on the telephone, I stared again at the horrific sight of millions of tons of shallow water ramming its way through the thirty-feet gap under the Ingolstadt railway bridge, and thought of the hazardous channel farther downstream.

The rain did not persist—instead it turned to snow and plunging temperatures again froze everything ashore from the high Alps to the Mediterranean. Again the river level dropped, and again we were faced with the prospects of a forty-mile smash-and-grab in waters only just deep enough for *Outward Leg*'s keel. We lightened our boat and sent the unloaded gear—two hundred charts, sails, cordage, booms —ahead, courtesy of one of the more human Deutsche Marine Kamerads. This raised our boat's hull about half an inch out of the water. That was, it turned out, a vital half inch. I had set 29 March as departure day.

One of the great disadvantages of leaving in a vessel with a lot of invited people in attendance is that you cannot leave at the best moment. You have to wait around, watching your advantages diminish or disappear, while the arrival of people is coordinated.

As we lightened our boat I told Thomas about the voyager's philosophy of lean and mean. "Get down to the narrowest margin possible. Involve the fewest people possible. Start when it suits *you* and move when it suits *you*, and take no notice of blandishments from the shore." But all the while I was instructing him (explaining the English as I did so) I myself was in the very circumstances I was warning him against.

We had moved about half a ton of gear off the boat on the day before we sailed and sent it ahead to Kelheim, where comparative safety lay.

"Do you think that's enough weight off her?" asked Thomas.

"I don't know." (Sign of a realistic skipper, when he can say that.)

"What if it isn't?"

"Then we'll keep unloading her as we need to, until she's light enough to float again, and pass over the shallowest gravel banks."

"How much can we take off her?"

"Well, let's see, there's the guardrails, the mast, the boom gallows, the anchors, the books, the bedding, clothes, food, the stove, the engine . . ."

"The engine?"

"Yes, Thomas, we'll take the bloody deck off if we have to. Our boat's getting out of here and out of Germany to where we can afford to wait, even if we've got to drag her on the shore and knock her bloody keel off!"

"Then I to the truck will take the kerosene spare, huh?"

"Ja, okay, *schön, aber schnell*, Thomas!"

On the morning of the twenty-ninth, at the set hour of departure, nine o'clock, no one was in sight but a few idlers on the bank. Fog had slowed down and even stopped traffic over the Jura range. As I told Thomas, "It's not the best-laid plans of mice and men that go agley; it's silly buggers not taking the vagaries of weather into account."

But by 10 A.M. people were beginning to turn up in cars and vans; the paparazzi in yellow TV trucks, the DLRG in yellow rescue trucks, their members in yellow oilskins, and onlookers by the dozen, soon to be hundreds. It all looked to me like the start of a Roman coliseum show, and as Thomas and I shortened our mooring lines to two (there had been six) I taught him the words to his first English song, "Where's that Tiger?" Out of the corner of my eye I caught sight of the DLRG squad unloading not *two* rubber rescue boats from their vans, but *four*. Various yellow-jacketed men rambled around holding portable radio sets, looking most important and efficient. Some of them, while they were being observed, even spoke into the radios, and held them to their ears to hear the replies, real or not.

One lady, bless her, brought us breakfast: *Wurst* sandwiches and coffee. It brought to mind the feeding of condemned men before a hanging. Someone on the riverbank was lugging a huge two-speaker radio, which blared hard-rock music. "Tell him to pipe that bastard down," I told Thomas. "We'll have enough hard rocks today."

My plan had been simple enough. I'd already laid out an anchor over *Outward Leg*'s port quarter. (She was lying facing upstream.) Ahead, from our bow, she was secured to our mooring tree with a long, stout line. I planned for our bowline to be *eased off* as the engine ran ahead, and with the wheel turned out into the stream. The current would, as it streamed past the rudder, steer our boat out slowly into the stream. Then, when our boat was far away from the bank to clear all hazards as she turned, the bowline would be steadily and quickly brought around the port side to the starboard quarter and eased out at the same time from the shore, so that in no time our boat would be anchored from the stern facing downstream, and held also by the former bowline which was now a stern line. Then, and only then, the anchor would be weighed, while the stern line on the tree took *Outward Leg*'s weight, and the engine steered her, in place, against the current, so holding her out from the bank. Then the stern line could be let go, and with engine ticking over in gear for steerage way, we could aim ourselves at the narrow, thirty-feet-wide gap below the railway bridge with the raging waters of half the lower Alps rushing through it.

Bear in mind that the railway bridge was a mere three hundred yards downstream, the gap under it only thirty feet wide, and the current through it at least *twenty knots*. It was all rather like maneuvering round, tail to head, a great lumbering war elephant, then firing a rocket to charge it down a steep mountain slope littered with boulders, to aim it through an enemy archway only a foot or two wider and higher than the elephant itself.

A German Army rubber dinghy turned up, with a thirty-six-horsepower engine. It was having trouble remaining inflated, and soon retired from the fray. That was the first untoward occurrence. Next, one of the DLRG boats, instead of holding off in the river current, insisted on coming alongside our starboard side just as we cast off our port stern line and eased off our long bowline. By now the operation was in full swing. In a strong current you are either moving or not, and once you start there's no stopping. I yelled at the DLRG craft to shove off. I was worried that when we turned around our boat might swing against the bank, and so crush it on the rocks, and probably kill the people in it, or severely injure them. They were having trouble starting their engine again, it seemed. By now (only split seconds are passing) my attention was on Peter Steinhausen and Horst Besler, handling our stern anchor line, Thomas at our bowline, and ashore a group of volunteers all tripping over each other to ease off our bowline from the bankside tree; also on the river current and on our distance from the shore. Without looking at the DLRG craft I shouted to Thomas to cast it off, away from the danger of clinging to *Outward Leg*'s side. Thomas, true to the last, immediately did cast off the DLRG craft. It went shooting off, out of control, but comparatively safely, downstream. Things happened so fast in the next few seconds that it is difficult for me to sort out what came next. I know that instead of easing off our bowline, the volunteers let it go. I know that at the same time Peter Steinhausen and Horst, seeing the situation, hauled mightily and miraculously on our anchor rode and brought our Bruce anchor, with a clang, on board as *Outward Leg* was swept over it by the current (try that one for size) and I know that Thomas gathered not only his wits but also our erstwhile bowline onto our foredeck. My eyes were riveted to the current and the distance of *Outward Leg* from the rocky river's edge. We were still facing upstream and, with our engine in gear, full ahead, *Outward Leg* was being swept stern first toward the railway bridge, slowly but surely to destruction on the bridge pillars.

I shoved the wheel hard to port and the current caught our rudder. *Outward Leg* swung round in her own length faster than it takes to say it. As soon as that rushing torrent got under *Outward Leg*'s wing decks and heaved on all three hulls, 117 feet of waterline, she ripped around. Even though she swept round as fast as an eye could blink, the current grabbed her, shoved her sideways on an eddy and thrust her, at a good fifteen knots, straight onto the nearest gravel bank. She hit with a crunch that shook all the teeth I have or that I've ever had. It all happened so fast that Peter and Horst were still on our stern deck, Thomas yet on our bow, and the DLRG craft . . . I yelled to Thomas. There was no sign of it. He rushed to our port side, and yelled something in German. Then, even as he yelled, two bodies shot up in the air out of the river on our port side, along with various bits of rescue gear from their boat. Fortunately, and *Gott mit uns*, the bodies were still alive and uninjured, it turned out. The two men, both very large, scrambled on board *Outward Leg*, which was listing well to port, being shoved sideways and over by the torrent. They were both in a state of shock. Everyone else looked bewildered, to say the least. Thomas gaped at me through water-spattered spectacles.

I yelled at the two survivors, as they shakily stood dripping on our port ama. *"Stay there."* I gestured with both arms so that they could not mistake my meaning, and Thomas told them what I meant. The men stood, with faces and hands pale and shaking with cold and fright, at attention.

I shook myself sternly. "Thomas," I ordered in as grave and authoritative a voice as I could muster over the noise of our engine and of the hundreds of people yelling on the shore, "Thomas, *go below and make a pot of tea.*"

In times of near-panic and shock, a return to the familiar will generally bring order out of chaos. The first thing I'd ever asked Thomas to do was to make tea, back in Nürnberg Docks, one minute after he joined *Outward Leg*. That would be familiar enough to him. "And don't forget the extra spoonful for the pot!"

"*Jawohl, mein Kapitan*," he replied, and dashed down our galley companionway, as Horst, Peter (who understood English very well, and who was telling the others what was happening) and the two DLRG men gazed at me in utter amazement. I decided to rub it in.

"And Thomas, put some music on the tape player; we need cheering up." All the while our boat's hull was pounding and pressing with a crunching noise on the loose gravel of the shoal. By this time I had weighed up that she was on a projecting corner of a shoal, and it wouldn't take much to lift her off.

Now Thomas was in the after cabin, standing by the tape player. His voice rose from aft, as I studied the situation around *Outward Leg*.

"What music, *Kapitan?*"

"The bagpipes, of course!" I turned to look down the hatch. Thomas was looking up into the daylight, perplexed. "Bagpipes," I repeated, "you know . . ." I made as if to squeeze with my arms and wailed, in a squeaky moan. My attention was elsewhere, as well it might be then with the boat teetering on the edge of a shoal in a fifteen-knot current.

Thomas's face lit up in enlightenment. "*Oh, ja, der Dudelsack*," he yelled: a minute later the strains of Donald McPherson playing "Lochaber Gathering" was blaring at full blast over the roaring Danube torrent.

After three or four minutes of studying the situation and gathering our wits, tea was ready. I handed a steaming cup each to our two freezing survivors. They made as if to come into the cockpit, but I waved them away. Manfred and Peter looked at me as though I were a heartless monster, but my motive was very clear to all a minute or two later, when tea was finished.

I waved the two huge DLRG men, still shaking, over toward the starboard side of *Outward Leg*, toward another DLRG craft that had arrived alongside to pick them up off our boat. The moment they moved their heavy, soggy bodies off over to our starboard side, which was up in the air, thirteen feet from the center-line of *Outward Leg* (and foot-poundage being one of the irrevocable Laws of Nature), *Outward Leg* tipped ever so slightly to starboard; her keel freed itself of the gravel bank, and she shot off downstream, her captain and crew committed to do or die, now or never, her ensigns and banners stiff in the breeze, her bagpipes bellowing the MacGregor reel out over all Ingolstadt. Off she shot, in a perfect *avalanche* of $H_2O$, at anything from eighteen to twenty-one knots, straight toward what, by any sober voyager's judgment, is a potential deathtrap.

# 13

## Gorgeous Gorges

I don't remember what I thought about as *Outward Leg* was rushed
headlong toward that Nemesis of a gap under the Ingolstadt railway
bridge. I could tell you that I remembered situations somewhat sim-
iliar. Such as when I'd navigated little *Sea Dart* down the roaring
Parana river, out of the hellish Matto Grosso over ten years before;
or when I'd seen an iceberg capsize over *Cresswell* in the arctic years
before that. I could say that through my mind's eye went visions from
the dozens of storms I've survived out in the ocean, or of the score
of other times when I was close to death. I could, I suppose, if I were
not me, say that all the good things in my life, the poetry, the music,
the good and wonderful people I have known, passed before my
memory's vision. I could say I thought of England, home and beauty.
But I didn't. The only clear thought I remember having, as I steered
the boat against the will of that awful current toward the center of
the gap, was *"Christ, I hope I don't shit myself!"*

I do remember, quite clearly, what I looked for, what I watched.
There had been one particular rivet on the bridge which I had seen
when we had been towed up to Ingolstadt a week before by the
German Army. It was directly above the very middle of the narrow
gap—as narrow as a country lane—under the bridge. There were
hundreds, perhaps thousands of rivets in the bridge structure, but
this one was different. It was of a darker hue than the rest, and it
had a streak of rust redder than all the others, running down from it,
like old, spilled blood. People might scoff at this, but when your life
depends on it you can recall the difference between one hair on a
human head and all the rest. So it was with that rivet. That rivet is

all I saw as *Outward Leg*, in as many seconds as it takes to tell you, was hurled downstream. That rivet was as much through my eyes as it was through the bridge girder. I saw no crowds of onlookers on the banks of the Danube; no television cameras, no cars, no weak sunshine, no capsized DLRG craft bobbing along ahead of us, no Horst, or Peter or Thomas on board *Outward Leg* gaping at what *Outward Leg* was rushing toward. I saw only that bloody rivet and aimed straight at the bastard. *When in danger or in doubt, sight the bugger and heft a clout!*

I remember what I heard, too, very well. It was the quiet gurgle of deceptive father Danube as he shoved us pell-mell to, it seemed, certain destruction, the purr of Yannie down below under my feet, and, above everything the highland bagpipes of Mr. McPherson rending the air with his rendering of "Lament for the Old Sword." If ever there was fit music to die to, this was it; glorious, heartbreaking, as Gaelic as a dashed hope, as Celtic as a broken dream.

Then we were under the bridge, riding a mass of broken, swollen liquid that seemed more like rusty blood than water. In a flash the bridge swooped darkly over us. The starboard ama scraped the top of the well-remembered rock, daylight broke asunder the momentary darkness over our heads, and we were out, free, and in a wider channel, now all of forty feet wide. The relief on board our boat was so deep that if my hand could have left the wheel for a second I could have touched it, fondled it, felt it and loved it. As it was, all I could do was try to ignore the sweat freezing under my three jerseys.

There was no stopping in this kind of current. All I could do was try to control the boat's distance away from the threatening rocks on the riverbanks and guide the direction her bows were pointing in the midst of that seething, boiling, irrepressible mass of moving water. The whole riverbed of the upper Danube is gravel, with now and again, to make matters more interesting, smooth but solid rocks sticking up through. Because it is gravel the navigation-channel bed is continually shifting, from one month to the next in high summer when the weather is fine and dry, and from one day to the next at any other time of the year. The Bundeswehr captain had told me earlier, "The channel cannot be marked in any way. It cannot be controlled or restricted with any method known to us, and even if we dug a new bed away from the old one it would still be the same, for the whole district is pure gravel for meters under the earth. We cannot even construct a canal; there's nothing solid to build it on. The best we can do with it is play around in it, like boys building sandcastles. We reinforce the banks one day, and the river washes our work away the next. This stretch of the Danube valley is the bottom of the old sea which existed here before the river forced its way through the Kelheim Gap.''

That had given me food for thought, as I'd picked a piece of gravel from the river's edge. It was small, round and shiny, no bigger than a man's fingernail. Yet it had defeated all man's ingenuity for centuries, and even now was defeating one of the most efficient nations.

Now, downstream from the bridge, the DLRG showed its mettle but, through no fault of its own, to little purpose. Four of their boats had been lugged from the river Main. They were all inflatable rubber launches, with outboard engines, each around twenty-five horsepower. Each boat had four men in it, except the one that had capsized; that, I believe, had a crew of two, but with their sizes you could have said four. In the departing debacle another of the four DLRG craft had lost engine power. That one was drifting helplessly ahead of us in the fast current, two of its occupants waving to us while the two others vainly tried to restart their drowned motor. These I steered for, carefully, and as we passed them with our engine gear in neutral, at about twelve knots, Thomas heaved them a line. In a flash they were slapped by the current alongside *Outward Leg*. Then we passed them a dry sparkplug.

All the time this was going on the two surviving DLRG craft were motoring about 550 yards ahead of *Outward Leg*, sounding with long poles as they went, toward each side of the river. At a momentary glimpse, just as a still photograph, the scene would have seemed one of placid endeavor; but the whole platform on which the scene was being enacted was moving through the surrounding countryside at about an average of fifteen knots and that's around twenty land miles an hour. It was also moving, like time and destiny, over a bed with unknown depths. Like a blind man in unfamiliar places, we had to poke and prod with our poles to feel our way forward while the river pushed us on inexorably, regardless of what was in our way.

It is impossible to sound with poles on a gravel bed from a rubber dinghy moving at over five knots. It defies all the known rules of hydrographic surveying. It cannot be done with poles, nor with line-leads. It can hardly be done with common echo sounders with any degree of accuracy. In that strong current the waters were shifting the gravel all the time, over and over, like a load of groundnuts in a washing machine. There was no way they could tell what was gravel, underwater, and what was not. I said nothing then, because these people had been asked to come to help, and they had willingly done so; but their labor, and it was heavy, cold, wet labor, and dangerous, was futile. They were courageous people with all the best hearts in the world, but they were wasting their time.

It boils down to a rule in the voyager's manual: *"In hazardous situations, the risks of disaster increase in direct proportion to the number of people present."* This automatically means that if people's presence is essential, then the number of people to deal with any hazard should be kept to the absolute minimum. That is the talisman of the solo-sailor.

The upper Danube has a very German character. Amid all the shifting gravel there are rocks, and bloody hard rocks. One of these we hit while my electronic sounder, which looks slightly ahead, registered five feet. We were making hardly anything with the engine, about ten knots with the current. A few more pieces of our poor old cooltubes went floating slowly astern, or seemed to, and *Outward Leg* staggered on.

As the river widened, which he did from time to time, from an average of two hundred yards width to three hundred or so, so the depth of water shallowed. In most parts the gravel banks took up much of the riverbed. All around were green fields, with cows browsing in the rain, neat farmhouses and dripping trees. On a nearby road, cars and trucks roared by, uncaring. To anyone passing through the area, even yards from the river, there could have been only a scene of rural winter peace, and no clue to the drama unfolding only a short distance away, no idea that there were men fighting for the life of a full-size ocean sailing craft.

The small town of Neustadt is fifteen miles downstream from Ingolstadt. Before we reached it we were shoved aground on gravel banks four times. On the bare face of the words this seems perhaps innocuous. But to experience it, to hear the roar, as loud as an express steam train rushing through a station, of the gravel on our hull as our boat hit at fifteen or so knots, and to listen, sick at heart, as the cruel gravel tried to skin her alive, and the mighty bully of a current smashed her rudder sideways like an abandoned child's toy, out of my hands with spiteful force, and to wonder how the devil we were ever going to get her off again against this bastard of a torrent of water, was a thing of sagas.

The first time, as *Outward Leg* lay at ten degrees over, with her port ama being rammed farther and farther into a shoal of greedy gravel, we ran the anchor line ashore and, after trying to tow her off with her own winches, her line secured to a stout tree, wound up dragging her bodily over and through the gravel with a big tractor, crabwise downstream, into the deeper water on the far side of the river.

This was a less shallow bank, and small fry compared to the next three. There, in our attempts to drag her clear, we broke three of our stoutest warps, all of two-inch nylon. The twang, as the tractor took the strain, jerkily moved forward, and as the lines stretched and snapped, is still in my ears. How the deck cleats stood these strains is explained in simple words. They were British-made of honest Birmingham stainless steel, courtesy of Brookes and Adams. Anything else would have, I expect, broken like pieces of dry cake, under such sadistic forces. Of course, all the while that the hawsers were in use and ready to haul, anyone standing nearby was warned away. They had to move. We would not take "no" for an answer. If they hadn't—if we had not forced them to move with threats, sometimes, of chucking them in the river if they didn't, they would probably have been decapitated, as the hawser's broken fangs whipped back.

Off Neustadt the Danube flows over a very shallow shoal and pours himself under a bridge. This was, for us, the worst of our obstacles. We hit the shoal at ten knots, even with the engine grinding astern at full revs, and with our bower anchor cast over the stern to slow us down. Then the current ground us farther and farther into the roaring gravel. If there had been no help for us, and if our boat could have stood the abrading of her skin for so long, we could have let the current shove her through the loose-gravel bank, slowly and inevitably. But on the downstream side of the bank, right beside the railway bridge support, there was a bloody great rock sticking out right in *Outward Leg*'s way exactly where she would end up when the shoving, heaving current had finally rammed her through the bank.

Dusk was falling by the time we had tried all our strength and failed to budge her away from the grasping grind of the gravel. Over and away from *Outward Leg* the scene was one of fluvial splendor. The sun dropped to the west, over the trees, and cast candescence over the river and seemingly from below the surface of the waters.

But below our hulls the grip of the gravel tightened inexorably as the current shoved us little by little, yard by yard, straight toward the rock under the bridge, only five yards downstream from us. The rock waited like a hangman on his scaffold, huge and black, gleaming in the wan light of the sunset.

The Bundeswehr was swift to answer my urgent message: "Dear colonel, I need you to help me get home, and fast. We have approximately one hour to save *Outward Leg*. We need to tow her against a fifteen-knot current, stern first."

Within twenty minutes a three-hundred-horsepower launch had been hauled by truck to the river's edge, launched, and in half an hour it was dragging *Outward Leg* bodily out of her trap. Within an hour we were safely shoved up onto a mudbank by the mouth of a little stream that runs thereabouts into the Danube. There, Thomas and Horst ate soggy *Wurst* sandwiches and fell into sleeping postures, whether they could sleep or not. Peter wearily left for his home in Nürnberg.

The captain commanding the Bundeswehr tug was not at all sure that *Outward Leg* would make it from Neustadt downstream to Kelheim. "I am accustomed to handling only bridge sections," he explained, "and those are towed mainly upstream, to cross rivers, and draw very little water, maybe an inch or two. I have no experience, nor does anyone else with me, of towing a deep-keeled craft downstream in this swift current. Ahead of you," the good captain told me in a deep, sonorous voice, "there are gravel banks for nineteen miles. Nowhere, that I know of, is the river deeper right now than five feet. Beyond the gravel banks is the Kelheim defile, where the river narrows to nothing, and the current averages twelve miles an hour." The captain was smartly uniformed, obviously efficient and businesslike, and spoke excellent English. I put his age at about thirty. He struck me as being the kind of man it is best to be friendly with, for as an enemy he would be quick, ruthless and victorious, even if he died being so.

"Now," he continued, "it's Saturday. You've broken into our quiet weekend rest. We're going back to base and we'll return on Monday at nine o'clock, *hein?*"

"*Hein*," I replied. What else could I say? You don't argue with a

Bundeswehr captain when he's speaking from his own deck.

Then the Army launch roared off in a cloud of exhaust fumes back upstream, and I collapsed onto my berth. "We're getting there," I told myself.

The following day the local newspaper hound was on board smartly at about 7 A.M. He was flustered and excited. To me he looked as if he would be more at home in a *Bierkeller*. He wore a black raincoat and beret, a red face and two icy eyes. He also wore a look of voracious hunger for sensation.

"Now you are stopped, and the Danube has delayed you . . ." he commenced to chortle in a strident voice.

I glared at him, silently, for a full minute.

"You must rest here until the late spring, when the ice on the Alps will melt." He went on, "How feel you, Herr Jones?"

"Who the hell is he calling Herr?" was my immediate thought, but I blurted out instead, "What do you mean, stopped. What do you mean, *Outward Leg* wait for the bloody Alps?"

"But you *are* stopped here in Neustadt," he maintained. "Stopped by the river . . ."

"Stopped by the river be buggered," I told him. "Don't you know it's Sunday?" (It *was* April Fool's Day.)

The newshawk looked nonplussed.

"Gentlemen never sail on Sundays," I told him. "That's for burglars, prostitutes and policemen." I went back to my tea. Thomas escorted the news-nosy ashore.

Sure enough, it was reported, next day, that the purpose of my voyage down the Rhine was to spread the Good Word on behalf of the British Lord's Day Observance Society.

Monday morning saw the Bundeswehr launch turn up exactly at nine o'clock. I explained the best method of dealing with the descent of *Outward Leg* down the Danube to Einem, where the cliffy defiles force the constrained waters to run so swiftly. They would not tow *Outward Leg* downstream; instead they would lower her down the torrential slide, just like lowering a big hogshead of beer down into a pub cellar. This they agreed to do.

Two of our stoutest warps, of three-inch nylon, were led from each of our ama sterns to the bow of the Bundeswehr launch. Each line was three hundred feet long. Then both boats, ours and theirs, were cast off at the same time into the swift current, and the launch held back while *Outward Leg* gathered speed, the engine at slow ahead.

Then the launch kept her three hundred-horsepower engine in reverse, braking the headlong progress of our boat with the current. Thus we could keep our speed-over-the-ground down to about eight knots. So both boats progressed through the south Bavarian lowlands, all innocent in the morning light, one after the other, both tied together with naval cords so tense that a violin string would seem a soggy thing beside them, and a ship's bobstay a drooping undertaker's hat scarf.

Over the first gravel bar, the offender of Saturday night past, our ship's log states coldly it took the Bundeswehr launch five hours to drag *Outward Leg* three hundred yards. After one hundred yards we were aground again. Another hour of dragging and swiveling our suffering keel through deep gravel. Free again and another grounding three hundred yards farther downstream. And so on, six times more, that afternoon and evening.

At last Einem Gorge came into view: a lovely sight observed in swift glimpses, for I was busy concentrating on the course. I have an impression of looming cliffs and brilliant colors in the sunset all around and above me, and riverside inns at the steep cliff's bottom, already open for tourist trade.

From my view at the wheel of *Outward Leg*, the Einem defile appeared a much softer prospect than that which we had overcome astern, even though there were jagged rocks all around and below our boat and even though the jealous current still gripped our longsuffering rudder with vicious eddies to try to force her onto the murderous cliffs on either side. Our sounder, in the middle of the Einem defile, showed a bottom at 120 feet. The width of the defile at its narrowest was, at a guess, forty yards. The strongest current, again at a guess gained by watching, grimly alarmed, the cliffs slide past quickly, was about twenty knots.

Suddenly, quite suddenly, as I was ruminating on what the whole scene must have looked like to the first caveman ever to penetrate through this dramatic, narrow split in the European continent, we were out and clear. The river widened, there were meadows all around, like a vision of the Elysian fields, and the depth was a good steady, sensible and civilized five feet.

Horst was cock-a-hoop. "We're through. We made it!" he shouted in German as he grabbed my hand. *"Alles gut!"* Einem Gorge was our Open Sesame to southeastern Europe.

"You're through. You made it, Horst. The rest of your ride with us, to Passau, is a piece of cake."

Horst didn't understand what I meant. I patiently got Thomas to explain. Then I said, "But Thomas and I still have another thirteen hundred and twenty miles to go before we're through to the Black Sea."

"Let's hope they're not all like the miles we made today," prayed Thomas, or words to that effect.

"Many of them won't be," I reassured him. "Most of them *won't* be . . ."

"Good," he broke in.

"But a few of them *might* be . . ." I completed my observation. "And some of them *will* be." I'd teach him English if it killed me.

By the time we reached the first lock on the Danube it was late evening. The German Bundeswehr launch, her captain and crew, shared a bottle of white fizzy wine with us, then roared off, hailing us farewell through the darkness over the river. They had worked like Trojans all day, hauling *Outward Leg* this way and that by her stern, so that she would avoid what gravel banks were ahead of her. The group of German friends, dear friends, who had helped *Outward Leg* most in her recent travails, all gathered there to celebrate with us her success in overcoming some of the worst physical obstacles and some of the worst human obstacles that are to be found on the Rhine–Danube track through Europe. There were a good dozen precious friends at Bad Abbach: Manfred Peter, Michael von Tülff and Horst Besler among them. They had been the three outriders of *Outward Leg* across the German Gap, and just as sure as her own three hulls had supported her soul, they had supported her heart and her purpose.

There were others present, too, but when Mars, Jupiter and Saturn are gleaming in the night sky, only the moon can outshine them, and our moonbeams were cast by the heart of *Outward Leg*, brightening all, bathing in light the black night of her skipper's darkened Celtic soul.

Horst returned north with the rest of them to the Main side of the Jura, to collect some odds and ends. Thomas and I returned to our boat. There he turned in, weary. He'd worked valiantly all day. It was the first night in the year when it was not too cold to sit for a while in the cockpit.

I, in the calmness of a windless night, bright and clear with starlight, listened with tears in my eyes to Beethoven's Pastoral Symphony. As the emotions ran over me I communed with the soul of an intently listening *something* all around me. I muffled myself up in my sailing jacket, reclined in the cockpit, grateful to what is beyond the watching stars, until sleep crept up on me and diffused the glare of reality, until there was no longer any distinction between it and the dreaming, so that there was no more pain.

# 14

## *Aspiring Spires*

All the gear that we had taken off our boat at Ingolstadt, to lighten her, we found safe in the lockhouse at Bad Abbach. I, more accustomed to traveling in the Third World, was amazed. Nothing had been borrowed, nothing stolen. Not one item was missing. In the early morning light Thomas and I lugged it all back on board; two hundred charts, sails, standing and running rigging, food stores and fuel for the galley. I silently thanked the best men in the Deutsche Marine Kameradschaftsbund for their help.

Horst was soon back from Bamberg and his family, his big, merry self. I had invited him to accompany *Outward Leg* as far as she would go through the rest of West Germany to Passau, the last town before the Austrian border. There was a problem inherent in Horst's presence on board. Thomas was new to swift-current work on rivers, such as mooring up a boat properly and quickly. That meant he had to undergo a very fast and hard training in single-handedly tying up alongside barges and the shore, before the time when below Passau, he *would* be singlehanded. Thus, no matter how much Horst volunteered, I could not allow him to touch a line or a fender all the time he was with us. This left Horst downcast at times, but I told him that had I been a guest in his boat, or anyone else's boat, I would never dream of handling any of the ship's gear unless I was asked to and it was imperative that Thomas undergo shock training as fast as possible.

Horst had been over-kind to all in *Outward Leg* during our cold spell in Bamberg. He and his wife had probably saved my life when I was sinking fast under bronchitis. So I let him clean up the rigging screws on the way to Passau. If it had been lines and fenders that he had been handling I would hardly have remembered it, but now, each time I look at any one of our rigging screws, I remember Horst, for he saved their lives, too. They had been left rotting all winter in three inches of water, and were seized up solid. It took him three days to free the thirteen screws.

When *Outward Leg* had shot out of Ingolstadt like a rocket from hell with her bagpipes playing, I had noticed—who would not?—that people in "rescue" craft even a quarter of a mile away had turned their heads to stare at us. People on the shore had turned toward us, from far away, as soon as, obviously, they heard the wail and drones of Mr. McPherson. I now realized that on board we had a very efficient continuous siren to use when we maneuvered in tight corners or heavily congested waters. It seems that the bagpipes, being an outdoor instrument, raise a row which is heard far and wide, and are of such sound wavelengths that they cut through any other noise, including heavy traffic and freight trains crossing iron bridges. I have no doubts about this. I have seen people turn their heads and notice us when the local noise-decibel level has been as much as the human ear can bear for even a short time. I have even seen the sound of bagpipes stir rivermen to look around when we have approached their barge (their engines are very noisy) from astern. So it was, to give warning to other shipping, that I decided whenever we left a dock or a lock, or passed round a sharp bend (and remember, the faster the current the sharper the bend), to slip our bagpipe tape into the cassette player and turn the volume up at full blast. We had a fine selection of strathspeys and reels on our tape, the reels for when we were feeling low and the strathspeys to make others feel low. We crept out of the lower end of Bad Abbach lock as the huge gates opened for our passage, to the stirring strains of "Mrs. McDougall," a highland reel. The whir and drone of the pipes rent the air, echoing from the vast vault of Bad Abbach lock over all it seemed of south Bavaria.

Beyond the locks was a long line of river ships, waiting for cargo, by all appearances at the head of the Danube's commercial navigation. There were ships of all the nations which line the Danube: West German, Austrian, Czech, Hungarian, Yugoslav, Rumanian and Bulgarian ensigns—and many, many Soviet blood-red banners.

To my trained sailor's eye it was obvious which of the ships were Soviet. Their arrays of electronic antennae would have been the envy of any naval frigate's skipper.

The current was about two knots and with us on this stretch. I decided, as there were small boats hovering around the long flotilla of river ships which stretched for one or two miles, to leave the bagpipes blaring. Somehow, as we slipped along quietly otherwise, our ensign and banners waving gently in the morning air, they suited the occasion.

As we neared the line of shipping I saw figures on their decks. When we were within a quarter of a mile, every one of the river ships was crowded with people. As we glided closer, with our Mr. McPherson's "Behind the Bushes" blaring away in dizzy highland style, we saw that they were mostly men, but there were quite a few women too, mainly on the Eastern Bloc craft, which had much bigger crews than the Western vessels. Everyone on the river ships, except on the Soviet craft, was cheering and waving madly as *Outward Leg* slid by. Even on some Soviet craft, tucked away out of sight of others, we saw men raise their hands in salute and women shyly smile. Two Hungarian ships dipped their ensigns to ours.

"They've been watching German television," said Thomas.

"And listening to German telephones, too, probably," I observed. "Look at that array of radio antennae on those Soviet ships. Christ, they must be eavesdropping on everything said for five hundred miles round."

"What makes you think that?" asked Horst.

"Well, Horst, since when did a river ship, registered on the lower Danube and obviously never meant to go to sea, need to have radio-direction antennae, and directional antennae, and such bloody great radar-reception dishes? Those things are never for other ships that might be around; they're for aircraft . . ."

It seemed to be true. The Soviets have a huge electronic listening post operating quite openly and legally forty miles or so on the western side of the Iron Curtain, the frontier between West Germany and Czechoslovakia on the western side of Czech Bohemia and open, electronically, to almost ground-level reception from the most sensitive area of Western defense in Germany, the Steigerwald, around Nürnberg. They were doing it, it seemed, quite brazenly, too.

On and on down the line of shipping passed *Outward Leg*, at a steady, easy rate. I tried to imagine what she must have looked like to the cheering crewmen on most of the ships. She was knocked about a bit, no doubt, but clean. Her mast was laid on deck, but her American ensign was raised twelve feet above our stern on a long bamboo pole, and her British and Welsh flags too were a good eight feet above her decks. Her little crewman now looked reasonably shipshape, with a woolly watch cap pulled down around the ears of his shaven head. There was Horst, too, a big, efficient-looking man in his yellow oilskin and Baltic cap, and her skipper, looking probably a bit worse for wear after a hard winter, but satisfied and smug enough, and quietly pleased at the reception these Danube craft were giving to the first ocean vessel they had ever met this high up on their river, if at all.

By noon, with Yannie at only a quarter revs (for the current was now our ally while we were under way), we passed Regensburg town. This was the place which *Outward Leg* had been aiming for when she had so hopefully, but belatedly, shoved her way up the Rhine and the Main the previous year. This was the place to which I would have had to struggle after retreating back to the North Sea, down the English Channel, across the Bay of Biscay, around Gibraltar, through the Mediterranean, Aegean and Black seas, and so up the Danube, to reach Regensburg, to keep my oath to Rittmeyer if the German autobahn authority had not backed down in the face of our demand for rightful passage. That would have been a passage of around 8,500 miles. And then I would have had to *walk* from that jetty, there, the seventy-five miles to Rittmeyer's office in Nürnberg with *Outward Leg*'s kedge anchor on my shoulder, before I could dump it, as I had sworn I would do, on his desk.

Below Regensburg, the Danube is tamed all the way to Vienna. He glides among forests, mountain valleys and farmlands, through some of the most beautiful country I have ever seen in a lifetime of wandering. All the way to Linz, about 150 miles, he is narrow, winding and fairly swift, but well buoyed, so there is little chance of the wary navigator striking the banks. On the upper Danube the general rule for river channels applies for much of the course: *the channel keeps to the longest course of the stream*. It is futile, and even hazardous in these stretches, to try to take shortcuts at long bends or short.

The looks on the faces of the fishermen by the riverbank between Regensburg and Straubing, our port of call that night, were of stark incredulity. Our little Yanmar makes hardly any noise even at full power; at half power none at all can be heard from outside the cockpit, and even from inside it, only if we listen carefully. We would round a bend in all our glory, and a fisherman, meditating on the state of the universe, would look up and see, lo and behold, a life-size ocean trimaran glide by only two feet away from him as he jerked his rod aloft for it to pass.

We secured for the night at Straubing with the anchor light on the guardrails of the starboard ama (shipping runs day and night on the river Danube) and the bower anchor (the Bruce) over the bow as a backup in case the heavy wash from passing barges should break the mooring lines or vandals pay us attention. That was to be our almost invariable routine from now on, all the way to the Black Sea.

The next morning's run took us to Deggendorf. It was a bright, calm journey through superb scenery of wood-clad hills, castles, spires, hamlets, and distant mountains. Horst and Thomas were proud of their castles, while I maintained that they were really only earlier versions of Rittmeyer's office, put there to stop people from passing by on their lawful business without first paying some bribe to the local bully.

In the afternoon *Outward Leg* pressed on downstream to Vilshofen. Now we were in our stride. Thomas was confidently handling the lines and the going was much easier, although the Danube winds more than any other river I have ever navigated. Beside the Danube, the Amazon and Mississippi are as straight as air-landing fields. We whizzed close by miles upon miles of tree-clad banks, mainly birch and elder, guided by regular buoys and shoreside ship-traffic signals.

# 15

# *Inquiring Choirs*

*Outward Leg* remained at Passau for two days. Here we not only would leave West Germany behind, but with it all the little detritus that still remained from the past miserable winter. Every sign of anything or anyone that reminded me of those weeks of struggle was eradicated from our boat. This was to be a new beginning, in new lands.

Thomas painted over the galley and the after cabin, with white gloss, to gain full benefit below of the sunshine peeping between April showers. Then he painted a sign in German pointing out that while we were grateful for the welcome we were receiving, and in our turn welcomed invited visitors on board, our boat was our home and would people please respect our privacy? The clamor of strangers to come on board was greater than I had ever known before, and this was to be the case all the rest of the way down the Danube.

As it was, although in Passau of course we did not know it, an estimated *three thousand* people of six different nationalities, and probably a few hundred of others, passed through the accommodation spaces in *Outward Leg* in the three months of the voyage between Passau and Constanta, in Rumania. Of those three thousand, a good eight hundred were people with one physical handicap or another. This was all the while that we were making our way through 1,240 miles of, for us, unknown, uncharted river, on resources which were, because of the previous winter's magazine-work agency debacle, very slim indeed.

Mainly, we tried to keep the visitors' hours to times when we were not working at maintaining the vessel and her gear, but this was almost always difficult. Quite often Thomas would be hunched over

the engine, doing routine maintenance work, while a crowd of atten-
tive schoolkids squeezed past him, under my shepherding, through
the passageway between my cabin and the forward cabin. Or I would
be writing to my agent or to an editor, while Thomas and a friend
helped some paraplegics to navigate the steep after cabin companionway.

There was no rodomontade about this. I was not showing anyone
what I had, or what I could do. I was showing them what might be
possible: many of them could do it if they chose to make their dreams
come true. That was all that mattered. The demonstration, alive and
kicking, that one person could, if he persisted, defy omnipotent governments, was incidental. That was the icing on our cake.

I was lucky in many ways, in my quest to reach the handicapped
people of the Danube valley. I was helped often by the media. I was
also helped in some ways by the World Trade Centres in Austria,
Hungary and Yugoslavia. In other countries I was assisted unwittingly
by the very governments who were trying to stop my passage, or hold
it up. In some instances I maneuvered the authorities into allowing
*Outward Leg* into areas not visited by a Western craft since the Second
World War. In all instances we kept our independence. In no instance
did we bow before seemingly all-powerful and, later, armed bureaucracy.

At Passau, as we limbered up swiftly for the passage to Vienna
and beyond, we had only an inkling of what was to lie ahead of us.
We were truly innocent, although I had an inchoate idea of Father
Danube's deviousness. There's no paradisical voyage on this earth,
never has been and never will be.

The West German customs authorities in Passau were a model of
efficiency and courtesy. In no time at all we had our passports stamped,
our ship's documents passed in order, and the good wishes of all the
officers who had made a special break from their various duties to
pile on board and wish us well. One of them also brought a bottle of
*schnapps*. This was the first time in thirty-three years of passing through
customs in a small craft that a customs officer ever brought me a drink.
Those officers usually expect the boot to be on the other foot, and
often demand that it should be. This was one for the book, as the
saying goes, and so it is.

In light rain we slid away from the lovely city of Passau, which
seems to hover in mists between three rivers, the *Drei-Flüss-Stadt* as

the German tourist brochures call it. The voyager needs to know that one of those rivers is the river Inn, and that's a biggie and causes the Danube to widen as the waters it brings down from the southern Alps join those of Paár, Isar and Vils, to give old Father Danube more muscle. As the river widened so the steering, for me, became less intense, much more relaxed. The river was anything up to a third of a mile wide now in places, but more often it was about 330 yards. Sometimes it narrowed, and then the current increased to six or even eight knots, especially at sharp bends.

The locks on the upper Danube are *big*. Into them can fit a whole clutch of barges—often a dozen at a time, under the shepherding of one tugboat. These tugboats do not tow the barges; they shove them, by means of two gigantic buffers fitted on their bluff, and often square, bows.

One of the clutches that passed through Jochenstein lock was of Rumanian barges, about eight of them, and they were a curious sight. The barges from Eastern Europe do not have engines, so they cannot propel themselves, unfortunately no doubt for some of their crews, who might otherwise take off on a dark night on their own. I would, with hindsight. All the Eastern Bloc barges have a crew of at least four people, it seems, and at least one of them is always a woman. These, I later learned, do the cooking and washing for the men. The Rumanian and Yugoslav barges, unlike the Bulgarian, Czech and other Easterners, are often rusty and scruffy. But these Rumanian barges, as they passed Jochenstein, seemed to be loaded with green plants all along their decks. It was like watching the hanging gardens of Babylon float by. This puzzled me greatly. I asked the Austrian lock-keeper what the barges were.

He replied through Thomas that President Ceausescu of Rumania had complained at a party meeting about all the space wasted in factory yards on growing flowers; from now only vegetables must be grown, to help feed the nation. What went for factories also went for barges. "But," said the lockkeeper, "each plant on the Rumanian vessels has to be accounted for to the flotilla commissar, and the number of fruit on it carefully noted each day and reported back to Bucharest."

Thus, at the Austrian frontier, we had a foretaste of what lay ahead. But that was a rather sweeter and funnier foretaste of what was to come much later.

Opposite Löwenmühl, just before the Jochenstein lock, immediately inside Austria, 1,400 miles up the Danube from the sea, the Austrian Customs were even more relaxed and friendly than the Germans had been at Passau. Only one young, smartly dressed man was on duty. He did not even bother to look at our passports, but waved at us lackadaisically to pass into his country. "Get them stamped at Vienna," he shouted. "I'm off to lunch!"

There were plenty of onlookers as *Outward Leg* slid past the small towns of Löwenmühl and Kernmühl. The northeastern Austrians were avid watchers of West German television ("because their own is so dull," sniffed Thomas) and they were expecting *Outward Leg* and knew their own versions of her struggle to reach the Danube and the reasons for it. They cheered and waved like crazy people. All the way downstream, all the way to Linz, cars stopped wherever a highway neared the river's edge, people alighted and waved us on, cheering. In many cases even buses stopped and hooted us on our way, and trains whistled long and loud for us more than a score of times as they rushed by, along the tracks on the bottom of the steep Danube valley.

Soon we realized that, mainly through the efforts of Manfred Peter in Nürnberg, we not only had practically the whole of West Germany with us, but half of Austria too and that in those countries *Outward Leg* was a household name. Everywhere, even in the smallest hamlets by the river's edge, people, men, women and kids alike, shouted her name as she passed by, with Mr. McPherson's bagpipes skirling away. It was a triumphal procession such as, I was told by one lockkeeper, had not been seen on the Danube since the days of the Emperor Hadrian.

Everywhere *Outward Leg* put in alongside Austria, people brought us little presents of food, or wine. This was without exception.

The next port of call past the frontier was Obermühl. All these town names ending in *-mühl* recall, of course, the days when they were sites of watermills, worked by the ever-flowing Danube waters. The miles before Obermühl on the Danube, and the vista from the little town-berth itself, struck me as among the most beautiful I had ever seen, rivaling the Hebrides scenery and that of the Chilean leads for pure loveliness and the cleanness of the air. It was raining still, April showers, but the mist around the mountaintops close-by added a poignant beauty to the ever-moving scene before our eyes as we glided downstream at a sedate rate.

Obermühl has some of the loveliest views, I think, that I ever saw from an inhabited place. I was sorrier to leave there than I had been to leave anywhere else on any other river in my life. But there were prospects of earning funds in Vienna, so we made for there, steadily, sliding downstream at about thirty miles a day on average. With a current of around two knots, and the engine merely ticking over for steerage way, that thirty miles took about seven and a half hours to cover, making allowance, too, for delays at locks. These averaged about an hour for each lock.

Our next port of call was the city of Linz. The river widens considerably north of Linz, where the Danube valley opens up into a wide plain. It rained and rained and rained. It rained this side of Linz, it rained that side of Linz, it rained all around Linz and it rained *in* Linz. The run to Linz was another beautiful stretch of mountains overlooking the river, with mists swirling around their peaks, all blue and silver. Now and again, when the weak sun shone through the clouds over the mountain chines or down a declivity to the river, the light changed the leaves on the trees from dark to Kelly green and enhaloed the trees themselves in soft diffusions of limpid opalescence. Then a cloud marched overhead and obtunded the light over the whole mountainside, so that it looked as if it was wishing us good-bye, in a study of retiring opacity, smaller and smaller, astern.

All the way down the Danube we saw plenty of birdlife, mostly ducks, wild and tame, larks, blackbirds, herons in the lonelier places, kingfishers supervising their own manors, and now and again, in the hillier stretches, hawks, magnificent in their haughty hovering.

The city public landings at Linz are at pontoons by the high river wall. There is plenty of water under the pontoons, which are well secured, and also plenty of current. That's one of the problems on the Danube. The towns are usually built where the river runs along the banks at his deepest, and that means where the current is at its strongest. On all the Danube, very rarely is there a town landing on the river where the current is less than three knots. At Linz it is about five knots. Here, and at many other places on the river, we had to keep an eye open, from time to time, for floating detritus, logs, big boxes and old oil cans heading downstream at a fast rate, sometimes straight for *Outward Leg*. Here the best plan for us was simple: we berthed our Dunlop twelve-foot dinghy across our three bows. That fended off the worst of the fallen trees in the now-swelling river.

The tenth of April saw us up and about early, just after a wet dawn, and on our way to Grein, where we berthed at late afternoon. But at Grein it was still raining, so, "in for a penny, in for a pound," we passed on another twelve miles to Ybbs, and berthed again there for the night. Both towns have public landing pontoons, plenty of water beneath them and lots of current. Note, at Abwinden, km 2121, there is a lock, unmarked on any chart or map that I have seen.

These pontoons that we tied to are the property of a private river ferry company, but they were not being used until the summer season, which extends from 1 May until 30 September. During the summer season, while the ferries are operating, there are three things that a small-craft navigator can do to secure a landing berth: the first is, as we did, berth at the pontoon, but be ready, day or night, to shove off and hold off when the ferry is sighted, until it departs; second, find an alternative berth, but this is usually far away from the town or village, and commute in the dinghy to and from the landing. Third, moor on a single bowline from the pontoon, but far enough down-stream from it to miss the pontoon mooring hawsers, thick, greasy things, as the boat yaws with the current eddies passing its rudder. The only secure way to do this would be to set a kedge anchor out astern to hold the boat steady in the current. A bows-to-pontoon mooring would also mean that the boat might be in danger of collision from arriving and departing ferries. It's up to the skipper to decide how much risk he's willing to take. He might also decide to run another after-mooring line from his stern to the shore, so as to hold the boat in toward the bank. But he would be remote from the moor-ing-line securing place, and vulnerable to passing vandals letting it go after bar-closing time. Until the local authorities see fit to construct special pontoons for visiting cruising vessels, it seems to me that the best alternative, in West Germany and Austria at any rate, would be to moor at a nearby local yacht club, although this usually might be miles from the town.

At Ybbs I went ashore for the first time even in Austria. This might illustrate one of the difficulties of handicapped people cruising. It's not the navigation of the vessel at sea or on a river that's the main problem for me and many others; it's navigating our bloody selves when we want to get anywhere ashore. Just getting onto the jetty can be a real pain in the neck as well as in certain other places. At Ybbs it was pouring hard and the night was as black as a Bible, but there was a brightly lit inn sign only a hundred yards from the boat. All I had to do was clamber over a barge between us and the jetty, climb down five feet from the barge onto the jetty, navigate my way over thirty yards of mud and broken concrete, then another seventy yards of slippery cobblestones, and . . . the place was only open for drinks. It was Cook's night off.

Back we went, Thomas and I, through the same obstacle course, to *Outward Leg*, to eat fast-cooked rice and stew on board. Booze and continuous voyaging don't mix.

Next day, a little less rain saw us cheerfully driven by Father Danube down to Tulln, a passage of sixty miles in twelve hours. The current on this stretch varies from nothing just downstream from the locks to three knots just upstream from them. That gives some idea of how much these mighty locks control the old bugger. The average depth in the fairway was fourteen feet, but this varied up to five feet either way, and our river was about one-quarter flood state.

For the rest of the passage to Tulln the river is overlooked by many fine old churches and castles, the most dramatic being at Dürnstein (km 2008). Not only are these old fortifications dramatic, but so was the speed with which we passed them. No sooner had we rounded the bend above the old town than Father Danube grabbed *Outward Leg* and fired her through the next mile in about three minutes. The channel between well-marked gravel banks narrows to about sixty feet and through it cataract half the waters of Central Europe. When our boat shot forward I almost lost my balance from the sudden thrust. I decided to turn her round beyond the narrows, so that Thomas might photograph the castle from downstream. When *Outward Leg* was finally facing upstream the current was such that, with our engine roaring ahead at full pelt, we were being pushed astern at about five knots. I soon got *Outward Leg* turned round again, and back on her delicate balance, between Father Danube's dishonorable intentions and her own virtuous wishes, facing downstream.

The next day saw us, in a half gale coming from upstream and astern of us, driving fast with the current and at full engine power, for Vienna. Word had reached us that the Bürgermeister of Vienna had invited *Outward Leg* to berth right in the city center at the Schwedenplatz, only a quarter of a mile or so from the Opera House.

All the lockkeepers had been warned by the River Police of our approach. All cheered us. We burst into the last lock above Vienna at km 1980 like a scared cat. We couldn't do anything else; even with the engine in neutral the wind was pushing our wide stern ahead at a good five knots, all the way down the lock, about three hundred yards. By this time Thomas was well trained in lock work, and with ultimate skill, as I prayed at the wheel (engine full astern to slow her . . . stop her), he looped his mooring line around the very last floating bollard before the far gates, and brought *Outward Leg*, with a mighty jolt, "up all standing," as yachtsmen say. She stopped dead in her tracks, only five yards from the great steel gates at the end of the lock.

Outside Vienna the City River Police arrived alongside to escort *Outward Leg* into the Donau Kanal which pierces right through the city, missing its very heart by only a third of a mile. Usually only very special vessels, with very special permission, were allowed into the Donau Kanal at Vienna, and we were honored indeed to have the privilege of being the first ocean vessel ever, in all the two-thousand-year history of that great city, to reach her heart.

It was a close-run thing, getting *Outward Leg* to the Schwedenplatz. The current through the Kanal is around six knots, and the channel is no more than about a hundred feet wide. Somehow, at the place indicated by the police launch crew, I managed to turn our boat in that small space and strong current. We hit the east side of the canal a couple of times, and bruised the after end of the port ama, but I thought afterward that the honor we had received was worth a few scratches.

The first message sent to the boat after we tied up in Vienna was from Sepp Schultz, Professor of Art at the university in Vienna. "Would you like to attend a service at which the world-famous Boys' Choir was to sing? Would you consider, in return, perhaps allowing the choir to look over *Outward Leg*?"

I sent back the invitation, to Sepp, with my reply scrawled alongside both inquiries. "Yes" and "Yes, by all means! Any time!"

# 16

## *From the Sublime to the Gorblime*

*Outward Leg*'s berth on the Donau Kanal in Vienna was about fifty yards downstream from the Schwedenbrücke. On all of the seven-mile-long canal as it runs through the city I doubt if there were more than six other craft. These were a couple of tourist-trip flyboats, a police launch and one or two small working dredgers. The canal was about a hundred feet wide at the Schwedenbrücke and the current ran fast even when the Danube was at low water. The rate never was less than five knots while we were in Vienna, and at times reached seven or more.

In the city center the canal ran under roads, then through little parks and high buildings from the last century. The canal sides themselves were quiet and peaceful, but above the high walls lining them on both sides and across the bridge the roar of street traffic was deafening at times, especially at rush hours. Then the clamor of cars and the clanging of streetcars made ordinary conversation on board almost impossible.

The mooring on the Urana Quai was very safe, day and night. There were a few evident human derelicts among the hundreds of strollers who passed us, but even their usually bottle-laden overcoats were darned and patched and their shoes clean. They had about them an air of genteel dissipation, of delicate dereliction, and they carried about with them, it seemed to me, a grander past which, while they might willingly let it slide into oblivion, still had them in its fond grip and would not let them go.

Most of the time I could not understand a word of what the passersby said. With my very basic understanding of German, the

143

Viennese accent is beyond me. But Thomas, with some difficulty, could understand them, and it appeared that they were wishing us well.

In the afternoon the schoolkids passed by, with their haversacks and bicycles. They were a lively, chirpy, bonny lot. Quite a few of them joined our afternoon visiting session, to look over our boat. The Viennese kids were almost the best behaved and politest I have ever come across.

In the evenings we usually went ashore when the rain desisted for a while. Then, when we left or returned to our boat, the quay was mainly the haunt of courting couples. They were everywhere; behind the trees, in dark doorways, hidden on the flyboat pontoons. Often we returned to find a young man and his lady friend in our cockpit, embracing. At first it was disconcerting, but they were harmless to the boat and wanted nothing but to be a little warmer and closer to each other, so we did not object, for who cannot love a lover?

Most of the time, day and night, there were small groups of men, mainly, drinking in dark corners, but these, it seemed, adopted *Outward Leg* and even appeared to guard her from ill. We slept well every night in Vienna.

Sepp Schultz had heard of *Outward Leg* through the World Trade Centre in London, and adopted us for our stay in Vienna. Sepp was a *bon vivant*, as well as a very human being. He showed us the secrets of good food and wine in the hidden *Heurigen* or wine taverns, sometimes huge, around the city, out among the vineyards. He also gave us the key to a studio in the city center where there was a hot shower and peace. For once in a lifetime of voyaging, I was in a civilized city, with my boat moored safely, and I was *clean*.

The ideal berth for a one-legged voyager in a city is near to the center, close to the public transport system, for obvious reasons. But this is almost an impossible attainment in most cities in the world. Except, as we shall see, in the Danube's three capital cities.

With my handicap, once I had found a safe berth, I had to probe ways and means of first getting to the transport system, and then using it. In a few hours I was being whisked around Vienna underground at a vast rate of knots by one of the most clean, efficient and pleasant public-transport systems on earth. First I went with Thomas, to explore the awkward places like steep escalators and steps, and then I was managing all alone; *no* stranger in Vienna ever offered to help me. Not that I wanted them to. Indeed my feelings were quite the reverse, for it was a tremendous triumph for me every time I negotiated, alone, under my own steam, a journey across the city. It was very different when I was in or near our boat, though. Then virtually everyone would, when they saw me awkwardly swinging ashore or aboard, rush to my assistance, while I would stave them off, saying things like "It's all right, I'm practicing for the Olympics. I'm going to jump for Wales!" Then the Viennese would laugh; their sense of humor was much sharper than the German.

I traveled all over Vienna, from the Südbahnhof to the Nordbahnhof and just about everywhere else in between. With Thomas I went to the Prater park and we rode on the Wheel made famous in the film of Graham Greene's *The Third Man*. We went to the Opera, and while we could not afford to attend the show, at least we saw the building, and like good sailors, could imagine the performance. In any case, we had attended a performance of the Vienna Boys' Choir, which had taken my ears as close to heaven as I suppose they'll ever reach, and any opera performance would be flat after that, at least to me. On the Kärntnerstrasse we found a cheap fish-and-chip joint. There we idled away an evening watching the parade of strollers and listening to the street musicians.

Very often Vienna brought to mind, suddenly, New York. There seemed to be a delicatessen on every corner. But there was something missing, and it was several days before I realized what it was. There were no Jews; it was as if ghosts walked the streets, as if every man, woman and child in Vienna had an ethereal *alter ego* walking with them, alongside them, everywhere, but gone, absent forever. Their places can never be filled by the East Indians, who now do much of the street selling. The work is done, but the ghost remains.

*Outward Leg* stayed moored in the heart of Vienna for nineteen days. There was a very practical reason for our delay; I was waiting for some money due for my writing. This was the princely sum of $500.00. After much prodding it was sent to me by a magazine editor. Then, with the $100.00 remaining from the winter, we had $600.00, a small fortune. With this we had to tackle the voyage down the Danube almost 1,240 miles to the Black Sea. There was a slight chance that some more income might be due by the time we reached Belgrade, over 430 miles downstream, but it was slight indeed. The next port of call where we could reasonably expect to collect some money would be, it seemed, Istanbul, and that was about 1,860 miles away. So with our $600.00 we would have to fuel the boat, feed ourselves and pay dues in six countries. There was no alternative but to take a leap in the dark, or outstay our welcome in Vienna, and that no good voyager ever does.

There were two other reasons for the delay in Vienna, though. We had to obtain Czechoslovak and Hungarian visas. With Sepp's help, this we did fairly easily, although it took several days of waiting around in gloomy consulates full of giants and dwarfs and other odd people and guarded by men who looked as if they would be more at home at the doorway of a Soho girlie joint.

The other reason was dear to my heart. *1 May was coming.*

In the days of the Celtic ascendancy in the Danube Basin, long before the Roman, the Teuton, or the Slav arrived, 1 May had been a day of rejoicing for the coming summer. Then the lads and lasses would gambol around the phallic Maypole (and still do on the upper Danube). When the Christian religion took over, 1 May became the feast of St. Joseph the Carpenter. It became identified with the men who worked with their hands. Now that another set of borrowers had taken over, at least on the middle and lower stretches of the river, 1 May was devoted to the commemoration of the brotherhood of workers the world over, including, presumably, ocean deckhands and peripatetic, penurious pen-pushing small-craft skippers.

What better day, then, to enter the Czechoslovak (Soviet) Socialist Republic with a U.S.-registered vessel, wearing the colors of George Washington, Thomas Jefferson and Abraham Lincoln? They were all of part-Celtic descent, all Christians and all, in their time, strugglers for the Rights of Man.

Besides, *Outward Leg* wore, too, the ensign of the British merchant navy, under whose colors so many British workers' fathers had died in the cause of the human dignity of all men. She wore, too, the Welsh Red Dragon, and who is going to lecture Wales on fighting for workers' rights? The Bavarian burgee she wore was her deckhand's, and about all he owned in the world, apart from the clothes he stood in. The bow burgee was from the Royal Naval Sailing Association, and the Royal Navy, the world's oldest fighting force, had lost many thousands of men in its century and more of struggle against the slave trade. That was not counting the men who had died to help free the Soviet homeland of Nazi invaders in the Second World War.

"Besides," I told Thomas, as he listened wide-eyed, "the Czech police's attention will probably be distracted with holiday shenanigans and we can slip quietly through the frontier post of the Czech border, and be through the hundred twenty miles of Czech Danube before they realize what's happening, see?"

Thomas, being methodical and sensible, didn't see, but it sounded good, and so we made it our plan.

The first thing to do was get *Outward Leg* back to the Danube from the Donau Kanal. That might on the surface seem easy, but with a six-knot current tearing through, and the canal too narrow to turn our boat safely, and a west wind usually blowing its head off straight downstream, merely planning the move was a headache in itself. I plotted all ways. Warps and anchors, police launches and even motorcars. I even considered making a stern board (backing her out stern first) all the rest of the four miles of the Donau Kanal, to where it joined the Danube farther downstream from Vienna.

In the last week in April the rains fell, raising the river level and the current to a flood, and the cold wind, straight off the peaks of the Alps, blew snow-dust in our eyes. On 24 April, it even *snowed* for a couple of hours.

By 30 April it looked as if my May Day plan was going to be thwarted by the weather and current. On May Day itself, however, the wind relented for just long enough, very early in the morning, for *Outward Leg* to just barely move ahead against the current the four miles upstream to Nussdorf. It took *five hours*. It was almost noon by the time we rejoined Old Father Danube, who was rolling along now, fortified by a couple of weeks of almost steady rainfall, in fine style. No sooner did I slide *Outward Leg* into his stream than he picked up our boat and hefted her, like a celluloid bath toy, at a good fifteen knots downstream. I slowed down the Yanmar to about a quarter revs, just enough to keep steerageway, and our boat settled down to being hustled by the randy Danube, as he fiddled with her nether parts with his busy fingers, at a speed of about twelve knots, away from Vienna. Down we shot, under all the Vienna Danube bridges, the Schnellbahnbrücke, the Reichsbrücke (flung across by Hitler, collapsed in 1972 and rebuilt exactly like the original), the Praterbrücke, and then we were in the clear and there were no more bridges, but lines of river ships in the Danube port of Vienna. To them, as we were wafted under the bridges by a romantically inclined Father Danube, we played "Lochaber Gathering" and "The Big Spree" on Mr. McPherson's bagpipes, and were cheered and waved at for our pains by passing Austrian, Czech, Bulgarian and Russian ships' crews alike. They all seemed to know us, they seemed to recognize that this was *Outward Leg*, on the move and bugger the begrudgers.

At Donauarm, km 1902, there was a small inlet leading off the Danube. There was situated the main Viennese Yacht Club. As we flashed by, the small craft were, it seems, all still laid up, but the banks and jetties were crowded with people who set up a mighty cheer as *Outward Leg* was rammed past them at a dozen knots by the Danube, and shoved away from them, toward Deutsch Altenburg, "Old German City," and a mile and a quarter below that, Hainburg, the last Austrian town, where lay the customs pontoon for vessels passing the frontier either way, in or out. Hainburg was no more than twenty-four miles from Vienna.

The two customs officers at Hainburg looked as if they would have been more at home as extras in a stage production of *The Student Prince*. When you get to the point of thinking that customs inspectors look positively cuddly, you *know* you're in for trouble. But all the way to Istanbul, that's how I remembered the two elderly gentlemen at Hainburg who charmed us with their good wishes as they stamped our passports in the rain and wished us "Godspeed."

Below Hainburg the riverbanks were scenes of damp, rural peace. Fishermen, sometimes alone, sometimes in groups of a dozen or more, silently sat contemplating the universe and Man's place in it. Here and there a family sat in a car parked by the river's edge and, through the oscillating, wet distortions of their windshield wipers, viewed the river and one vessel passing.

"*One* vessel?" I suddenly realized in consternation that we *were* the only vessel moving on the river. I struck my wet forehead with my wet fist. I stared upstream and downstream at the empty river.

"Christ!" I blurted to Thomas.

"*Was ist los?*"

"It's a holiday . . ."

"Well, of course, that's why you said we'd enter Czechoslovakia today, so they wouldn't notice us."

"But it's also an Austrian holiday, Thomas, and a German holiday, and a Rumanian holiday and a Bulgarian holiday, and we're the only . . . bloody . . . ship . . . moving!"

We knew from the Austrians that this frontier was a hot spot. Several Czechs had been shot by Czech frontier guards and by robot rifles aimed along the narrow paths between minefields in recent weeks. We knew that all along the Iron Curtain thousands of young East Europeans are stationed, armed to the teeth, to guard their countries, not from Western European intrusions so much as to prevent their own countrymen from escaping from a political system which has become, to them, no longer bearable.

As *Outward Leg* approached the Curtain, the Czechs couldn't help but notice us arriving. On the whole river Danube, from Regensburg to the Black Sea, *Outward Leg*, with her American ensign, her British, Welsh and Bavarian flags, was the one and only vessel not tied up, moored, berthed, anchored, or sunk. Then it all fell into place. No wonder all the crews of the river ships in Vienna had cheered like mad; no wonder the yacht-club members at Donauarm had congregated to wave us a rousing farewell; no wonder the reserve staff of retired customs veterans had stamped us cheerfully out of Austria. *Outward Leg* was the only vessel, ship, craft, boat, yacht, or marine vehicle of any kind on the move. She stuck out like a sore thumb. It was too late to return to Austria against this current.

I saw a wide black slash of raped earth right across the tops of the nearing hills, and a high fence that followed it, and knew it was the Iron Curtain, and that we were being thrown at it by the force of half Central Europe's water rushing to the sea, regardless of man's divisions, directly and very quickly toward and through it.

Even as I stared at the slash of black earth over the hills, I sighted a tall tower among the trees by the Czech edge of the river March which joins the Danube at km 1880. I grabbed the binoculars and stared at it through the rain. I wiped the lenses twice, hardly believing my eyes. I stared and stared. Then as I steered I muttered to myself, "God . . . blind . . . my . . . bloody . . . eyes." (Which is what "Gorblime" really means.)

# 17

# *The Bear's Paw*

By now, even the most bovine among us, from the most bucolic places in the West, must know that when we are descending a fast escalator, say in a department store, and have somehow managed to find ourselves facing backward on it, by the time the escalator reaches the bottom of its travel we had better be facing forward, or we'll probably be in for a spill. That's a bit like being on a small craft heading down a fast river. We must start turning to face upstream well before we reach abreast of the place where we intend to stop.

On the Danube, when the current was running at about six knots, this meant that we in *Outward Leg* generally started, as a matter of course, to turn her about a half-mile upstream from her destination. That, I should think, is reasonable enough, logical enough, to satisfy even the most contrary mind among us. Before we go farther that must be clear to all.

Once that inarguable fact is established you will more easily follow what happened in the next two days as *Outward Leg* plunged headlong through the Worker's Paradise of the Czechoslovak Soviet Socialist Republic.

The sight that had shaken my usual imperturbability on board our boat was a stark contrast to what had been the customary peaceful scene farther upstream in Austria and in West Germany. Atop the Czechoslovak tower, painted a light yellowy-green the color of a choleric baby's kaka, were four soldiers, wearing uniforms of the same color. Each one of them was sighting and pointing a machine gun directly at *Outward Leg* and aiming it to follow her progress downstream. Below the tower a line of khaki-clad figures was hurrying

151

toward a low bunker at the base of the tower. Each one of them lugged a rifle.

Momentarily I stared back through the clearing rain at the Austrian side of the frontier. I could clearly see three fishermen on the north bank of the river March, waiting patiently for a bite. On the western bank of the Danube a gypsy family was taking shelter from the drizzle under a wide plastic sheet which had once been red or pink and was now fading to gray. The plastic sheet was suspended on one side from their truck.

I swung my head back to check if I had imagined what I had seen on the Czech side, but no, the soldiers were now all deployed to defend their homeland from the threat descending swiftly upon it; a small ocean yacht containing a one-legged man of sixty and a slight little youngster of twenty wearing spectacles because he was near-sighted.

I decided to send Thomas below, where he would not be topside when we passed the tower. I had no way of telling how he would behave when he finally saw what I had seen. Some youngsters, as I well know, get very nervous or excited when four machine guns and ten Kalashnikovs are pointed at them.

Thomas slid below to put the kettle on for tea. Even as he did so I sighted two small powerboats heading for us at speed. These turned out to be a light gray color, each about eighteen feet in length, each with an inboard engine which must have been very powerful. They made at least ten knots even against Old Father Danube's six. Then, with one eye on the crowded tower, now rapidly sliding past to port, and one eye on the current eddies, strong thereabouts, and one eye on the approaching craft (that's right, it's surprising how many eyes you have, crossing the Iron Curtain), I waited, as *Outward Leg* hurtled forward at a good nine knots, for come-what-may.

Come-what-may turned out to be seven little sailor boys in each speedboat, all wearing green tops on their sailor's hats, and green collars on their uniforms, and not one good shave between the whole lot of them, except for their helmsman, who was pointing a Kalash-nikov rifle straight at me. As they came closer and closer before my disbelieving eyes, I saw that they mostly had cherubic faces, but all wore stern expressions, rather like small boys who have been refused another toffee, but cannot kick up a row because Uncle is visiting.

They glowered at me. One or two nudged their rifles in my direction.

Suddenly, as they slowed down and bobbed alongside, one green-hatted sailor raised his head above the others and shouted. His boat had by now swung right around the stern of ours and was on our starboard side, while the other boat had taken station on our port side. The standing sailor seemed, from his bearing, to be a little farther up the scale between the rest and Mr. Gorbachev. I can't say he was in command; he hardly seemed old enough to be in command of himself. I gawped at this puerile announcer. He repeated his shout and held up two fingers. At first I thought this was a sort of gesture of welcome, like a victory sign, and in reply I, too, held up two fingers, even though I knew that the Solidarity people, whose signal this was, were hundreds of miles away, north of us in Poland.

The leader of this crew of armed adolescents immediately closed his fist and shook it at me. I threw out my hands, to signal that I didn't understand what he wanted. The motorboat engines were making a very loud roar all the while. The lad, who reminded me of a chorister we had seen singing a high falsetto with the Boys' Choir back in Vienna, lugged his Kalashnikov to shoulder level and aimed it directly at me. Even as he did this Thomas stuck his head out of the galley hatch. As soon as he saw Thomas, the "chorister" swung his rifle over to aim at my deckhand. When Thomas saw this congregation of armed-to-the-teeth chorus boys he almost fell back down the galley hatch.

"Speak to the bugger in *deutsch*, Thomas. Nip over to the ama, but go slowly." I broke into Spanish—"*Andaremos con pies de plumo*"—but then I realized Thomas wouldn't understand what I'd said. "Let us walk with feet of feathers," I repeated in English.

"*Was wollt ihr?*" "What do you want?" shouted Thomas. His voice was thin in the wind, but I suspected it was not only the wind that made it thin, but the sight of all the guns aimed at him.

The chorister pulled another sulky face, then jerked his thumb downstream, time and again, with violent thrusts of his arm.

Thomas turned to me. "He wants us to follow him downstream," shouted my faithful crew, interpreting as accurately as ever. "No one speaks German!"

"Ask them, do they speak English," I called out as I steered.

Thomas shouted something to them. "*Sprechen sie Englisch?*" probably, but received in reply only hard glares from everyone on board our escort. Thomas turned to me and again shouted, "We must go downstream, at this speed, with them."

"That's fair enough," I told him. With the river running at six knots there was hardly anything else I could do but head downstream at "this speed." And so *Outward Leg*, like a graceful lady who has been accosted by two dockside pimply pimps, shaking her stern end now and again, as Old Father Danube gave her bustle a little twitch, was hustled into the Great Proletarian Future, to see if it worked or not.

Before we reached the customs control point at Karlova Ves we passed the little town of Devin, immediately inside the Czech–Austrian border. As we progressed, at a fair speed, so the rain became stickier and stickier, so the colors all around us faded more and more. There is nothing ideological in this (I had left London with a miner's pick at my masthead); it is an incontrovertible fact that as we entered the C.S.S.R. colors faded and even perspectives became flatter and flatter. By the time the watchtower and the great iron fence had more clearly come into view, erected along the side of that long, obscene slash of naked, raped and barren soil across the face of our Earth, all the world seemed gray and flat. Soon there were no more colors—only shades of gray. Everything was gray, gray, gray. Trees, houses, earth, sky, faces, river, plants; good God, even the flowers looked gray, what few there were, and I spent much time in the next three days wondering to myself, over and over again, who, in the name of humanity, had ever allowed this to happen?

I am running ahead of myself, but if I don't you will not see Czechoslovakia as we in *Outward Leg* saw it, and so I must prime you. It did not happen gradually; it happened with a sudden change in the primal colors of the universe, like passing from sunshine into shade. It was something of the feeling I've had when I've walked into a butcher's freezer. Suddenly I was divorced from the faulty, dear world of color and dimension that I knew, and cast into something else; something cold, gray, sinister and seething with downright wickedness, that was full of all that insults and threatens the very existence of the immortal human soul; something that distorts and changes, for its own ends, the eternal verities of faith and hope and love.

Devin town was imprisoned from the Danube by an eight-foot-high, rusting barbed-wire fence. On it there had blown scraps of cloth and paper and fluff. Behind these fluttering reminders of the living world, all looked gray and dead and *flat*. The houses mainly of wood were slowly collapsing. Every lick of paint in sight was gray and peeling. In the gardens of the houses only gray weeds grew. It was like a ghost town, yet gray people lived there, because we could plainly see that every house was occupied; there were gray people in the gardens, in the windows, and on the paths between the houses, yet not one of them showed any expression as they turned to look at our little convoy. I had the feeling that I was a live man being carried to the graveyard to be buried. The whole town seemed to have the look I have seen in the eyes of mugging victims in New York. It seemed to say, "Look what they've done to me."

Devin is at km 1879 from the Black Sea. The Czech stretch of the Danube runs downstream for just under a hundred miles. This is, in fact, the Russian Bear's Paw on the upper Danube. This is where it sticks its heavy paw onto and over a main European artery.

In the old days, robber barons used to build castles on rivers, and they had many sweet-sounding excuses for doing so. One of them was that the castles were there to protect the surrounding countryside from marauders. But the reality was very different from what most history books and tourist brochures will tell you. The castles were there to block the rivers, so that passing merchants on ships had to pay a bribe in order to make their way past the robber baron.

The only operating "robber baron river castles" that I saw in Europe were all in Eastern Europe, and the biggest one was Czechoslovakia itself. Its real owner is the biggest bully of all the robber barons past and present. He doesn't demand only money, though. He does not protect the property of his neighbors. Instead he demands their hearts and souls, and builds fences around the peasantry to lock them in his fief while he grinds them down. He does this, he says, for the peasant's own good. Life is going to be good, even if it kills life itself, he says.

At km 1872 our pubescent escorts gestured us to go into a small inlet. The chorister gave no warning, and so by the time I had turned the boat and punched back to the inlet against the current, which took some time, he was fuming. Inside the inlet of Karlova Ves we sighted a decrepit pontoon, again all peeling paint. On it was a big painted sign, *"Lovhaft."* This looked a bit like "Love Haven" and cheered us up. But not for long. We were brusquely waved over to yet another pontoon, by yet more armed brats, and tied up alongside. There, two more uniformed, green-hatted saplings sulked above us with Kalashnikov rifles. I offered them tea. They grimaced and looked away, but not for long. By gestures they gave us to understand that we must wait for their officers. They did this by pointing at the boat, then at us, prodding their fingers, then lightly touching their right shoulders with the same finger. We later realized that this, all through the Russian Southeast European Empire, means "officials."

While we waited in the clearing rain, several kayaks appeared from behind the "*Lovhaft*" pontoon. They were all being paddled by strapping young men and women in tank tops of different colors. They had all trained hard, that was obvious, for they handled their craft with great skill.

Suddenly, as we waited under the guarded pontoon, and as our juvenile guards talked quietly among themselves, I heard the first English words to reach my ears behind the Iron Curtain. "Hey, mister!"

I spun around and looked down to see a red-headed youngster of about twenty-two sitting motionlessly in his kayak. He looked as "clean-cut" and healthy as many Western parents would wish a son to be. On his white vest was a red star and sickle, with an anchor.

"Hi!" said I, more in consternation than surprise.

"How much did your boat cost?" he asked. With relief I realized swiftly that the world would save itself. When a youngster asks how much something costs, that means that he wants to have that something, one day, if not sooner, and that means that he has personal ambition.

"A lot of sweat," I told him, the same as I tell anyone.

"You must be a millionaire," he observed. Then as he drifted past our stern he added, "I bet you have a ranch in California!"

"That's right. I do," I lied, thinking, "If he only knew . . ."

But then one of our young Lords of the Flies stamped over the pontoon and waved our English-speaking kayaker away with the muzzle of his gun.

We waited an hour and a half for the officials to arrive. It appeared, from what we could gather from our guards' grunts, that Czechoslovakia was competing in a World Championship ice-hockey match with the U.S.S.R. in Canada, and everyone who had access to a television was watching their progress. Luckily for us, I suspect, Czechoslovakia won the match against the Soviet Union. Every one of the officials was in comparatively good spirits when they finally turned up. All except one of them, the only woman. She had eyes like boiled currants in her fat red face over her dumpy body and looked about the most unappetizing female creature I'd clapped eyes on many a long year, anywhere on Earth or at sea. She was too dumpy to negotiate the climb down from the pontoon, so she had to be content with glaring her currants at us from in front of her hair-bun and from under the red star on her peaked cap. I had been hoping to hell they hadn't sent her down to seduce me from my own allegiances, and now thanked God that she couldn't have in any case. All the while she was staring down at me, *Outward Leg* seemed to shudder at her proximity, and I stroked her cockpit coaming to calm the boat down a mite.

The other officials were all, it seemed to me, men. There were three of them. The leader or spokesman, who spoke German with Thomas, had a devil-may-care look about him. He wore no hat and his tie was eased off. He was a good-looking man and about thirty-seven or so, and would have been at home, appearance-wise, in any bar, pub or disco even in the Western world. He looked like the kind of man who would play a good and jolly game of darts or equally charm the ladies. This was deceptive. He soon showed his mettle. He brusquely demanded our passports, and rammed them in the pockets of his uniform jacket.

One of the other two men was, I supposed, what political writers would describe as a party hack. He too was dressed in a gray uniform. He was of late middle age and looked as if there had once been a fire somewhere in the dead hearth of his soul. Now the only bright thing about him was the red star on his cap.

The other man in the party was dressed in civilian clothes which looked as if they had been bought, as fashionable relics of the forties, from a secondhand stall in Petticoat Lane. This one pretended not to understand one word of English or German, yet, as he rifled through my books and papers, seemed to know very well what he read. He was in his fifties, and looked like a schoolmaster.

Playboy, Jack and Squinting Squeers (as I had respectively christened them) made a thorough job of searching our boat's middle hull. They just about took everything from its stowage, inspected it, noted it down in a book, and took the name and number of everything removable. This took about two hours or so. All the while, whenever I poked my head topside, Boiled Currants glared at me from under the low peak of her commissar's cap.

Finally, at the end of their inspection, Playboy told Thomas in German, "Well, you can go through, but you must spend twenty dollars a day each while you are in Czechoslovakia. You must stop only where you are told to stop, and you must sail only when you are told you can sail, and there must be no landings anywhere in between the places where you are allowed to stop, and no communicating with people ashore from your boat while you are under way. You must go from here to Bratislava Port and there report to the Police Control Office. Then you must carry out their orders. You must not use any of your transmitters while you are in Czechoslovakia, nor must you take any photographs from your boat without permission from the soldiers in the watchtowers, understood?" He thrust our passports at me. I took them and carefully laid them on my table.

I nodded. "Sounds fair enough," I lied. Then the three men, with curt nods, left the boat to join Boiled Currants on the pontoon. *Outward Leg* was then freed from the berth and slid astern, to be escorted by yet another adolescent armed boat outing, downstream and around the long bend that the Danube sweeps through on his way past Bratislava.

"They never even noticed the amas," I told Thomas. "We could have had six CIA blokes in 'em."

The May Day celebrations were in full swing in the big park opposite the Bratislava city center, just by one of the two bridges across the Danube (there are only three in all Czechoslovakia). Among the dripping trees thousands of workers and soldiers milled under hundreds of streaming blood-red banners. Even the ferris wheel was decorated with a red star at its axis. The graceful bridge itself was bedecked with two long lines of Soviet flags alternating with Czech tricolors. On the bridge and over the bridge and at each end of the bridge and under each end of the bridge, out of the rain, stood dozens of better-dressed officials and officers. We could see them all very clearly, for the Danube is only two hundred feet wide off Bratislava.

As soon as I saw what was happening ahead of us, as soon as those flags and figures were at all obvious for what they were, I quietly and quickly ordered Thomas, "Play the pipes, old son, play the bloody pipes!"

Thomas, like the good sailor he is, sprang immediately to my order. In seconds the rousing air of "Lochaber Gathering" was blasting out at full volume all over Bratislava, over its red-flag-festooned wet park, over the officials and officers under the bridge ends, and over our escorts, who now looked, at least to me, positively defeated. Then, as ten thousand workers, peasants, soldiers and party members of Bratislava stopped their milling and stood stock-still, the officials like dolmens, the soldiers like lined-up ramrods, and gawped at her, *Outward Leg* with her bagpipes blaring over everything, and her American ensign, her British and Welsh flags, her RNSA burgee at her bow, *and* her Bavarian burgee, flapping stiff in the breeze, steamed past the whole shindig in review order, sedately and bursting with *élan*, like Her Majesty's royal yacht *Britannia* at a Spithead Review.

Beside me, Thomas was staring about him, wordlessly ecstatic. I muttered to him, as the thousands of workers, peasants, soldiers and party members dropped astern in the rain, still all standing stock-still, "That'll show the buggers."

Then I thought to myself for a minute or two and added, as Bratislava Port Control watchtower came into view, "It doesn't matter what they do to us now, it doesn't matter what happens to us, it doesn't matter about last winter: that five minutes just passed was bloody well worth it!"

"Do you think we'll get through all right?" asked Thomas.

"We'll scuttle through Czechoslovakia like a rat through a drain-pipe, Thomas, never you fear. Now, get your mooring lines and fenders ready . . ."

But I wished I had felt as confident inside myself as Thomas evidently imagined I was. It had sounded good, anyway, and when there's nothing to lose but your freedom, or perhaps your boat or even your life, *anything* sounds good.

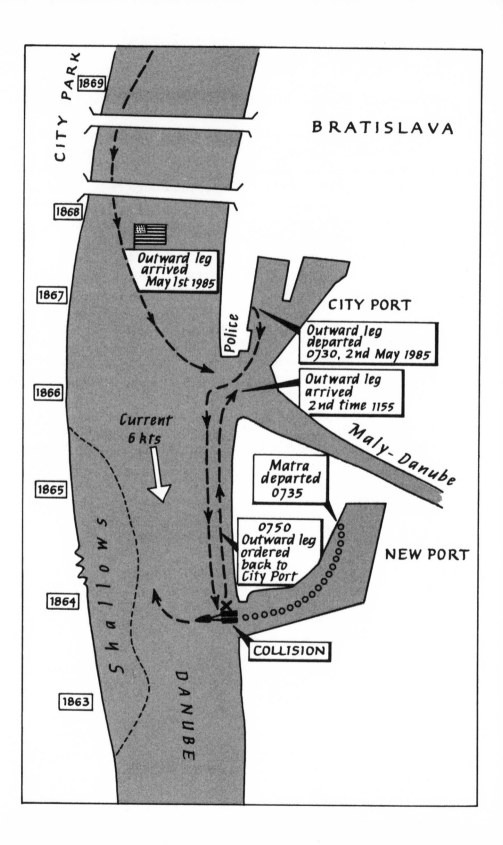

# 18

## *The Setup*

All the rest of the year except May Day, the Danube at Bratislava is busy with shipping. The city is Czechoslovakia's main water outlet to the Black Sea. Its only other outlet by water is the river Elbe, which flows north from near Prague to the North Sea at Hamburg.

Past Bratislava, on 364 days a year, there streams a continual procession of ships, barges, tugs and working craft of eight nations; U.S.S.R., Bulgaria, Rumania, Yugoslavia, Hungary, Czechoslovakia, Austria and West Germany, up and down the river, day and night.

Although by now all the ships of the river seemed to recognize *Outward Leg* and most of them greeted us familiarly, it was to be the less frequently met ships of West Germany and Austria, and especially the Austrians, that we were to be most pleased to see. Then we were to know that our continued progress downstream would be reported back to their home ports and our friends would know that we were still in business. We could not use our radio legally, and anyway the mast antenna was down.

It was to be from these river ships of Austria and West Germany that we were to have the most rousing welcome that I can remember from fellow shipping since the days of the Allied convoys of World War Two. Then, we British used to meet up with surviving ships from a transatlantic running battle with U-boats, and cheer them. Or others would cheer us. Now, ironically, it was to be the Germans greeting our ship as though she was a survivor, and this was to be so all the way downstream to the Black Sea. As we reached Bratislava we little realized how much of a survivor she was going to be.

It was early evening when *Outward Leg* swung around in Old Father

Danube's strong stream and poked her way into Bratislava city port, on that rainy May Day, escorted still by seventeen brats of Bratislava in their pretty green hats, holding their Kalashnikovs.

Inside the mouth of the harbor, which ran back parallel almost with the river for half a mile or so, was a gloomy vista of police barracks, watchtowers, cranes, silos, watchtowers, tall, grimy docks and jetties, a high wall with watchtowers surrounding all, and rows and rows of concrete workers' flats peeping over the grim walls like faceless prisoners peering over a fence. Over all, from above, a thin, cold, sticky rain descended on and permeated everything. As we crept through the port, now out of the current, I watched, as usually I do when entering any port, for a suitable place to berth our boat.

I looked astern. The river-patrol craft was now hove to across the entrance of the port, its gang of lads still glaring at us. They gave no signals as to where we should head our boat. I peered around the port again, the rain dripping off my oilskin hood. To me it looked one of the most dreary prospects I had seen since the Soviet port of Murmansk during World War Two. It had the same hopeless, suffering, miserable, *crying* air about it. There were shadows moving behind the windows of the police barracks at the entrance to the port, and there was an armed soldier hovering, vulture-like, on each of the watchtowers, but for the rest, the port seemed to be deserted to the rain. Then I saw, in the middle of this industrial desert, a full-blown ocean yacht wearing a Czechoslovak ensign: It was like seeing a rose on a garbage heap.

The yacht was about fifty feet in length, ketch rigged, and as I steered *Outward Leg* closer I saw that she was built, it seemed, entirely of steel. I mean not just the hull, but the mast, the guardrails, the wind generator on her stern, she was all welded steel. Even her mooring warps were of steel, padlocked firmly to the bollards with steel padlocks. As we approached closer I noticed the name on her stern: *Kondor*. She was painted gray. Everything in her or about her was painted gray, warship gray. This made her look as if she was a government sail-training ship, and this indeed is what I thought she was.

I considered going alongside her to tie up. She was moored by steel cables fore and aft to the sloping dock wall below the police office watchtower. I made a gesture to the soldier on the tower to ask if I could go alongside *Kondor*. I pointed at the yacht and slowly clapped my hands together, which is the usual signal for this the world over. His answer was to turn his back on us and stare the opposite way. I debated with myself, as anyone does in the short seconds before fixing on a berth, and decided that as sailors are sailors the world over, no matter what the politics of their people ashore might be, I would tie up to the steel vessel. In two minutes we were snugly moored to her.

There was no movement ashore or in *Kondor* except for falling rain. Until suppertime we waited for officials to arrive, but none did, so Thomas and I set to on canned meat and potatoes from Vienna. It was pointless for us to go ashore, even had it been earlier, for 1 May was a national holiday and the banks would be closed. They would stay closed, we knew from the officials in Karlova Ves, until 4 May. There was no way we could legally change money in Czechoslovakia, and yet our visas gave us only a two-day sojourn in that unhappy land. My intention in this matter was to get through anyway, and if necessary hand over the $80 at our departure from Czechoslovakia, if they were adamant that we should pay this extortion. I naturally assumed that two days would be enough time to cover the passage of 120 miles of Czech Danube until the exit port of Komarno, from whence we could exit for Hungary.

About an hour after we had eaten, two officials, one policeman and one immigration sergeant, came on board. We must, they said, leave Bratislava at *exactly* 0730 next day. We were allowed ashore, they said. The nearest hotel where tourists were allowed was about four miles away. Thomas asked if there was a bus stop nearby. They were not operating that evening, it was May Day. Thomas then inquired if there were any taxis. The officials both snorted, first reminding us that we *must leave at exactly 0730*, and left.

When the guards had left our boat, and as we were making ready to turn in, I noticed, through my cabin window, someone moving about on *Kondor*'s deck. I poked my head out of the companionway hatch, and stared over at our mysterious neighbor. He was a man of about my age, white-haired, clean-shaven and cleanly dressed in overalls, with a tidy jacket to protect him from the cold rain. I greeted him with "Hi!," and he spoke back in what seemed to be German. I called for Thomas to talk to him, and invite him on board our boat.

"My name," he said through Thomas, "is Zdenek Polasek, and I am a retired miner from Brno. I built *Kondor* myself." He opened his palms, and showed hard calluses. "It took me ten years, and finding materials and parts was very, very difficult. I completed the boat, in Brno, in 1982, and had her hauled here, to Bratislava, where I launched her, and all my friends came to the launching."

"1982?" I asked him. "But that's three years ago!"

"Yes, I want to go down the Danube, of course, to the sea, but the government says I must pay a deposit of eighty percent of the boat's value before I can sail out of here."

"What for?" The boat must have been worth a good $100,000 in any Western country and more in the U.S.A.

"To guarantee my return to my country."

"Can you do it? I mean pay the deposit?"

"No. I'm sixty-three now. My miner's pension would not pay it if I saved it all for thirty years."

"Then what will you do?" I asked him.

He grinned wanly and threw his hands out. I noticed again his calluses. "Stay here, I suppose, and wait."

Later Thomas and I looked over *Kondor*. She was superbly built and full of the latest ideas in ocean-craft comfort. Zdenek had even built an on-board washing machine for his wife, a saturnine woman who spoke not one word with us but sat watching a small television in the main cabin. His engine installation was first class, and his electric wiring system was one of the neatest I have ever seen. Because of the near-impossibility of obtaining boat gear or chandlery in Czechoslovakia, Zdenek had been forced to construct his own mast out of steel pipe, and his own winch system. There were many original ideas in his craft that I had never before seen put to practice, and I could only admire this craftsman for his persistence, his obvious longing for the sea, and for his patience.

"Why not just take off?" the old Welsh buccaneer in me inquired.

He looked at me again with a wan smile. "Oh, but I love my country. I'd have to return here, you see, to die . . ."

And this was a man whose son, he told me, had been shot dead by his own countrymen while trying to escape from Czechoslovakia into Austria over the frontier fence. He told me this with no bitterness, no rancor. He told it as a sad fact of life. A fact of death. His own eldest son's death. He told me this calmly, as if his son had deserved to die for trying to leave his country.

Next morning we were up at seven, ready to shove off at exactly

0730 as our gruff officials of the previous evening had instructed us. At exactly half past seven we eased our boat away from *Kondor* and soon one of the most forlorn yacht berths I have ever seen in my long life at sea disappeared into the misty rain astern of us.

As we passed out of the port entrance, under the police barracks, I noticed that dozens of uniformed people were crowded on its balconies to watch us go. I thought this natural enough. *Outward Leg* was, after all, the very first American ocean vessel ever to enter their harbor, and probably our ensign was the first American Stars and Stripes they had ever seen in real life, except outside the United States Embassy in Prague, or over a barbed-wire fence. There were no cheers, no well-wishing. They all stood there, men and women, in their khaki and gray uniforms and watched us, glumly. Some of them had binoculars, and I had the feeling of being an insect under close focus and about to be swatted.

I should explain here that so far as anyone could tell me there are no charts available for the Czechoslovak stretch of the Danube. They probably do exist, but like the old charts of the Roman empire, the Spanish empire, the Portuguese empire, the charts of the Russian empire evidently are state secrets and not available to those who, in the eyes of the creatures of the Kremlin, do not merit them. Once a vessel is past the Austrian frontier, and until she reaches the Hungarian frontier, her pilot, unless he be a sycophant of the Soviets, or knows one, is blind. There are some very basic road maps, but these show no river depths, only blue ribbons, with little yellow islands all along them. They give no idea of the deviousness and trickery of Old Father Danube in league with Soviet servants' treachery.

*Outward Leg* emerged from Bratislava city port under the gaze of several dozen port and frontier police officials, as we passed out into the Danube. The city port is at km 1866.5. What no one had mentioned to us, what we had no way of knowing, was that at km 1864.8 there was another port, much frequented by commercial traffic. In the visibility though the thin rain, which was about a hundred yards, and sighting along the foreshortened river wall, there was no sign of any harbor exit. The current downstream from Bratislava city port was strong, about seven knots, and with our Yanmar twenty-two-horsepower engine ticking over, we were making about eight knots over-the-ground. Up to now, everything navigation-wise was about normal for a rainy morning on the Danube, heading downstream.

Thomas was on deck, clearing away mooring lines, and I was at the wheel, keeping a good, careful lookout ahead, through the rain, astern and to each side on the bows.

Suddenly, as fast as I can write it, from the river bank apparently, there shot out a great looming shadow in the rain. I shoved the wheel over hard, to pass under its stern. Then I realized that the dark mass ahead was a tug with a tow steaming straight out into the river and not yet turning. It was lumbering directly ahead of and across our course, and it was, I saw to my horror, towing two barges, side by side, out of the harbor. Now I could plainly see directly ahead of us the long, deadly hawsers snaking out from the ship's stern low over the water. They were swiftly nearing *Outward Leg* as we bore down on them. The only thing I could do was try to dash our boat for the narrow gap between the emerging barge and the harbor entrance. A split-second reckoning told me that there was perhaps a one percent chance that we might clear the space between the barge and the wall. But in the same micro-second I determined that if we could not clear the barge and its murderous warp I would then aim *Outward Leg* straight at the river-side wall, which sloped gradually upward and back from the water's edge. That way I would run the bows hard onto the wall, and although she would be damaged, it might save our ship.

If your eyesight is average, and your reading too, all this was taking place much faster than it takes you to read about it. I rammed the wheel over to port, hard, and aimed our boat right at the high concrete river-retaining wall. But Old Father Danube was having none of that. His speed increased, he picked us up, as we turned, and hurled us at ten knots, broadside onto the barge. I jammed the engine throttle down hard ahead, so that we would escape the hawser, and collide instead with the cliff-like steel sides of the barge. *Outward Leg* hit the barge just abaft (behind) the barge's bow. Had we hit the wires, the hawsers would have sliced her horizontally in half, and probably cut in half or decapitated, or churned to mincemeat both Thomas and me in the process.

Our gallant little Yannie screamed as I shoved down on the throttle. The barge bore down on us so that the whole starboard ama was under water; our guard-rails snapped like matchsticks or bent like reeds all along our starboard side, and our boat almost capsized to starboard, under the barge. Somehow the engine shoved her inch by inch forward, to scrape and scuttle and scrabble along the side of the barge, almost under it, until at last *Outward Leg* reached slower river current, and with a mighty heave sprang out sideways upstream from the murderous sides of the barge. All the while this was going on, the tug, the barge, and *Outward Leg* were being pushed downstream by the Danube at about ten knots.

I am positive that if *Outward Leg* had been a monohull, without the tremendous buoyancy of her starboard ama stopping her capsize, she would have been driven under the barge by the force of the current, and sunk. I am absolutely certain that if she had not been a trimaran with her great transverse strength, she would have been broken up as she sank and I would not have been alive now to tell this true tale.

Once *Outward Leg* was on an even keel, I shoved her inch by grinding inch with our engine all the way along the eighty feet of rusty iron barge until we were at last clear of her stern. Then, with our engine still hammering like a hound of Hades, I rammed the bows round to face upstream, to escape from the threat of imminent and instant and undoubtable death. There was no way I, if we had foundered, with my one leg, could have escaped death or near-death.

The first things I saw, when I took rapid sight all around, were the tugs' and barge's crew all standing still in shock, it seemed, and a Czechoslovak patrol craft only yards away from us, with her crew of striplings gesticulating upstream with their Kalashnikovs, back toward Bratislava.

The first thing I said to Thomas, after I made sure that he was uninjured, was "The bloody bastards! The shit-faced, devious, mean-minded assholes!" Thomas was already hoisting back in place the American ensign's pole which had been snapped off the stern rail.

It was quite obvious to me what had occurred. It was immediately evident, with no doubts at all, that we had been set up for a collision, and it was the Czech police who set us up.

When we had left Bratislava city port that morning I had watched regularly astern through the foggy rain. I had seen the port police barracks disappear when we were no more than 220 yards from the port exit. The only way they could have watched us farther down-stream was either by radar or from a patrol craft shadowing us just out of sight in the rain astern. Having witnessed the Czechoslovak official standards of care for small-craft voyagers, I could by no means imagine that their patrol craft might be shadowing us for our own welfare.

No ship leaves a Czech dock, jetty, riverbank or anchorage without official permission to do so at a certain, exact time. The Hungarian ship *Matra* (which is what the tug turned out to be) *must* have been instructed to leave the lower port at the precise time when, upon emerging into the river, we would be bearing down on her. The authorities must have known where the Hungarian ship with her long tow, a total of about 220 yards, was heading, out of the port and across the river channel to turn upstream. The patrol craft was on the scene far too quickly for its control not to have known that something was going to occur.

I had been afloat at sea, on oceans, rivers, canals, docks, lakes, waterways, marinas, harbors, ports, havens, rivulets and bloody bathtubs for forty-seven years, almost full time. For thirty-two of those years I had been mostly at the helm of my own command, and *always* at the helm in crowded or hazardous waters. I had *never* been involved in any kind of serious collision. I'd had a few scratches and close calls here and there, but never had I ever collided with my vessel against another. If I did not know a setup when I saw it, it was time I dropped my hook permanently.

Now the patrol craft's snotty-nosed little bastards in green hats shot alongside *Outward Leg*, all grinning as they shoved their Kalashnikovs out from them and pointed them upstream. Now I muttered at them through slit eyelids as I peered against the rain and as our boat, with all her starboard side battered and gashed and all her guardrails on that side bent and broken, and we started to shove, slowly, so slowly against the mighty Danube current.

I muttered steadily and quietly. I called them every foul name ever used in the English language, the Welsh, and the Spanish, the French, the Portuguese, and threw in some Swahili, for good measure, too. I cursed them, those little boys in the boat, their families, their future progeny, their officers and their antecedents and descendants for the past and the next thousand years, and their bosses, and their offices, and their secretaries and their limousines and their country villas and their mothers and their fathers and their offspring and their special schools and their party and its members and their cadres and their commissars and their red stars and their goddam frontier guards and their blood-soaked fences that stop honest men and true from going down in their worthy ships, down to the bleeding sea.

All the while, as *Outward Leg* made all of one-eighth of a knot with the engine at full blast against the current, Thomas, as he inspected the damage and rehoisted all our flags on broken poles, stared at me in open-eyed wonder as he heard my bitter tirade against whoever had tried to sink my vessel and kill my crew and me.

As slowly, so slowly, the bank passed us yard by yard, and Bratislava port police barracks came into view, I sighted our bow stem on them again and again and wished, oh, how I wished, each single time the barracks were dead ahead I had a couple of Whitehead torpedoes slung under our wing decks. I imagined to myself how I'd make those bastards jump. I'd give 'em kilometers, all right, and they'd all be bloody upward!

There they were, now the rain had eased off again, all lined up on their balconies, all grinning and waving now, as *Outward Leg* limped back, looking probably to them with their shoddy-minded brains, severely wounded.

So far, Thomas had been mostly silent. I suppose he'd thought that any conversation would be futile, considering my anger. Then he turned to me and said, "Did you see that gash we put into the side of the barge?"

I looked at him for a split second, away from gazing at the hateful dreariness of Bratislava port, and the watchtowers all around. Even the sentries were smiling now. "No—well, I saw that there was a bit of a dent in the barge when we escaped from it. You mean we put it there?"

"We caved those iron sides in this much," said Thomas, and made a curve with his palm. "We pushed it in five centimeters at least. Our own side isn't dented or cracked at all."

"Good for Leo Surtees." I thought of *Outward Leg*'s builder as I maneuvered her alongside a small jetty. "Good for Leo. The buggers tried to sink us, and didn't realize that they might as well piss on the Rock of Gibraltar!"

As we pulled alongside, we were met by the two same officials as the night before. The sergeant, all grins, told Thomas quietly in German, "Welcome back to Bratislava. Your boat and both of you are under arrest!"

# 19

## *Running the Gauntlet*

The first rule in the voyager's creed always was, is, and always must
be, *defend yourself*. The second rule is *defend the vessel*. Defend her no
matter where she is, no matter how much at fault she might be or
against what or whom she is defended; no matter how omnipotent or
omniscient, omnidextrous or omniomni whosoever or whatever is
threatening her might appear.

"What do you mean, under arrest?" I asked the sergeant through
Thomas. "We are navigating an International Waterway."

"Czechoslovakia," replied the sergeant, fixing me from under his
eyelids, "administers the law on the Danube where it goes through
Czechoslovakia."

"Why are we under arrest?" I asked him. "If we are?"

"You must not move from here until we know who was responsible
for the collision," he replied. All the while the immigration officer
looked at me as though I were on a slowly turning spit.

"Then what you mean is not that we are under arrest," I sug-
gested, "but that our presence here is requested for the time being?"

The sergeant blustered at this for a few seconds, then, turning
redder, exploded, "Well, that's one way to put it!"

"One of the times I've been under arrest," I told him, truthfully,
"was in Bolivia. There I was arrested because I had a red British
ensign on the boat and they accused me of being a communist. It
was ridiculous, of course."

"We are not savage Indians here," said the sergeant.

Even as he said this an officer of the River Authority arrived on
board. He was in a gray uniform, like the others, but he looked much

171

less ox-like, much more amenable to reason. He was accompanied
by two civilians, dressed in working overalls, who appeared distraught.
These turned out to be the captain and pilot of the Hungarian tugboat
*Matra*. In their hands they carried a sheaf of forms so thick that you
would think they were the file clerks of some government being
evacuated in the face of an invading army. Both the skipper and his
mate were obviously hardworking, honest family men, who had been
manipulated into a situation not of their own making, and who had
been completely unaware of what they were being led into. A few
minutes of conversation with them convinced me of that.

The forms, explained the officer, were for me to make my official
complaint, if I had any, against the good skipper of the *Matra*. The
skipper stood quietly quaking in his shoes before these two uniformed
morons and the river-police officer. I turned to him. I would get the
skipper off the hook, if he had any skipper's brains at all.

"I didn't hear your siren," I stated. It was true. He hadn't
blown it.

The tug skipper at first started to say something, then thought
deeply, screwing up his brow for a few seconds, as I carried on, in a
slightly louder voice, "although mind you, I had my engine doors
open and there was a loud racket on board." Thomas had to have
this explained to him twice so that he would understand clearly what
the words meant. Even then, he had to repeat it three times in German
so that the officials and the skipper would understand what were the
lies I was telling them.

The skipper suddenly eased off his frown and stated, "But I did
blow my siren, three or four times, a few seconds apart." Now he'd
caught on. Now he was lying, too.

The officer broke in. "Do you," he said to me, "want to sign this
official complaint?"

"I have no complaint," I said, between tight lips. "It was all my
fault, if there was any fault," I lied through my teeth. There was
tension in my cabin. "Mea culpa."

"But you must still sign the form, in any case," stated the officer,
"to state what you have just told me."

"Right," said I. And so I did. For the first time ever in my life I
wrote a lie on an official document. I wrote that it was I and I alone
who was responsible for the collision of *Outward Leg* and *Matra*'s barge.

I did this because I had calculated what the officer's very next words would be:

"Good," he said, reluctantly. All correct. "Now you can leave Bratislava." He did his best to sound nonchalant about it, at least on the surface, but the sergeant of the frontier police and the immigration official were quietly fuming. By letting them punch empty air I had *Outward Leg* off their particular hook. There was no reason that would be recognized in any court in the world why they could now detain our boat. There simply was nothing to have a court case about. She was obviously still worthy of a river passage and we ourselves were uninjured.

If I had told the truth on that official document *Outward Leg* could have been detained in Bratislava for as long as it took the Czechoslovak Soviet Socialist Republic's courts to finally get around to reviewing the case. If *Kondor* was anything to go by, we'd have still been sitting in Bratislava even as I write. I had very quickly seen the red light and made up my mind. *Outward Leg* was no *Kondor*. An albatross, maybe, but not a condor. She was going to sea again if I had to *carry* her. So for her sake, to defend her and her passage to the sea, I lied. I'd do the same again in the same circumstances. In my signing that piece of paper I told the world that I had caused a collision, but as God is my judge, and as I plead his mercy for my lies then, I swear that we were set up, and I will swear so until my dying day.

As I signed that odious paper the relief of the Hungarian skipper and his mate, who were standing behind me, was almost tangible. It was as if it filled my cabin so thickly that I could have taken out my knife, cut it in little pieces and sent it to every left-wing half-assed "peacenik" on earth. The poor men almost fell over themselves after I had signed, grabbing my hand and shaking it with both of theirs. I'm sure that if the two Czech morons and the river-police officer had not been present they would have kissed my feet.

The two gray-uniformed morons turned and stamped their way up my ladder, across the deck and off our boat, without one more word. The Hungarians, speaking cheerfully to Thomas and me in their unintelligible language, followed them, shaking their heads and clucking sympathetically over our damaged guardrail stanchions and ship's side as they went. Only the river-authority officer remained behind now. I knew he liked my style. He knew the score all right.

"It's almost noon," I observed, "and we won't have enough daylight now to reach Komarno and the frontier. We have only two days' visa-permit to stay in Czechoslovakia. If I'm to be out of your country by the time our two days are up I have to move off now. But we were told we could only stop here and in Komarno. We have no chart and the river winds like crazy among many islands . . ."

"So you must stop somewhere overnight," the officer added for me in German. He thought for a minute, then said, "Make for Hrusov." He spoke the name as if he were blowing out his breath suddenly.

I must have looked puzzled. Thomas grabbed a sheet of paper and a pencil, and passed them to the officer. He, a human being, wrote the name down. "It's about seventeen miles downstream," he explained. "There's a little river joins the Danube. It's called Cilitovski Rameno. You can anchor there, just off the Danube. I'll signal ahead to the frontier guards there that you are coming. Otherwise they might shoot at you." He said this as though he were saying, in another world, "Otherwise the gate might be locked," or "Otherwise you might be refused admittance."

Then, as the officer stood alone on the jetty and silently watched us leave, *Outward Leg* for the second time that day, 2 May, pushed out slowly through the wet dreariness of Bratislava port, past her forlorn, imprisoned sister-craft *Kondor*, past the watchtowers and soggy red bunting drooping from a dozen dirty barges, and so back again into the bounding river Danube. As we passed the brick port-police barracks, there was not one living soul standing on the balconies to watch as our forward wind speed picked up the Stars and Stripes, the Red Ensign, the Draigh-a-goch and the RNSA burgee, all on their broken standard poles, and whipped them out stiffly, so that, besides our turquoise decks, they were the only moving bits of color in the whole damp, miserable, sad, gray scene. But there were dark shadows behind the curtained windows of the police office. They were watching all right.

"That'll larn 'em," I called to Thomas.

He was keeping an extra eye out as we made downstream. He stared down at me and screwed his ears over the blast of a factory hooter somewhere. "What's that?" he inquired. *"Was ist das?"*

I said, "Shove some bagpipes on the tape player!" He did, quickly.

Before they lost sight of us the Bloody Bastards of Bratislava heard the loud strains of "Delvinside" and "Dougie Gillies" reaching out over their miserable manor, blaring over the soggy, drooping red banners all around and, once we were out of sight of the sentries, raising even a few hand waves from barges and lone cyclists on the river wall road, as we faded in the drizzle into the distance.

This, I knew, was now no longer a mere exploratory voyage; no longer a mere attempt to pass on a little hope to all the handicapped folk who might see or hear us; this was now a demonstration, a long drawn-out procession, if you like, to show the Pretenders to the Danubian throne that river Danube was not a private Russian river, but that it could, and should, be navigated by all voyagers, from wherever, and no matter what their political stripe might be.

Some people might say that it was now to become a provocation. So it might have been, but a rightful one for all that, and an unanswerable one in the bargain. I would show everyone, on both sides of the river Danube, and as far-flung from the banks as we could possibly reach, what everyone can do, if they have the faith to know that what they are doing is right and is on the side of mankind's self-evident, sacred rights.

Later, I knew that some fogies, old and young, might protest that I might have made things awkward, or even as bad, or worse, for voyagers that followed me, but I would reply that Zola and Dickens, and Dostoyevsky too, had struggled against mighty adversaries for the dignity of the human individual, and while I could not ever claim to be in their company as a writer, by God I would, like them, try to create a little catharsis against all the sullen bullying and repression that I saw down the Danube valley, all the hidden resentment and all the screaming silences in the face of a sinister, brute force. It is only *hidden* repression, in the long run, that survives and thrives. It cannot stand the continual daylight of exposure. What I would expose would be mere drops in an ocean of wrong, but it was my human duty to expose them and hang them out for all to see and feel and hear and know about. I would not merely warn my fellow sailors; I would say to them "This kind of thing has got to be countered" and I would say it as loudly and clearly as I could.

There must be a limit to government bullying and interference. If anything threatens human freedom of movement or expression within the limits of social responsibility it should be removed or changed as soon as possible. If anything or anyone tries to stop or delay the passage of any vessel on her lawful occasions, then we should counter whatever it might be, by any and all means in our power. Where it has been impossible for me to counter it, then I have exposed it for what it usually is: someone trying to get something that isn't theirs from someone else by force or by threat.

If anybody thinks that I received any special or different treatment from officialdom in the Eastern Bloc countries of Europe because I earn my living by writing, they could not be more mistaken. Practically any writer worth his salt in Czechoslovakia or Rumania, for example, is either behind bars or silenced. This is common knowledge in those countries by the Danube, and instead of the mite of respect the writer might have in some Western countries, there he is treated by officialdom with contemptuous suspicion, unless, of course, they know that he has come to tread the party line and suck up to them in return for gold, booze and board. I'd rather starve in a dog shelter.

The river from Bratislava to Hrusov wound tortuously between shoals and islands. At some places the channel was marked; at others it was a matter of by-guess-and-by-God. At one or two stretches we managed to sight a descending tug convoy before it disappeared into the mist or rain ahead of us and these gave us some clues as to where the safe passages lay.

All the way from Bratislava to Hrusov, each bend in the river had its military watchtower, even though both banks of the Danube are in Czechoslovak territory for much of the way. All the way to km 1837, where Hrusov is marked by a row of ruined riverside chalets, there was nothing but trees, rows and rows of them, all the same height and color, a greeny gray. There was nothing between the trees but, now and again, a glimpse of armed patrols making their way along the river banks. On the good side, all the way, we found the channel to be of twelve-foot average depth.

At last we sighted the creek Rameno, or rather the bank that pokes downstream out into the Danube parallel to it. Immediately, I started to turn our boat, and she swung so that as we passed the creek we were facing upstream. The Danube current here was about six knots, so we entered the creek slowly. Inside the creek the depth suddenly dropped off to five feet, but by then *Outward Leg* was out of the current. The depth then dropped off again to ten feet and we knew that we were over the bar at the creek entrance. We dropped the Bruce anchor into sandy bottom. It was the first time that *Outward Leg* had anchored solely on a hook since she had left Hole Haven, in Essex. It was also the only time on the whole voyage across Europe that I wished myself back in that otherwise most unattractive anchorage in the Thomas Estuary. As we anchored, an Austrian ship passed us, heading upstream.

"*Alles gut?*" they cried.

"*Alles gut!*" was our lying reply, but they had seen us, which was a comfort.

Thomas and I had discussed our plan on the way downstream from Bratislava. Even though we had escaped death or near-fatal injury earlier that day, most of our talk had been of how we could change a few of our deutschmarks into local currency and perhaps obtain some fresh food at the village. Such innocents we were. Such is the way of true adventure.

Apart from the ruined chalets the only other building in Hrusov was a wooden hut, with signs hanging by the door, under a red Soviet banner. This was obviously a restaurant. Hopefully we headed for it. We rowed to the bank and dragged the Dunlop dinghy onto the beach so that it would not float away and leave us stranded. We passed many people on the way to the restaurant, couples and families walking along the muddy riverside dirt track. Not one person we passed looked at us. They all avoided our eyes, and children who did stare at me had their hands gripped tighter and their little paces quickened until they were past us. I told Thomas that these people seemed to be afraid of talking to, or even looking at, us.

"They are afraid of us," he said. "Our values are not theirs. They are afraid we will contaminate their children with our ideas of individual freedom of choice. Our ways are not theirs."

"Then," I asked him as we sloshed along, "what makes them think that we are too dangerous to know?"

"Well," he replied, "they are taught that way, taught to be afraid of us and the way we think."

"Then anything that makes anyone afraid of anyone or anything else, simply because it is different, is wrong. Absolutely, utterly, indefensibly wrong!" People still avoided passing too close to us. I continued, "Fear governs these people's lives. It might not be fear of their own government, but obviously they are afraid to speak to us, or to know us, and if they are, then something has made them afraid, and therefore that something is controlling their lives, and doing it by making them afraid. So they are governed by fear."

At the restaurant I asked the headwaiter, in sign language, if we could pay for a meal in deutschmarks. The waiter, in a shiny black suit, was short and stubby, with a dark complexion. He threw his chubby hands in the air and rushed for the nearby telephone, waving his soft fists at us. We hurriedly made back for our boat at anchor. As we pushed the dinghy from the muddy foreshore we sighted, on the one hand a car full of be-suited middle-aged men arriving, and on the other yet more armed children in baggy uniforms patrolling the riverside.

We kept our counsel as we ferried ourselves back aboard *Outward Leg*, and dived down below, to prepare a meal of Austrian canned and dried goods. No sooner was the pan on the stove than I, poking my head through the companionway like a sniper in a trench, observed a small motor craft descending the Danube and making for our creek. As I watched, I saw that in it there were four big men.

When the motorboat came closer, and made to tie up alongside *Outward Leg*, I saw that it was apparently a homemade boat of very rough fiberglass construction. The stout helmsman and his bald mate, who was handling a tiny mooring line on their boat's bow, greeted me in a very friendly fashion, in German. I hollered for Thomas to interpret for us.

"We are from the Bratislava Yacht Club," said Helmsman, "and we saw you pass farther on upstream, so we thought we'd pay you a visit. It's not often we see a foreign pleasure craft, and we've *never* seen an American one before."

That was true, what he'd said about seeing us upstream, for I, too, had sighted them, with their boat drawn up on a beach about three miles upstream. There had been other people on the foreshore, but no other craft. Indeed, it occurred to me, this was the only other "pleasure" craft we had sighted anywhere else in Czechoslovakia, apart from the kayaks at Karlova Ves, and *Kondor*, if that sad vessel could be considered a "pleasure" craft.

"We are from Bratislava Yacht Club," repeated Helmsman, a big, jolly-looking fellow of about forty with a paunch and the look about him of a bon vivant. His mate, who had now finished tying up the mooring line with a hitch I'd never seen before, joined in, "Yes, our clubhouse is in the Neuen Hafenbecken." That, he explained, was the second port downstream from Bratislava, the one from which our Hungarian friends on *Matra* had emerged. He had a bald head which glinted.

A red light, as bright and extensive as sunset over Galway Bay, lit up in my little Welsh head. I'd heard of no yacht club in Bratislava.

"My friends, here," said Baldy, "are also from the club." He gestured toward the two others, both big, serious-looking men in casual sports clothes, who sat silently weighing up every little thing about me, Thomas, my cabin, my charts (one was inclining his head to read the legends on them) and my desk. I studied the two men as I shook hands and thought, "Well, one of you (the thin one) might be a yacht-club member out for a spin, but if this here thick one is, then I'm the Bishop of Portsmouth." Aloud I greeted them in German: "Grüss Gott."

Thick-One was dressed in a white shirt, rolled up at the sleeves, black trousers and shoes. His belt showed wear on one side more than the other, where he had kept putting one hand or something in his pocket. "Pleased to meet you," said I, while Thomas made suitable German noises. "Always pleased to meet fellow yachtsmen." We plied all four of them with some hard stuff.

The upshot was that when we had explained our predicament, that the banks were closed for the May Day holidays, and the waiter had refused to change us money, they offered to accompany us to the restaurant, with us paying them in deutschmarks which they (they said) would change at a bank, while they paid for the meal in Czech korunas.

To the restaurant we did go, all six of us now, with hard stuff in us, all intelligent and handsome. The fink waiter almost dropped dead in subservience when he saw Thick-One with us, and spent most of the evening tripping over his own feet in a hurry to serve us. At supper we spoke mainly of boats and sailing. They told us that they could boat only a few occasions in the year, and the May Day holidays were the longest, so they came to the river to get away from their families and to drink. I had pocketed, as we had left the boat, the last box of cigars on board. They had been a Christmas present from someone in Nürnberg. There had been about twenty cigars in the box. As I placed them on the restaurant table there was a general grab for them, and in a flash there were none. Thick-One silently reached for the empty cigar box and shoved it into his capacious trousers pocket. All around us the other diners, who obviously knew who we were and what we were doing, avoided us with their eyes, although they greeted each other loudly across the room.

At the end of the meal, of devilishly hot soup, fish and vegetables, but no afters and no coffee, the four horsemen of the *Apocalypse*, as I had persuaded them to name their vessel among much amusement, saw us back to our dinghy and we thankfully gained again the decks of *Outward Leg*. They then shoved off in their tiny, now crowded and noisy boat.

"That was bloody hard work," I observed to Thomas, when they were out of earshot, as he went below to turn in.

"*Ja*, and it was very funny, too," he replied.

Now, when a German says something is funny, it immediately arouses my curiosity. "Funny? Why do you say that, Thomas?"

"You know what that label on the cigar box said?"

I shook my head.

He grinned. "Germany United." "*Deutsche Einheit.*"

"Oh, suffering Jesus!"

"*Ja*, and they're all party members, they told me!"

I went to sleep wondering, "Were they really yacht-club members?" As I write I still have not solved that one. But if Thick-One was not a police functionary, then I am not a small-craft navigator. Of that something very deep inside me is convinced. That is what it means to be voyaging through a police state, the worrying, incessant wondering about everybody.

The rest of the voyage through Czechoslovakia, of seventy-five miles from Hrusov to Komarno, took *Outward Leg* most of the next day, starting from early dawn. Even as we weighed the anchor two armed youths, lugging Kalashnikovs, so close that we could see the down on their cheeks, glared at us from the beach. Again, the scenery was uniformly dreary in the rain. Now, on the one side, was Hungarian territory, while our side, the east side, the one we must stick to, was Czechoslovak. Each bend again had its pale khaki watchtower among the trees, and each glade among the trees its patrol of be-rifled brainwashed youths. On the Hungarian side there was only one building the whole way from Hrusov to Komarno. That was a river-control post. The lone Hungarian at its window waved to us as we passed. Otherwise Hungary seemed to us, from the deck of *Outward Leg*, to be one vast, flat, empty plain of waving grass. There were no people, no animals, nothing but a few stumpy trees here and there.

At Komarno, understandably enough, for there was nothing to indicate otherwise, we made our way into the town's commercial port. This was a very large, smoky basin surrounded by dirty concrete jetties, watchtowers, a high wall and huge, noisy barges, most of them wearing droopy red hammer-and-sickle ensigns. We were, of course, immediately ordered out by puerile green-hats waving rifles, and sent alongside a pontoon under the bridge where Komarno meets the river. Opposite, only two hundred yards away, was Komarom in Hungary.

Hard by the pontoon we were escorted by an armed sailor into the office of a very tall man who looked like a young Boris Karloff. He looked sideways at us through crazy eyes as we entered. This was the duty customs officer. His radio was blaring out a soccer commentary, we understood. It took him about an hour, after studying our faces and clothes minutely with his maniacal eyes as he listened to his radio, to get round to talking at us.

He examined our passports on the table before him. Then he intoned in thick German, "You have broken the law." Thomas interpreted again for us.

"What law?" I asked him, as innocently as I could. On the wall a picture of Lenin listened.

"You have not spent your twenty dollars a day each, and you will be one day over the expiration of your visas after midnight tonight," he replied. There was the look and the sound of an incipient schizoid about him. Sure enough, he continued, "Do you like soccer?" He smiled; it was awful.

"I'm from Liverpool," I lied, as if that answered the question. That was what my passport said, because I was born on a Liverpool ship.

"We're the best soccer players in Europe," Boris went on.

"Liverpool's in England," I countered. Anywhere else in the world I would have explained, "but England isn't Europe," but in a Czech madman's office it's best to keep things short.

"I think I'll keep your boat here," he went on. "Until the Chief arrives in three days. Let him decide what to do about it."

I thought fast. Reverse psychology was the only solution, it seemed. "Oh, great," I crowed to Thomas in German, in my kind of German, *"Ach, das ist schön, und wir can gesehen alles das Stadt, und das bars, und den frauleins und den cinemas"* . . . "Then we can see all the city, and the bars, and the young ladies, and the cinemas . . ." is what I was trying to convey; which I did convey, obviously, because then Boris Karloff Junior stood up to his full seven feet, looked down at me and said, "No, I will not allow you to stay in Czechoslovakia." He thrust our passports into my face. "Now get on your boat and leave, immediately." It must have been quite a change from stopping Czechs from leaving the country.

We both, Thomas and I, tried not to show any relief at all. We meekly did as Boris had ordered us to do, clambered aboard, started the engine, and shoved off. We could hardly believe our luck. We rejoiced inwardly, while outwardly pretending to look hard-done-by. Elated, we let the Danube current sweep us rapidly midstream and into Hungarian waters.

As soon as we were out of Czechoslovakia and officially in Hungarian waters, with our Hungarian courtesy flag flying from a bent starboard stanchion over our wounded starboard side, I gave Thomas a nod. He was waiting for my nod, expectantly grinning. He swung down the after hatch and pushed the button of our tape player. Soon "Lament for the Old Sword" was echoing over the river, over our badly wounded boat, right across to where the mad Czech customs officer stood, all alone in the drizzle, on the pontoon, staring after us as we chugged away for Hungary and comparative freedom and light after the danger, gloom, depression and despondency of the Czechoslovak Soviet Socialist Republic and all its works.

# 20

# *The Green Fields Beyond*

Komarom had two very good things going for it: it was outside of Czechoslovakia and it was inside Hungary. As *Outward Leg* crossed the Danube to the Hungarian side we were waved to by a small thin soldier on the third pontoon upstream from the bridge. Although there was no marking on it, this was the customs pontoon, we were assured by the small, thin soldier who seemed to be in charge of it. Three minutes after being snugly tied up, we were ordered to the next pontoon upstream by a large customs officer, dressed in a light-blue uniform. There was twenty feet of water off both pontoons.

As soon as we had tied up there, the large customs officer spoke rapidly to the small, thin soldier. The soldier gestured to us with his rifle to follow him ashore. I was already exhausted with my efforts in Czechoslovakia. Thomas asked the large customs man, who understood very little German, if he alone could take the ship's documents and our passports to the police office, which the officer indicated was at the top of a steep hill.

No, that wasn't allowed. *"Der Kapitän müssen kom. Alles müssen kom."* The customs officer was quite gentle in his manner. But then after the Czechoslovaks even a Great White Shark would seem kind and gentle. But he was also firm, and so I soon found myself struggling to my feet after having clambered up over the cliff-like pontoon side, then, accompanied by Thomas and the small, thin soldier, hobbling along yet another long, dusty dock road to the back of a warehouse. From there a steep flight of very narrow steps led between official buildings and through a high barbed-wire fence. So far it all looked depressingly similar to the scenes on the Czech side of the Danube.

At the top of the narrow steps, the similarity to Czechoslovakia ended. We emerged into a little lane lined with flower-bedecked cottages. Someone actually smiled a greeting as I hobbled by. Just around the corner at the top of the steps was the Port Police Office. I had headed for it full of trepidation, but when we were ushered inside I had to pinch myself mentally to see if I was dreaming. The place was *palatial*. It was clean, light, spacious, well furnished and the walls were decorated with pictures, mostly in fair taste. It was also thronged with uniformed men and a few women. They milled around, it seemed, in no order, like people do at a cocktail party. There must have been at least a hundred of them, and they were all, it appeared, dressed differently. There were blue uniforms and gray uniforms, khaki, dark brown, white, beige and black. Loud music played from a radio somewhere, some sort of Western country tune. Everybody wandered around, from open office to open office, and gossiped loudly in a language which bore no relation to anything I'd ever heard before.

On the table of the general interviewing room, where we were led, was a big vase of flowers. Very high on one wall was a large picture of Lenin. He was leering through the picture windows across the river toward Czechoslovakia, and seemed to be ignoring Hungary altogether. His steady, slit-eyed gaze shot straight over the heads of everyone in the room.

Around the table were leather armchairs; real leather armchairs, and I sat back in one, disbelieving my senses and wondering what kind of subtle trap we had been led into. But there didn't seem to be any trap at all. Of the hundred or so officers who addressed us as they wandered past, only one or two spoke any German. Our large blue man collared one of these, to be our interpreter-interviewer. White-Shirt turned out to be a very civil gentleman, but even he could not enter us into Hungary without seeing the Ship's Builder's Certificate, as well as the Ship's Manifest, the Ship's Deratization Certificate, and the Ship's Crew List (in quadruplicate) together with our passports and visas, also our proof of financial solvency. I showed him our bankroll of $550.00. He nodded. I sent Thomas back to our boat to bring her Ship's Builder's Certificate. He would be much quicker than I, along the lane, down the steps, along the dock, over the pontoon and back again to the Police Office. Cheerfully, Thomas took off. I was left in the real leather armchair to twiddle my thumbs, stare up at Lenin and try to exchange pleasantries in bad German with White-Shirt and with a dozen other officers of all sizes, ages, shapes and color of uniform.

After a half-hour of banter and meditation in alternating spasms, it was obvious to me that something must be delaying Thomas. I hauled myself over to the window, which overlooked the river. Around the corner of the next building, if I leaned right out of the window, I could just see the pontoon where our boat . . . was swung out into the river with her bows pointing out to midstream and her stern hitting the iron pontoon! My heart almost stopped. I headed for the door. A half-dozen officers in various uniforms tried to detain me on the way out but I shouted at them in plain English to kindly allow me to get back to my boat as she was in grave danger of pounding to pieces if a river ship passed by and sent a huge bow wave under her. Actually what I said was something like, "Gangway, you bastards, my ship's in the shit!" Good job they knew no English; they all gave way.

I made it along the lane, down the steep steps and the quarter-mile along the dock in about three minutes. I had never walked so fast since my leg had been lopped off in New York three years before. As I swung along, praying for my boat, I could feel every pebble, every rough nodule on the surfaces of those concrete steps and rough dockside railtracks. Pain shot through my stump as I pushed myself to the uttermost limit of my agony-endurance. A large barge convoy heading upstream, deep and loaded, was the cause of my hurry. I made it in time to scramble on two arms and one leg onto our dinghy, with the help of Thomas, hop over the deck and throw a line ashore to Thomas, now on the pontoon, from the bow, so that when the stern line, which was still holding, was let go, *Outward Leg* could drift back on the current and lay herself safely again alongside the pontoon. The whole rescue took me no more than six minutes. Danger is a fine therapist.

Thomas had been straining at the spring line, which was almost at breaking point, for a half hour, to ease the tension off it. For half an hour he had been, alone, holding three tons from being swept downstream by an eight-knot current. He had not dared to leave the spring line in case it snapped.

We soon had our boat tied up like Gulliver among the Lilliputians. We had lines from and to everywhere within sight. Then she was comparatively safe again.

There are temptations, when something like this happens, to

wonder immediately what happened, to ponder on it, to cast recriminations or blame. I've always guarded against these. The first thing is to safeguard the vessel, let everyone calm down, let good humor and compassion take their course, and then hold the postmortem.

Later, it appeared that in the confusion of conflicting orders from the soldier and the customs official, and the rush to get ashore as they hustled us to the police office, both Thomas and I had forgotten to secure our boat's bow with *two* lines, which was our usual rule on the Danube. When a passing river ship had sent a big bow wave under *Outward Leg* she had risen, fallen down again, and the force of her drop had broken the single bow warp, which was of two-inch nylon line. Old Father Danube's current, always quick to take advantage, had pushed the bows away from the pontoon. This had brought the full force of dozens of tons of Danube water onto *Outward Leg*'s sides, and as her spring line took the strain she had been thrusting her three sterns into the pontoon, for her port ama was then the fulcrum of her agony. That was enough said; by the time we had figured out what had happened we had learned our lesson. Never again, no matter how many officials, soldiers or machine pistols there were to be on any jetty, would we ever let *Outward Leg* lay in Danubian waters to one bowline. Never again would we, in the customary mad rush of arrival, forget to throw out the bower anchor, either.

By the time we got back to the police office, sorted out our entry into Hungary and shaken the proffered hands of practically everyone in the building, we had put the broken bowline out of our minds, so great was our relief at being out and clear of Czechoslovakia. The customs officers who searched our boat were interested only in bottles and sampling their contents.

Komarom town was half a mile or so away from the port. We found one small hotel where the lady in charge spoke good German. We changed some deutschmarks illegally with a bundled-up little man who sidled alongside us on the street. There was a restaurant on a street corner in the middle of Komarom where loud gypsy music issued from the door. There we went, for a good, solid meal which cost us $4.00 each and that included some potent wine. The place was half-crowded with people in all sorts of conditions, well-off, middling and poor. Their clothes styles were from the mid-forties. Most of the people, we noticed, drank beer. The "gypsy" band was composed of a youngish man, who in his overalls looked like a truck driver, an elderly lady with white hair, who, like me, had only one leg, and a very old man with a long, gray beard. The truck driver played a wheezy squeezebox, the lady an off-tune grand piano which looked as if it might have once graced the halls of Emperor Franz Joseph, and the longbeard played a fiddle. This he did very well, except that his beard often got caught up with his bow. Then the effect made me sputter over my goulash. Many uniformed frontier guards and soldiers entered and left the restaurant while we were there. They seemed to be on most friendly and familiar terms with everyone, and they removed their caps when they entered, and kept them doffed until they left. Service was offhand but efficient enough, considering language problems.

There was only one bridge between Hungary and Czechoslovakia. That crosses the Danube at Hungarian Komarom and goes to Czech Komarno. One friendly customs officer told me that the reason the names are so similar is because in the days of the Austro-Hungarian empire it was all one town, on both sides of the river. Then when Czechoslovakia gained its independence it also gained the city center, and posh side of town, while Hungary was left with the poorer suburbs. "But now," he continued, "now we have the posh side of town."

"Why is this the posh side?" I asked him.

"Because it's in Hungary," he replied as if he were telling a child that fishes swim because they can't walk.

The bridge between Hungary and Czechoslovakia was shut at night except for trains on one of its levels. This meant that there were no traffic headlights, and no streetlamps lit at night near the river, which was also the frontier. Near and on the darkened bridge the shadows of frontier guards flitted from one doorway to another. I somehow felt closer to the early thirties here than I have done anywhere else. All the while I was in Komarom I had a strange feeling that time had stood still since I was a small boy. Even the lamplight in the town center had had a weird, grained effect, like a flickering old film.

The next day was fine and sunny. It was the first dry spell we had seen since we had left Vienna. *Outward Leg* shoved off in mid-forenoon after Thomas had shopped for fresh food, which he found very cheap after Austria.

The Komarom police instructed me to inform the local police whenever and wherever we berthed in Hungary. Apart from that there were few restrictions or onerous regulations all the way through the country. Almost invariably the police were friendly, and if they could speak no German, French or English, would send for someone who could.

We headed the thirty miles or so downstream to Esztergom. On this stretch we still had Czechoslovakia to one side of us, and Hungary was to the other, but our Hungarian courtesy flag was hoisted, and we were officially in Hungarian waters, and so our fear of treachery or danger from men and boys was much less.

As we passed downstream we saw that there were few habitations on the Czech bank of the Danube, but many villages and towns on the Hungarian bank. From these Hungarian villages, as we passed them, we received rousing cheers and waves all the way. Cars on the roads stopped and blew their horns for minutes at a time, while their occupants waved at our scarred boat from their windows. Many, many workmen, on barges and on the riverside, as we passed raised both their arms over their head and shook both hands. This was to become a perpetual rite all the way through Hungary and Yugoslavia, and much of Bulgaria, too.

"They must know of us, the way they're greeting *Outward Leg*," I observed to Thomas.

"How can they?" he replied, "They don't get any Western papers or television here." It was a puzzle which was soon to solve itself.

A big Soviet river tug appeared pushing upstream, all bustle and importance. It was followed immediately astern by a small convoy of large Czechoslovak river gunboats. Spying the case through my binoculars I nodded to Thomas, and on went our bagpipes. As we reached the convoy we were making all of twelve knots with Yannie at three-quarter power; all of the ships, the Soviet tug and the three Czechoslovak navy gunboats, slowed down for us, to lessen their bow waves, and everyone it seemed as we sped past, on their bridges and decks, cheered us. For that I told Thomas to dip our ensign, not so much to theirs, but to their gesture of consideration for *Outward Leg*. Saying "thank you" never hurt anyone.

About halfway between Komarom and Esztergom were some islands on the Danube. These belonged to Hungary, and the ship channel passed between them and the Czechoslovak bank. The Hungarian islands were lined with little weekend chalets, and this still being May Day weekend, they were crowded with Hungarians enjoying themselves. We had only just passed the tug and the gunboats, and Mr. McPherson's reels were still blaring out over the Danube as we tore through the narrow channel between the islands and Czechoslovakia. I will never forget the scene that followed as long as I live. On the one side was the Czech shore deserted except for a watchtower every mile or so, with an armed soldier atop it. On the other hand was a line of holiday chalets on the shores between the trees, stretching for about six miles. Outside the holiday chalets and from behind them and standing up in front of them, and climbing up to their roofs, suddenly there were hundreds of Hungarians, old and young, all shapes and sizes, dressed and undressed, excited and calm, loud and silent, and all of them waving like mad at *Outward Leg* as she ripped into their view, all her flags flying over her damaged starboard side. When I saw the people by the hundreds rushing down to the river, and many of them even into the water to be nearer to us, I slowed the engine right down, so that we now steered at the speed of the current, about four knots. Then I heard it, again, again and again, a sort of wild, thin cry over the twenty yards or so of distance on average between our cockpit and them: *"America! America! America!"* The cry came through to us from the tree-lined shores softly and stridently, clearly and indistinct, bass and tenor, man, woman and child, over and over and over again, all the way through that island passage, for a good hour, one voice at a time, one hundred voices at a time, calling, calling, across the water, *"America! America!"* They waved towels, jackets, handbags, beach balls, shirts; some even waved pillows and air mattresses at us as we passed by them, unable to stop, unable to do anything but wave back and steer the boat. For one minute or perhaps two as I watched them over the wrecked ruins of our starboard guardrails I thought it was raining again, but then I realized that what these people were calling for was not the America which we know *is*, but the idea of it, and the idea, the dream was our cargo, shown to the world about us in our ensign. They were recognizing, I realized, their own dream of peace and well-being and liberty, and the freedom to be safe from bullies and brainwashers.

I was very nearly overwhelmed by this reception by complete strangers. I was not to know, how could I, that this scene would be repeated time and time again, dozens of times, all the way down the Danube, wherever there were no policemen or armed skinheads to prevent it. When there was armed prevention, then there would be, it turned out, nothing but a silent look and perhaps a shy wave of a hand, or the holding up, suddenly, of a small child, to watch us as we passed while quiet words were whispered in the little one's ear, so that it, too, waved a little hand.

I only hope and pray that through these words they will be heard afar, right around the world!

Esztergom turned out to be beautiful. It was a fine, clean well-maintained town, seen from the river, overlooked by a fine, clean, well-maintained cathedral whose huge gold cross shone across the Danube, clear over to the banks of godless Czechoslovakia. "Long live Hungary," I whispered to myself when I saw that. It occurred to me how much easier it was for us in *Outward Leg* to pass through the Danube valley with our own symbols of respect for humanity and its immortal soul. We would, we knew, be here today and gone tomorrow, and one day, God willing, we would regain the sea and the freedom of the ocean. But the brave souls who kept that cross shining in Esztergom would be there all the time, day after day, night after night, month after month, year after year of Eastern European twilight. I promised myself that I would remember them when I had regained the freedom of the oceans, wherever I was.

When I think of courage and patience, the two necessities for any voyage, I shall remember the golden cross of Esztergom, where the Danube turns south in a great bend, away from Central Europe, to pass through the vast, ocean-like Magyar plain, and I shall remember the men who guard that cross gleaming golden in the sunlight, silver under the moon, for these are surely, in their own way, voyagers too.

There was a little river leading off the Danube, at Esztergom. Just inside it was a police pontoon. We berthed downstream a hundred yards from the inlet and ferried ourselves in the dinghy to the police post. We took along half a dozen empty water containers. The police, all in civilian clothes, were helpful and even carried a full can of water for us on our return from the tap at the café close by, across a pretty little park alive with excited children and spring blossoms.

By late afternoon I decided I'd had enough of being overlooked by the Czechoslovak frontier only a hundred yards over the river. I saw on a tourist map that the Czech frontier left the river only a few miles downstream, to head inland. Below that, the river Danube flowed only through Hungarian territory.

We headed downstream, cheered all the way from the Hungarian shore, and glared at by eight Kalashnikov-armed young louts at the very last Czech frontier-guard post. It seemed that we had crept down on them unawares. Their gray patrol craft was bobbing outside their gray pontoon post, but they were not ready to pile on board and head out to us. We tore silently round the bend, caught them napping, then a quarter of a mile downstream from them, in wholly Hungarian waters, switched on Mr. McPherson's "The Big Spree," a stirring pibroch from the good Scottish highlands. It is known to every Scots soldier from Glengarry to the Gorbals as "If you catch me you can fuck me." I could plainly see the Czechoslovak robot-boys jump up and gawp as we cleared away from them in the dying sunshine and left their shore entirely and irrevocably beyond our stern.

Now we were wholly in Hungary. Now we could, to a great extent, relax and enjoy the trip down the Danube as I'd always dreamed of doing.

Nagymaros at km 1694 was the first place where *Outward Leg* had tied up that had no policemen or armed guards since Vienna, 150 miles upstream. There were two ferry pontoons there, with twelve feet of water under them, but a strong current, about eight knots, because the channel here is only about 220 yards wide.

Here we found, in conversation with Hungarian riverboat men, that they despised the Soviet tugboat captains and crews. This was because, they said, all the Russian ships carried political officers who were in charge of the crew, and the captain was on board merely to steer the ship. The Soviet ships spent nothing, according to them, all the time they were on the river, because they brought with them from Ismail, the only real Soviet Danube port, all the stores and fuel they would need for the whole voyage up and down the river, no matter how far they went. When it came to food, for example, on board the Russian ships, if the meals were bad it wouldn't matter one bit. The cook was a party member. There was nothing the captain could do about it. The same went for any other activity on board the Russian ships, according to the Hungarians. Because of the crewmen's affiliation to the party their whole responsibility was to the party commissar, and not to the captain.

"So why don't they make the commissar the captain?" I asked.

"Captain? They'd be better with Donald Duck in charge!" was the reply. "At least he knows how to wear a sailor's hat!"

What we were told next surprised us even more. The river ships'
skippers talk to each other on their radios, as seamen do on VHF. It
seemed that our near-sinking in Bratislava, and our passage through
and out of Czechoslovakia, was now common knowledge among all
the ships of all the eight Danube nations. So too was my disclaimer
for damages from the tug *Matra*. Thus the tremendous cheers and
vigorous waves we were raising whenever we passed a ship coming
upstream, or were ourselves overtaken by one heading downstream.
We were part of a far-flung family now, strung from West Germany to
the Black Sea, from the Soviet Union to the Adriatic. Now, it seemed,
*Outward Leg* was bearing her own legend beside her own dream. That
suited me well, for legends fly much farther than gossip, and last for
much longer.

Outside the Danube valley, no one knew where we were nor what
was happening. I could not tell them, except in the most general
terms, in case other powers should lay their hands on us to stop our
voyage, delay our progress, or diminish our triumph.

As this was now the "tourist season," the river ferries were operating. We had passed a few, of a wonderful age, coming downstream. We asked if any were due to arrive at our pontoon that night.
No one knew, or everybody knew, but differently. I decided to take
a chance and go ashore with Thomas for an evening meal. It was
cheap enough to do that on many occasions in Hungary. Close to the
pontoon there was a restaurant with modern music blaring all evening.
It was crowded. There were hundreds of people milling about inside,
and on a clearing the size of a postage stamp several couples were
jitterbugging. All wore casual leisure clothes, and all looked moder-
ately well off. We waited an hour to be served by the harried waiters.
Thomas had steak tartare, I had wiener schnitzel and we shared a
bottle of good white wine. The meal cost a total of $10.00.

I am not comfortable in crowded places, especially since my leg
was amputated, and especially where people get tipsy or drunk. Some
clumsy drunk might fall backward and knock me flying. We left the
restaurant fairly early and returned across the square to the pontoon,
to find a considerable crowd gathered round, staring at *Outward Leg*
as her turquoise decks reflected the riverside lamplight. Of the hundred
or so onlookers, old and young but mostly young, at least half of them
asked us for an American flag. We could, we found in the next few
weeks, have distributed thousands of them all the way down the

Danube. This was the first request, but from Nagymaros onward, wherever we berthed, it was a continuous refrain.

From Nagymaros to Budapest, the capital city of Hungary, was a twenty-six-mile run. The Danube current was strong in Hungary, and with the help of its four knots average we could have made the trip in a couple of hours had we hurried. But the day was fine; it was a Sunday; and all the Hungarians were out on the river's edge fishing or sunbathing or just promenading. We passed several weekend resorts and many villages and towns, and all the way we were cheered and waved at.

At the village of Venceramos we stopped for lunch. There was fifteen feet of water by the pontoon and *no current*. Here many people came to the ferry pontoon to greet us. Many youngsters toured through the boat. A student who spoke good English, a young man of twenty, talked with me for a few minutes. It was a polite exchange about our voyage, the weather, and supplies available in the local shops. These were good and plentiful, he said. But to me it meant much more. His was the first English I had heard, except from Thomas, since Vienna, over 125 miles upstream. The village policeman, hatless, tie undone, wearing no gun, broke off his Sunday lunch to come and greet us. A group of children, who earlier had visited the boat, returned bearing gifts from their parents, of wine and cheese, and an invitation to their homes in the town, for coffee. But I wanted to enter Budapest on that Sunday afternoon, when the river would be less busy from working traffic, and so we wished them farewell and told them we would not forget them, as they had begged us not to.

So we steamed on, past the fabled Margit Island and into the most beautiful riverside city I have ever seen, Budapest.

As we passed under the Margit Island bridge, staring around us over our scars and wounds in wonder at the architecture, the parks, the churches, cathedrals, chapels, parliament buildings, castles and monuments, Thomas asked, "Where are we going to berth, Tristan?"

"In the middle, old son, right in the very heart!"

"Do you think they'll let us stay there?" he inquired.

"It's like old Admiral Nelson said, Thomas."

He looked at me seriously. I was always telling him what Nelson had said about this, that or the other.

I intoned, *"A good captain can do no wrong if he lays his ship alongside the enemy."*

"The enemy?"

"That's right. Big Brother. We're going to moor right in front of the Ministry of the Interior."

Thomas hopped up onto the foredeck to ready the mooring lines, as all around us tugs, barges, tankers, ferries and even water-taxis sounded their sirens off at our coming, arrival and our passing.

As we tied up at the first pontoon upstream from Adam Clark's famous British chain bridge, a police launch bore down on us, its siren blowing. A policeman on deck was waving us away.

Thomas looked at me.

"Well, even Nelson couldn't be right *all* the time," I told him, as we made to shift.

# 21

# *A Tale of Two Cities*

The capital of Hungary, Budapest, is made up of two cities: Buda, on the "west" bank of the Danube, and Pest, on the "east."

When *Outward Leg* had tied up at Pest city center pontoon a youngish man, who had been riding a bicycle along the riverside road, stopped, rushed down the pontoon gangway and hailed us in English, "Hi, good evening!" He was fair-haired, fresh-complexioned and tidily dressed.

Even while our boat was still bumping the pontoon and Thomas tying up, I did something I very rarely do. I took notice of the man while the boat's security was yet at hazard. Normally I ignore any kind of calls or chat from jetties or docks until our boat is safely and snugly berthed. Only then do I exchange words with people ashore. The reason for that is because most of the snarl-ups and errors that occur in berthing and unberthing small craft do so when the skipper's attention is distracted by exchanges with onlookers ashore or in other craft. But at Budapest on our first arrival I had been so pleased that someone spoke a language that both Thomas and I could understand that I broke my custom for that occasion. "Good evening!" I called out to the cyclist.

"Welcome to Budapest!" He sang out over the noise of traffic crossing the bridge immediately upstream from our pontoon. "If there is anything I can do to help you, please let me know . . ." He had just shouted those words when the police patrol boat roared alongside, its siren blaring, and waved me to move *Outward Leg* off the pontoon.

I told Thomas, as soon as it was obvious from the patrol craft crew's gestures that we must move, to let go of the lines. Our Yanmar

195

was already running. Indeed, there had been no time to stop it. All
the complement of the patrol craft, four men, were in the gray uniform
of the Hungarian river police. They did not glare at us, nor wave
their guns at us, as had the Czechs, but they were quite firm about
us having to move right then, and right away from there. The sergeant
pointed a finger upstream and then waved it from side to side, as if
he were telling us that we could berth anywhere up there, outside
the city, but not here, outside the Ministry of the Interior.

By now the cyclist had turned away, silent, and was walking along
the pontoon gangway. As he did so and as I watched in glances, for
I was busy, I saw that he was escorted by two men in civilian clothes.
They took his elbows and escorted him behind a low tree on the river
bank walk, where they were obviously questioning him.

*Outward Leg* moved away from the pontoon slowly, against the
Danube current, which is strong through Budapest.

The two cities of Buda and Pest were built where they are because
the river there is narrow. The water flow from half Central Europe is
forced through a defile only 220 yards or so wide. That means a fast
current. We could make hardly two knots against it. I told Thomas
to play the bagpipes, because I wanted as many people as possible
to know that *Outward Leg* was in the area, and had been made to
return upstream, out again from the city. "We'll be back," I told
myself and Thomas.

To cut a long story sideways, the next two days were spent shifting
*Outward Leg* from one unsafe berth to another. This was mainly off
the island of Romai, about five miles upstream from Budapest, where
there is a sportscraft club and some small pontoons of sorts, muddy
lanes and the only surly local people we met in Hungary. Even for
agile young people the task of getting ashore and back on board was
strenuous and hazardous, made so by slippery mud on the whole river
bank. Even for monohulls, anything over a half-ton displacement
would be at risk off Romai. The pontoons were small, fragile and
weakly moored by hawsers more fit for knitting wool. The current
there was a relentless six to nine knots, depending on the rainfall
farther upstream. Anchors, any anchors, simply would not hold in the
soft mud river bottom.

The day after we had been chucked out of Budapest on our first
call, the English-speaking cyclist turned up, along with his wife, in
a car. We invited them to sup with us. He told us that the two men

in civilian clothes had been security police, and they had at first asked him why he was talking to us. He had told them he had offered to interpret for us. They then asked him for his identity passport, which, he said, all Hungarians must carry with them all the time. He did not have his passport with him. The police had taken him to the police post nearby and fined him 1,000 forints ($20.00) on the spot. It made me wonder how many times Hungary voted at the United Nations against South Africa, which has similar stupid laws for its citizens.

All the while *Outward Leg* was in exile from Budapest at the, for me, remote island of Romai, an unknown friend had been busy making arrangements to get us back into the city. This was Peter Kerenyi, of Radio Budapest. He, as he later told us, had been trying to track us down ever since he had first heard of a mysterious, legendary boat, with a strange, three-hulled shape, turquoise and gray, which was progressing down the Hungarian Danube playing loud bagpipe music. Eventually, after a marathon of phone calls and car drives, he tracked us down at Romai.

With him we met a group of young ladies on holiday from their work at a textile factory in the south of Hungary. There were twenty-five of them, who all worked together, and who all stayed together, even on holiday. They were staying at a factory-owned villa near where we were moored at a public ferry pontoon. We were having to shift *Outward Leg* every time a ferry arrived during the daytime. But that evening we were free to go ashore to the young maidens' villa, and there, over a simple meal of fried ham and bread with good wine I told them, around their garden campfire, what I knew of dolphins, for evidently there are no dolphins in Hungary. Peter interpreted for me and they listened, bright-eyed and ecstatic as I described the leapings and lovings of our sea dogs so far away. They were all very pretty, all between the ages of seventeen and twenty-two, all charming to be with, even though we did not understand one word of what they said.

As the fire gleamed in their eyes in the shade from the moonlight under the high fir trees, I thought of the thousands of sailors who were dreaming of such nights as this. They were thousands of miles away, in their crowded, smoky, noisy yacht marinas in Tahiti and St. Thomas, Ibiza and Rhodes, and I silently rejoiced inside me at our fabulous fortune. Those young women from the great Magyar plains obviously worshipped the waters that Thomas and even I voyaged upon. Next day we took them all for a ride a few miles upstream on board *Outward Leg*, and they looked as though they would never forget it as long as they lived. I certainly won't. I thought that the place we took them to, the island of Lupus, on the river Duna, was one of the most idyllic, quietly beautiful places I have ever been to in a long life of wandering, and made up my mind to return there one day, perhaps to write. It was all high trees, singing birds and little villas with carefully tended gardens. Lupus was lovely.

Next morning, still homeless, we tried once more to get our anchor to hold at several places on the Danube, but the old bugger wouldn't let us rest. He wanted us to go to Budapest and his current and mud bottom kept making our anchor drag. I was tempted to head upstream again for Lupus island and berth there. It would have been illegal, because of course the island is not on the International Waterway of the Danube. But at least the boat would have been safe there. Thomas was just beginning to haul up the anchor rode yet again when a police launch zoomed in on us. It was not the same as the one that had made us retreat upstream from Budapest. The sergeant in charge was a big, jolly-looking man who spoke good German. "Get your anchor up quick!" he shouted, as his boat bumped alongside ours on our gashed and broken starboard side. At first I thought we were in trouble for being in the entrance to the river Duna with our anchor down, but it turned out that he wanted us to go back downstream.

I got out our chart—a roadmap of Budapest. "*Wohin?* Where?" I asked him as I traced the Danube course with a grubby finger.

"*Dort*, there!" he pointed a chubby thumb at central Pest. It was laid directly over the pontoon just off the Ministry of the Interior, immediately upstream from the Adam Clark chain bridge, the one we had been unceremoniously chucked off two days before. The open space by it was marked "Roosevelt Square." I was elated. As the sergeant, by then well-fortified, left *Outward Leg*, I nodded to Thomas, who had stowed away the anchor line. *Outward Leg* drifted midstream for a moment, until the police launch cleared away. Then, with Mr. McPherson's tootlesacs blasting away at full volume, our Yanmar engine at full revolutions, and all our flags and burgees whipping in the breeze, *Outward Leg* reentered the city of Budapest at a good fifteen knots. I kept up this speed until she was opposite the

Parliament Building, when I slowed her down to six knots. All the way into the city she was greeted with shouts of welcome; cars blew their horns for her and ships their sirens. We tied her up at exactly noon and stayed there, with our large Stars and Stripes waving aloft in the sunshine, for *three weeks*.

There were several reasons for our long stay in Budapest, but the main is such an extraordinary story that I would hesitate to even consider such an episode for inclusion in a novel. Certainly, if I read it in a novel I should think it so contrived as to believe that the author must have been running short of original solutions to his problem. But this account is true, and there are, this time, many witnesses to one of the most glaring instances of "synchronistic destiny" that I have ever encountered.

Five minutes after *Outward Leg* had tied up at the "Min-Int" pontoon in Pest by Roosevelt Square, a grubby green van stopped at the head of the gangway. Out of it stepped a large young man, dark and handsome, in filthy black overalls. He wandered down the gangway, and for a moment or two, along with a dozen other silent onlookers, stared down at *Outward Leg*. Then he caught my eye.

"Me artist," he claimed proudly as he stuck a grubby thumb at his chest. His overalls were open several buttons. His black chest hair showed.

"Oh, good for you," I called back. I'd heard that one before at a thousand docks and jetties the world over. But there was something very different about this one. For one thing, his hands were dirty. There are very few painters or writers with dirty hands that I've met. Another thing that was different about him were his eyes. He had voyager's eyes. I decided to be curious. "And what do you do?"

This puzzled him. His English seemed to be very basic indeed. I closed my fingers and thumb together and waved my wrist up and down: "Painter? Do you paint?"

He wagged his head. "Artist!" he repeated, poking at his chest.

I pressed my forefinger and thumb together and made as if I were scribbling. "Writer? Do you write?"

"No, no!" He closed both fists and held one above the other and made a hissing sound with his lips. I thought he looked as though he was miming a fireman, playing at being a water hose.

"*Schweissen!*" shouted Thomas, loudly, as he too stared at the man miming on the pontoon. I thought my crewman was cursing. I turned to Thomas with a querying look.

Thomas explained, "You know, *schweissen*—when you stick two pieces of iron together and . . ." Now he too made the hissing noise. The man on the pontoon, as Thomas did this, grinned hugely and nodded his head vigorously. I turned back to my crewman, and even as I did so the penny dropped in my head. Daylight flooded the world. It couldn't be true? I said quietly, "You don't mean welding metal, do you?"

Thomas nodded. "*Ja*, welding metal, that's it!"

"Ask him what *kind* of metal," I said, then I remembered that Thomas was in a worse situation than I as language went with English speakers. I turned my face up again to the man on the pontoon.

"Metal?" I felt like a six-year-old moron. "Iron?" The man nodded. "Steel?"

Again the man nodded and said something in Magyar.

I decided to take the plunge. My throat constricted. The words came out like those of a small child asking his Daddy for an ice cream on a hot day.

"*Stainless* steel?"

There was a flood of liquid-sounding vowels and consonants from the man which must have made Old Father Danube himself envious as he burbled by, underneath my feet. But one of the words I caught in this flow was a word understood by sailors from Khartoum to Connecticut, from San Francisco to Sydney, from Birmingham to Budapest . . . *inoxidizable*. It came out of him like burbles of water running over a stony brook.

The moment I heard that word I moved faster than I had since our boat was breaking free in Komarom the week before. (Was it only the week before?) I clambered out on deck, skitted and clattered over the wing deck and so to the starboard ama, which was hard against the pontoon. I almost fell into the vent netting as I bent down and picked up one of our broken guardrail stanchions, dangling still on the guardrail wire. I tried to hold it up to the man on the pontoon, but the wire would not let it free. "*Inoxidizable?*" I spluttered, hardly daring to believe what was being said, or what I understood was being said.

"Inoxidizable!" shouted the young man. He was grinning hugely now, and pushing again his chest with his thumb, then at our broken stanchion.

I stared at him, his black, greasy overalls, his dark hair, his dreamer's eyes for a full minute, like an idiot. Then I said to him quietly, gesturing down the pontoon side as I did so, and over our deck, "Come aboard. Come aboard, my friend." I felt like a spider who had just trapped a great big fly.

Within ten days all our heavy stainless steel guardrail stanchions, one-inch-diameter tubes of strong metal, otherwise unavailable to private citizens anywhere in Eastern Europe, were rebuilt or made anew.

Out of the millions of people who might have been in Budapest when *Outward Leg* arrived we had met the one and only one who could heal our wounds from the Czechoslovak setup. Or perhaps something directed him to us. He said he had "just been passing by" and didn't see our damaged guardrails until I showed him one. He swore he knew nothing about our near-sinking in Bratislava, and that indeed he knew nothing at all about us, until he had sighted our big American ensign fluttering in the breeze outside the Ministry of the Interior. He had been in a hurry to go home, but his curiosity had got the better of him, as it should of any true artist, and he had stopped his car to stroll over and see what the flag was all about.

Biro Tamas was an artist, working under the auspices of the University of Budapest, sculpting in metal. His ambition was, one day, to build his own seagoing boat in stainless steel. He already had plans for it. In return for his repairing and remaking our starboard side, I pored over his plans with him, of a Bruce Robertson forty-footer, checking and suggesting. It was all I could do, for he would take no money. I also wrote to the London World Trade Centre, recommending Tamas's work for display there. I don't know what came of that.

During the time that Tamas healed our wounded side, I explored the waterfront of Pest. Although public transport was frequent, convenient to the berth and cheap, I preferred to do it on my foot, for the walk was one of the most beautiful city walks anywhere that I knew of, and I had seen cities on six continents and many on ocean islands. I still don't know of one that is more beautiful than the two cities of Budapest together. In the seaside cities of the world, such as Hong Kong, Sydney, Cape Town or Rio, there is generally only one shore to see. Here in Budapest there were two, each one vying with the other for interest, charm and lovely perspectives. The great statue to the Red Army that dominates both cities reminded me of the tremendous sacrifices made by the Soviets to defeat Hitler, but it also reminded me that they had no right to colonize with their ideology the lands they had liberated.

The most pleasant walk I found was along the Pest riverside promenade that led in front of the International Hotel. Even when it was raining, which was not often, I could still walk under the drawn-out awnings. Just beyond the Hotel International was a corner shop, where most groceries, fresh and canned, were available at about one third of the cost in England or in the U.S.A. Right opposite the corner shop was the Restaurant Neopolitano, where a good Italian meal with wine cost Thomas and me about $6.00 for the two of us.

Closer to the Min-Int pontoon on Roosevelt Square is the Hotel Atrium. Most voyagers would find its costs reasonable but it was too expensive for us to eat there more than once or twice. English newspapers were available in the foyer. In the Atrium Hotel there was also a business office, and from there we could, with no problems of language or procedure at all, telephone abroad, to England, West Germany and the United States. Telephone calls abroad were expensive, but we always wrote down beforehand what we were to say, in cryptic short form, so that we did not waste time and money.

The staff at the business office in the Hotel Atrium were very helpful and sympathetic to all our problems. Their English was the best I'd heard in Hungary. One of the young ladies had an uncle who had sailed his own boat from Australia in 1956 to Pula, in the Adriatic. This, no doubt, helped *Outward Leg* no end, and again goes to show, as I observed to Thomas about voyagers, "We Are Everywhere."

In Budapest the taxi drivers were reluctant to take us on rides of less than two miles. Some of them were downright insulting. They were the only rude people I met in Budapest itself.

From Budapest I was trying to raise interest in our progress in New York and London respectively. Thomas was trying to raise a reserve of $500 from his parents in Munich in case of unforeseen delays or disaster farther down the Danube, in Yugoslavia, Bulgaria, or Rumania. I felt bitter about being reduced to trying to raise a loan at this stage. I had foreseen a need for a reserve fund during the winter in Germany, but all the articles I had written then to earn it had been laid aside and evidently forgotten, and so now we were paying the price of someone else's negligence or slow-mindedness. Thomas's mother, bless her, knew something of the vagaries of a writer's income, and promised to lay aside $500 for us, which she would send out to us should we need it.

In Budapest, as in Vienna, we traveled around the city by subway train. On one visit to Moscow Square station I suddenly felt a tremor run through the crowd of people around me in the station foyer. It seemed that everyone had instantly hushed. Then I heard behind me a sinister sound, like a rustling, shuffling noise, and low murmurs, as of animals passing into an abattoir. I looked around to see what it was. There, passing within feet of us, was a battalion of very scruffy troops. They were wearing dirty battle dress and big leather boots which shapelessly reached to their calves. The boots seemed to be all the same size, regardless of the build of their wearer. The young men's jackets were of cotton, and shapeless too, like cheap shirts worn outside their khaki trousers and tied over the waist by a thick leather belt. Their faces were very sunburned and they were of many racial types: European, Mediterranean, Teutonic, Slavic, some even Scandinavian in appearance, many Asiatic, with some of Turkish, some of Mongol, and some of purely Chinese aspect. They all wore a baggy forage cap fronted with a red star, for these were soldiers of the Soviet Red Army on the move, and my heart bled for such waste.

Every one of the Hungarians around us, as the Soviet battalion shuffled and straggled past, turned his or her back on the sight, and studiously and silently ignored it.

There is no doubt in my mind that the Budapest Hungarians still are among the most elegant people in Europe. Their elegance is not merely on the surface; it reaches right down inside them. They have a fine sensitivity that shows in everything they make, do or say. All the Hungarian people that I encountered (with the exception of the taxi drivers) were among the most charming and courteous folk I have ever come across. In this they vyed with the Western Irish and the Paraguayans. There is an artistic flair in all of them that shows even to the way a tablecloth is set out, even to the way a streetcar ticket is inspected.

Both Thomas and I spent our birthdays in Budapest. Mine was 8 May. The whole riverside was lit up for the anniversary of Victory in Europe. His was 20 May, and we celebrated it in what turned out to be a most expensive Chinese restaurant in the city.

This meal was a special occasion, as all our meals ashore were. Even though in Eastern Europe meals ashore were much cheaper, on average, than they would have been in similar restaurants in the West, we were not well off, so most meals were cooked and eaten on board. We skipped breakfast every day, to save money in case of breakdowns or accidents.

Our visits to the Rumanian and Bulgarian embassies to secure visas were expensive, both in taxis and fees, and tiresome, because of interminable waits in dreary rooms. It took two weeks of intricate negotiation to secure our visas for Rumania. It took fifty-six of our few dollars to grab the Bulgarian visas.

During our stay in Budapest we met officials from the city's handicapped-people's rehabilitation center. With them we arranged to take a party of wheelchair cases, mostly with no legs, and recently amputated one-legged cases for a trip upstream to Lupus island. There were seven wheelchairs strapped to the deck of *Outward Leg* and nine people on crutches. They were all ages, from seven to seventy, and enjoyed themselves, we think, thoroughly. The weather was sunny and we played Handel's "Water Music" on our tape player as we shoved upstream to Lupus and then back down again in the evening.

During our stay in the city an estimated average of forty people a day visited *Outward Leg*. These included parties of schookids and the cast of the local city children's theater as well as handicapped people. It was hard going, sometimes, with a crowded vessel, and trying to make preparations for the further one thousand miles to the shores of the Black Sea and for the sea passage beyond, but with good humor and patience Thomas managed to show everybody around the boat. The kids in particular were thrilled by our pictures of the whale which had tried to play with the boat off the Azores, and with my wooden leg that Larry Pardy had so kindly made for me. A few handicapped people, men, women and youngsters, also managed to negotiate the clamber down from the pontoon as our boat rocked and rolled continually in the wash of passing craft. But many of them lingered on the pontoon and inspected us and our boat from their wheelchairs and, on three moving occasions, from the stretchers to which they were condemned for the rest of their lives. I like to think that even they gathered a mite of hope from *Outward Leg*. I certainly prayed so.

During the whole of our Danube voyage, only four things were stolen from us, all in Budapest. They were: one small hand-digital timer, which I used for navigational timing; one U.S. ensign, the one we'd had since the boat had been commissioned and which was embroidered and usually hung from the stern staff; one British Red Ensign, and one Royal Naval Sailing Association burgee.

We made a new rule on *Outward Leg*. We would never leave our boat with no one on board or watching her at nighttime with her ensigns or flags hoisted. I know that the old fuddy-duddies will say, "Serves him right; he should have lowered his ensign at sunset," but in actual fact we were navigating on an International Waterway, and the laws state that vessels must show, day and night, their nationality, under way or not. But we could not now afford to lose the ragged and tattered flags that remained. They were the only ones we had, and the nearest replacement, at least of Old Glory, would be at Istanbul. I had begged friends for spares, but none had arrived.

People sitting at home in some Western country's suburb, or in someone's yacht in some marina in the Antilles or the Mediterranean, might wonder why all the fuss about a few pieces of colored cloth? But from the deck of an ocean vessel surrounded by hundreds of miles of Soviet-dominated territory on one side, and thousands on the other, the view was different indeed. In the weeks to come, those pieces of ragged cloth would be almost all that defended us, in some instances, from arrest, imprisonment, or even worse.

One day, before *Outward Leg* left Budapest, I hobbled ashore to see the Soviet consul in his lair. I wondered innocently enough, what would be his reaction to a request for permission to voyage on the Black Sea once we had emerged from the Danube to ports in the Soviet Union. He asked me what the purpose of my visit was, and I told him: to visit handicapped people, because an amputation to a Russian is just as painful and problematical as it is to anyone else. I was especially interested in meeting amputated veterans from the Soviet Arctic fleet, who had shared such arduous and hazardous warfare with us British matelots during World War Two. I had heard they had a special hospital for those men in the Crimea. Could I please have permission to go and see them? He, a large gentleman with the face of a gentle bloodhound, was very noncommittal. He coughed quietly and was sympathetic and understanding, as he told me he was being, and referred me to his colleagues in Yugoslavia. Hungary, he said had no seacoast, and so the Soviet government had no naval attaché in Budapest. I told him that I had seen Soviet vessels on the Danube which looked, to me, very much like naval ships, with antennae sprouting everywhere and strengthened deck sections just right for guns or missile launchers to be mounted on. He again coughed and repeated that he knew nothing about maritime matters, and would I go to Belgrade? He told me that he would not pass my request on to Moscow, as the reply would take "too long." But he would contact his colleague in Belgrade and notify him of my request.

As for the United States Consulate in Budapest, I sent Thomas to tell them where *Outward Leg*, a U.S.-registered vessel, was berthed, along with an invitation to anyone interested to visit her. The reply was a great fat silence, which said to me, loudly and clearly, "Buddy, you're on your own!"

# 22

# *The Naked Truth*

Lazlo was an official of the Bank of Hungary, and a leading light of its sailing club on Lake Balaton. He arranged to take us there in his car for a weekend, before *Outward Leg* was due to depart from Budapest. His car, Russian made, soon whizzed Thomas and me along the motorway that leads out of Buda, through the attractive city of Székesfehérvár, and then we were out in some of the prettiest countryside I had seen since I visited Clare Francis's family home in Buckinghamshire, eight months before. It was mid-May, well into Central European spring, and the plants, as usual, were recognizing it before people did. All the trees were in blossom and the grass was as green as anything this side of Ireland.

Lazlo's car motored more slowly through the twisting lanes on the north shore of the lake, and I was glad of it. Now and again we could see the lake, wide, wide and deep blue among the shoreside trees. Everything seemed to be blooming most recklessly; if the colors had been voices there would have been an unbelievable din. I realized the difference between motoring in a car through the countryside, and boating. In a car, you passed through the land. In a boat, the land glides by you. On roads, everything is set up for your coming; the traffic signals, the signs over shop doorways, the roadside façades of the houses, even the people are aware, it seems, that a car is coming around the bend. In a boat it is very different. There you see the backs of shoreside houses, there you catch the people ashore unawares. In a car you are either driver or passenger; on the river you are a *traveler*. On the river you are as close to travel before the age of steam as modern man can be, unless he walks. There is no way better to know a land you travel through than by doing it on a river. There, in the main, the people are natural, their own selves, and the subconscious urge to be "up-to-date" does not seem to affect them. When the land travelers come to the riverbanks, they come relaxed and again revert to what people were before the invention and spread of the internal combustion engine.

On the shores of Lake Balaton we saw many sailing centers. Some were for youth organizations; they sailed mainly *Optimists*, *Soling* and *Lasar* dinghies, and there were many old *Snipes* about, too. At Balaton we met the busiest yacht builder in Hungary—a private concern because the state-owned fiberglass yacht factory had been closed down for some reason that was not made clear to me. I could guess what the reason was. No state can build anything as individual as a small sailing craft efficiently and well. The private concern was operating in the garden of a house by the lake edge. There were two twenty-eight-footers under construction, one recently out of the hull-molding stage, and one with her hull almost completely furnished, ready for launching. The office of the concern was in the cabin of an old river launch now high and dry in the garden. The whole thing was run by a big, jolly man in his mid-forties, who worked single-handed, with help now and again from members of his congregation, for he was the local Catholic priest. His workmanship was as good as most that I have seen in coastal boatyards, and far better than the general run.

Nearby the private boatyard was the Tihany peninsula. This was a major Hungarian holiday resort, and there were visitors from some Western countries as well as thousands of East Europeans. Bus after bus of East Germans passed through while we waited for the ferry that crosses the lake. Some spoke with Thomas, but it was obvious that apart from their language they had nothing at all in common with him. Thomas told me that the East German youngsters talked as if by litany. Most of them lectured him on "International peace and the brotherhood of man," and "Socialist solidarity." By the looks of them, they believed it all too.

We stopped with Lazlo at a fish-fry stall near the ferry, for lunch. There were nationals of half-a-dozen Eastern Bloc lands standing around, eating fried perch, which was very cheap and delicious, and drinking beer or cola. The Russians, easily spotted by their old-fashioned clothes, remained strictly apart and spoke among themselves in low murmurs.

The yacht club was at Tihany itself, by the yacht haven. There we were shown many beautifully preserved and still-operating sailing yachts from the nineteen-thirties, a few from the twenties, and one or two of pre-World War One vintage. We were told that the boat building and sailing activity on Lake Balaton had been started in the 1870s. It appears that in the days of the Austro-Hungarian empire there was much rivalry between the two capitals, Vienna and Budapest.

The Viennese wanted to send their own boat builders to Lake Balaton from the shores of the Adriatic, which then belonged to Austro-Hungary. But the Budapest yachtsmen forestalled them by sending to Britain for craftsmen to build their own boats on Lake Balaton, and the whole thing was started by an Englishman from Essex and a Welshman from Swansea.

The two Britons' influence still showed very much on the lake. The Hungarian sailing yachts bore the unmistakable marks of nineteenth-century British design: narrow beams, fine bows, rounded sterns, masts well forward. The workmanship in these craft was precious, and I was pleased to see them still in use.

The night I spent at Tihany in the local yacht club dormitory was the first I had slept off *Outward Leg* since I had left London. I could not sleep. I missed her little tinkles and jiggles, and her whispers to me in the dark.

We should have stayed at Lake Balaton another day. The world sailing championships were taking place there. But I could not be easy in my mind away from *Outward Leg*, even though I knew the Bank yacht club members were keeping a wary eye on her back in Budapest. It is not easy to explain the relationship between a voyager and his craft without appearing to landsmen perhaps a little touched by the sun. A voyager's boat is not a *thing*, like a car or a motorcycle, or even a weekend yacht, or a runabout. A voyaging craft is the sum total of all the emotions and influences of all the people who have ever had anything to do with her, just as is, for the most part, a human being. In that way a voyager's craft is imbued with a personality of her own in the voyager's mind, until, at some magic moment, she does actually become like a person. This anthropomorphism, this transmutation of my vessel from a thing to a person, has never occurred in my mind until we, the vessel and I, have overcome some great risk. I could never think of a newly built craft as anything more than a collection of bits and pieces of different materials, no matter how skillfully they were designed and put together as a whole. Because of that, and because of the limitations of her own abilities to think and act for herself, it was my duty to care for *Outward Leg*, and to be with her whenever I was able. She was no longer a piece of property; she was a living soul. She was no longer a reflection of my needs, my ambitions, my preferences; now she herself had needs, was ambitious, and reflected her own preferences. It wasn't only with my own boat. I could tell a happy voyage ship as soon as I stepped foot on her, whether I knew the owner or not, even if there was no one around for miles.

For these reasons, although I could have stayed on the shores of Lake Balaton as long as I liked, we headed back to Budapest and *Outward Leg*, to continue our voyage down the Danube valley for another thousand-odd miles.

We departed from Budapest to the air of "Arniston Castle," played by Mr. McPherson on his tootlesacs. It was a fine day, 24 May, as we sedately wafted past all the big tourist ships off the Pest pontoons. They were mostly Soviet and Bulgarian flag vessels, and crowded with passengers and crew, who waved us a cheery send-off. We passed under four bridges and then kept our eyes skinned for ships emerging from the Budapest commercial haven at km 1640.

South of Budapest the scenery was, at first, industrial, but not too dreary in the warm sun. For the first time that year we erected our canvas dodger over the cockpit, not to shelter us from cold wind, snow, hail or rain, but from the sun. There were many groins in the km 1950s and 1940s, and ferries crossing the Danube from side to side were sometimes suspended from wire cables strung high across the river to prevent them from being thrust downstream by the strong current. This was a common practice on the Danube, the whole way down. Another common ferry-securing method was to have two gigantic anchors laid in the riverbed about midstream, marked by buoys, which could be seen readily from the monstrous "bow wave" they set up. The ferry, secured by its "bows" to the anchors, was let go from its mooring, and on its immense "anchor rode" swung across the river, mainly powered by the speed of the current, but with a little auxiliary engine, usually mounted on the ferry's side, to enable it to maneuver over the slackish water by the river's edge on the bank it was aiming for. The high-wire ferries were generally employed where the riverbed was not suitable for anchors. And that meant our anchor, too.

South of Budapest, for about eighteen miles, the river-side scenery quickly became highly cultured and remained civilized. Cozy villas and cottages straggled over the green, green hillsides among trees blossoming with clouds of lilac. Now and again there were shepherds tending small flocks of sheep, and sometimes they brought them down to the river to drink. We were so close to them that we could plainly hear the thin bleating of the day-old lambs.

Birdlife was much more common south of Budapest than north of the city. Sometimes, toward evening, great flights of wild geese took off or landed within yards of our boat, and the fluttering of their massive wings was loud enough to drown Chopin on the tape player. There were enough ducks by the river's edge to keep the Chinese restaurant in Roosevelt Square supplied for years to come.

We had left Budapest late in the day, so our first stop south was at Adony, a small village where gravel dredged from the Danube bottom was off-loaded from the dredger barges, and sent away in long trains of freight cars. It was early evening when we arrived. I had imagined that men would knock off work at about seven o'clock, but there were none of those capitalist-countries' trade union rules here. The clattering and banging went on and on all night. Pontoons were scarce south of Budapest. I had sighted an old dredger-barge canted up and stranded on the bank. Sure enough, when we felt our way alongside it, there was enough water on its lower, river side. We settled down for the evening and night. Thomas brought out some canned food from Budapest, and I rested from my hours at the wheel. There was no way that either of us could get ashore from the barge. The space between it and dry land was a sea of thick mud, kept soft and wet by the wash of a hundred passing ships a day. Soon after we tied up on the barge at Adony, news of our arrival must have reached the village, which is set back from the Danube about three miles. For three hours we held a shouted conversation in bad English and German with about fifty people—men, women and children, gathered to see us from behind a spiked iron fence that surrounded the gravel pit, about fifty yards from where we stood in the cockpit. The people beckoned us ashore. One gang of men even turned up with a wooden plank, about thirty feet long, which must have weighed half a ton, so that we might cross over the barge gap. But the wash from ships passing up and down the Danube was so heavy, and the boat rose and fell so much, that we dared not leave her in case our mooring lines again snapped, as they had before.

All the while this friendly bantering back and forth was taking place we were under heavy attack from clouds of mosquitoes. They were so thick at times, just before sunset, that they darkened the sky. We had bought a can of repellent in Vienna, which was all we could afford at the time. This I slung over to the villagers, who were dancing up and down like crazies, battling off the mosquitoes. I didn't sling the can hard enough. It fell into the sea of mud between the barge and bank, and before Thomas could rush around with our fishnet-pole, it was lost irretrievably in the mud. We were resigned to smearing kerosene on ourselves to fend off the mozzies until we reached Mohacs, where we managed to find another can.

Like friendly and inquisitive locals, mosquitoes came out on the middle and lower reaches of the Danube valley from about an hour and a half before sunset to about an hour after, but unlike the civilians they made our life a torment. Nowhere was free of them, although in the larger towns and cities they zoomed in only ones and twos. But one was enough in a hot cabin at night. In the villages and along the remoter berthing jetties, they were a plague. One answer for the odd mozzy that decided to lodge in the boat overnight might have been a chameleon or a gecko on board as a pet. But for us it was mosquito nets (which never worked perfectly and which prevented air circulation around the sleeper), mosquito repellent, expensive in Eastern Europe and hardly available anywhere except in a very few better-stocked pharmacies, or kerosene or diesel oil. Plain lemon juice would have worked too, but it would have meant an awful lot of lemons and an awful lot of squeezing.

We left Adony, at km 1598, very early next morning. Again the scene on the west bank of the Danube was of villas set among lilac trees in the early morning light. The young sun shone on the lilac blooms horizontally as he rose in the east. The effect was stupendously beautiful; clouds of glowing pink lilac above waving sheets of bright green grass over the shining silver-blue river. It was so beautiful that it moved me to play Beethoven's Pastoral Symphony on the tape player. Then, as we drank our breakfast tea and ate our marmalade sandwiches, we were as close to Nirvana as I ever approached.

The most beautiful open stretch of the Hungarian Danube was probably that off Kulcs, near the Racalmas Dunaag stream which flowed into the Danube thereabouts. That was about forty miles south of Budapest.

Near Kulcs we sighted the biggest gypsy encampment we had seen in Hungary, and we had seen many. Some of those farther upstream were scenes of almost unimaginable squalor, others seemed better off, a few positively rich. This large camp was a mixture of all three, it seemed in equal proportions, as we flashed by. No one waved at us. No gypsies ever did. The women tended the horses, washed clothes, or prepared meals. The children lugged heavy loads around or fished. The men sat and smoked in the shade of trees. This is the way, it appears, it has always been.

Through most of his course across the Magyar plain, the Danube is about 330 yards wide, but he is fast. His course is much straighter than farther upstream from the great Esztergom bend, and there are few bends to delay his headlong rush toward the Carpathian Mountains and the Iron Gates.

Overhead, all day, as we steamed steadily on toward Mohacs, there were flights of Soviet planes, fighters, bombers and troop carriers. It was plain that a big air exercise was taking place. The contrast between the peaceful, lovely scenery around us and this noisy, bombastic nonsense and waste going on above us was unreal, or so real as to be frightening.

I saw a lot of military installations and equipment in Eastern Europe, some of it belonging to local forces, most of it Soviet. Where it didn't impose on *Outward Leg*'s peace of passage, I forbear to mention it. But where it did, I do, because what they were doing, flying at that height over us, was trying to terrorize people, and the answer to government terror is exposure. Besides, I was getting tired of witnessing grown men, who should have known better, rushing around like small boys, playing at being soldiers and not realizing probably that they were holding a lighted wick near a pile of dynamite.

Kis Duna River, at km 1570, would have been a fine place to anchor at, but for the fact that its mouth was encumbered with flooded trees. It was just upstream from a Soviet Army training area, around km 1566, where Red Army river-crossing exercises were taking place. There was much smoke and noise from squads, battalions, regiments of khaki-clad Red Army soldiers running, walking, standing, lying, and just *being*, everywhere on both banks. There were several landing craft, which almost lost their way when their helmsmen saw *Outward Leg* tearing down on them, all her flags flying, and heard her bagpipes blaring. The troops on both banks, those that had been moving, stopped dead in their tracks as if in paralyzed disbelief as we shoved by them, small and peaceful and indomitable. The soldiers who had been lying down on the grass stood up, looking dumbstruck.

A group of officers, wearing peaked caps and red-and-white armbands, stood on the west bank in long overcoats of whitish gray, looking elite and important. They stood and stared as we flashed by.

The only other town of any size on the Danube in Hungary south of Budapest and north of Mohacs was Paks. This is now a large city, although before Hungary's only atomic power plant was built there a few years ago, it had been a sleepy little market town. As almost always is the case where new cities have been built overnight, Paks was a mess, at least as seen from the river. It might have been clean and well run, it might have been convenient for workers getting to and from their jobs, it might have been a thousand times better than what they had had before, but it was still a mess. It mainly seemed to consist of thousands upon thousands of apartments piled together into a few dozen faceless complexes of concrete.

From Paks south, in the mid- and late afternoon, we passed hills and meadows by the river's edge crowded with naked Hungarians. There were *thousands* of them. Not all in one place, of course, but spread out for the whole forty miles or so from Paks to Mohacs. They were all ages, shapes, sexes and sizes, and all as naked as on the day that they were born. Even naked, they all had an air of elegance about them. They did not hide themselves or anything about them as we passed close to them. Many of them ran down to the water's edge when they saw what was approaching, and waved at us in a most friendly and welcoming fashion.

Mostly, they had cars waiting nearby, away from the banks, these naked Hungarians, but sometimes there was a clubhouse too, and we saw naked customers, naked waiters, even naked cooks. We knew, on one unforgettable occasion, that the man we were looking at was a cook, because his tall white chef's hat was all he was wearing outside his skin and hair. He stood in a doorway, waving his big ladle at us as we passed, playing "Behind the Bushes," courtesy of Mr. Mc-Pherson.

The only times that the naked Hungarians hid themselves or grabbed a towel, or dropped down into the long grass, was when a Soviet ship passed by. I know this looks like an ideological fancy. I assure you on my mother's memory, that on the two occasions when we were being passed by Soviet river vessels heading downstream, overtaking us and therefore with us for some minutes, the vast majority of the Hungarians ashore hid themselves from view, naked or not. When we were passed by river ships of nations other than the Soviets, the naked (or not) Hungarians stayed where they were and waved to us. That is a fact, and that, too, is another reason why the Russian empire creaks, at least what we saw of it.

Dunaszekcsö, at km 1460, was a pretty little town with an ancient riverside wall and a pontoon. We might as well push onto Mohacs, we thought. The late afternoon was fine and warm and there were only another eight miles to go, downstream between rolling hills and bathing beaches covered, for the most part, with naked Hungarians. So we made the most of it while the going was good.

Mohacs (pronounced "Mohach"), at km 1447, turned out to be a busy river port. Every ship heading into or out of Hungary had to stop there, for customs inspection. This means about a hundred ships a day, many with a tow of up to a dozen barges. I had meant to stay in Mohacs over the weekend.

It would have been, we had been forewarned, expensive to go on into Yugoslavia on a weekend; Yugoslavia has a sea coast and its customs service has learned to charge overtime for weekend attendance.

An account of the next two days spent shifting from one berth to another every few hours would wear out any reader's patience, as it almost did mine. But Hungarian charm and courtesy made the whole traipse around, back and forth from one bank to the other and back again, an exercise in good humor. The Hungarians did it so that we were never far from a bar or restaurant, and always berthed so that somehow I could get ashore with minimum clambering.

On the last night in Hungary, Sunday, 26 May, Thomas and I ate at a large upstairs restaurant overlooking the port. There was the usual gypsy band in attendance. The owner, who spoke German well, took us in his car to a gypsy nightclub about two miles outside the town. There we got rid of our Hungarian forints. It would be no good taking them into Yugoslavia, we had been told in Mohacs, since they would not be exchanged for local currency. Poor though we were, we thought we had good reason to celebrate: we were now just 620 miles from Ingolstadt and its memories. When people use the (often in error) term "spending like a sailor" it must mean something like spending as we did our last 100 forints in Mohacs.

The gypsies in the nightclub, in between playing their instruments, told me that while gypsies comprise a fairly high and rapidly increasing percentage of the population of Hungary, they found great difficulty in being accepted by the non-gypsy population. They admitted that this might be due in part to their general reputation for being, shall we say, "light-fingered" but that it was more because of the difference of their complexions and physical coloring from the rest of the people. But with Thomas and me they were rigidly fair. This might have been because I told them that I had been a three-day guest in the tent of their World King, himself a Hungarian, on the pampas of Argentina back in 1975. This thrilled them, so that instead of the gypsies entertaining their customers, the shoe was, so to speak, on my one foot for a change. I also told them that East European sociologists who had lately been criticizing Australian treatment of its aborigines might just as well serve humanity by helping the plight of East European gypsies, not only in Hungary, but in Yugoslavia and Rumania as well. As they told me, their fellows there were far worse off than they when it came to acceptance as first-class citizens of the lands they had inhabited for centuries. They agreed with me wholeheartedly that the "brotherhood of man" should include gypsies, although up until then they had seen few signs that it did.

Our restaurant owner had to return to town early, and we didn't want to, so we wound up about midnight walking back the two miles.

No taxi would accept us. The good cheer inside us made it seem less than two miles though.

The only time on the whole Danube voyage when Thomas and I had a little spare money for drinking was at Mohacs. We enjoyed it to the full, partly to hide from ourselves the fact that we were leaving behind us, the next day, a people who (apart from the taxi drivers) were honest, friendly, helpful and charming.

# 23

# *When You Go, You Go Yugoslavia*

Toward the end of May the chromatic cries of spring in the Danube valley had become a changing harmony of colors each day, opening with crystal mornings after red dawns that made the calm, cool face of the river appear like glass. Then, looking downstream, it was difficult to see where the river ended and the sky began. Now that the river was widening there were, in the early morning light, *fata morgana* effects to the south of Mohacs, which showed us strange islands where there were supposed to be none. Each of the islands had curled-up ends, so that they looked like great *Ra II* rafts floating on a sea of pearl.

Off Mohacs, that morning after the night before, there were several strings of barges awaiting customs inspection before pushing on upstream into or through Hungary. *Outward Leg* shifted to the customs pontoon before breakfast, so that we would get through inspection early and cover as much distance toward Belgrade as we could that day.

After Thomas and I had finished breakfast in the cockpit now in the warm sunshine, the officials arrived. There were six of them, a positive platoon. They were, it seemed, in good humor. We asked them if they could clear us through soon. Their chief, a heavyset man with a fat, red face and light blue eyes, smart in his khaki suit, waved his hand in front of him. "After breakfast," he fobbed us off.

"But there's all these ships and barges waiting to come through," I expostulated. "We don't want to be in the way when their tugs come alongside . . ."

"No problem," he replied. "You stay as long as you like. Let them wait. They're only Rumanians after all!"

All the Hungarians I had met, of whatever age or degree, either despised Rumanians or showed some fear of them. In the north of Hungary it was the Czechs they glared at over the Danube at Komarom. Here in the south the Rumanians and Hungarians were correct with each other, but sullen. In the middle, the Yugoslav crews passed through, hardly noticed in their scruffier ships, more often than not rusty and with peeling sides. Bulgarians seemed to ignore everyone from their smart tug convoys and tourist ships, while Soviet ships had, it looked to us, priority over everybody else. By now the Austrian and West German ships were few and far between, but when they passed *Outward Leg* they hailed us so familiarly that you would have thought they had known us for years, even though we had never seen most of them before.

"*Alles gut?*" they cried.

"*Alles gut!*" we replied.

By mid-forenoon we were still waiting to clear Hungary. By lunchtime, when the officials retired to their homes or somewhere with their briefcases, we decided to emulate them, crossed the Danube, and ate a good cheap lunch at a small outdoor restaurant which had its own pontoon. The restaurant was overshadowed by tall trees which showered us, every time a breeze passed through their branches, with little white, fluffy seeds, like cotton. They were so many and so thick that they made it seem as if it was snowing, and made me shiver to remember the previous winter. For the next few hundred miles, these fluffy seeds blew all over the river, and sometimes the decks would be an inch thick in them. Sometimes they stuck in my beard and around my mouth so that Thomas laughed and said I looked more like an Arctic explorer than an old crock drifting down a river.

Immediately after lunch *Outward Leg* returned to the customs pontoon to await the return of the officials to clear us out. At 2:30 they returned with their important-looking briefcases, obviously well-lunched. They wanted to look busy, so by 3:30 they were waving us off as we pulled away downstream toward Yugoslavia.

By midafternoon the sun was blazing hot, and I steered in the shade of the dodger, as we let the Danube add his five-knot contribution to our ten-knot speed between flat banks and low islands. By the time we had threaded our way the thirty-five miles of river no-man's-land between Hungary and Yugoslavia I had figured out why everything was now taking so long. There was an indolence, even, about the passage of time. Then it came to me; we were gradually but steadily approaching the Middle East. These areas showed, in strange little ways at first, signs of having been under Turkish tutelage for centuries. Now and again there would be a woman washing clothes in the river. This we had not seen on the Danube before. Then again, there might be a young shepherd lad sitting on his haunches as he tended his flock. They were small signs, but many and unmistakable.

I had no charts for the river farther on, and not even a road map now. Buoyage in northern Yugoslavia was either poor or very obviously absent. What few buoys there were looked like the remnants of some wreck, all rust, so there was no way of knowing, most of the time, where the channel was. Often I slowed down and even stopped, stock-still, bows upstream, to let shipping appear in the hazy distance, to give me some sign of safety. It was to be like this much of the way through Yugoslavia and later, through much of the Rumanian–Bulgarian Danube.

In Budapest I had been told that the Soviets had surveyed the whole river in their domain quite recently, and had issued some of the new charts to their friends. But to the public, or to those whom they mistrusted, the charts were simply not available. We might as well look for a plan of their missile sites.

Toward late afternoon we sighted the Yugoslav town of Batina. It was a pretty little place of low, whitewashed cottages set in flowery gardens under the shade of elm trees which seemed to be unafflicted by blight. On the opposite bank from the town is a hamlet, of a few cottages and a couple of restaurants with outdoor terraces. The terraces were crowded with lingering diners. As soon as we were within seeing distance of the restaurant terraces, everybody on them, about a hundred people, stood up and cheered *Outward Leg*. Many of the diners waved napkins and even bottles at us, inviting us to stop alongside. As *Outward Leg*'s ensign and flags caught the breeze they yelled and danced where they were, while youngsters ran down to the riverbank to wave at us. Anyone would have thought we had just arrived from some stirring epic venture, instead of waiting most of the day at a tardily attended customs pontoon.

The Yugoslav customs officials at Batina were even more tardy than the Hungarians had been at Mohacs. The rule in Yugoslavia is that when the boat arrives voyagers must wait until the officials come on board. They must not go ashore and look for officialdom in its lair. The Yugoslavs, we had been told, were adamant about that. So we waited, waited and waited. It was not unpleasant, listening to Mozart, drinking late afternoon tea, looking at the peacefulness of Batina town, opposite. There was plenty of wildlife, ducks, geese, herons, kingfishers, to distract us as evening approached.

Some time later, I can't remember how long, for time is different in different places, but it seemed like a year later, a Yugoslav tug pulled upstream and hooted us off the pontoon so that she could berth alongside, in our stead. The tug was very noisy, had a big crew, including an English-speaking engineer who had worked in Canada for some years. With his help we raised the customs officials' attention enough for them to step aboard and share another cup of tea with us. They liked the bagpipe music we had been playing when we arrived, they said. They were young, in their mid-twenties perhaps, and had a carefree appearance about them. As I went below to play their request, another official arrived, as if from another world. He was about sixty, perhaps more, and of a very dark aspect. He was dressed in a plain brown uniform and cap, and on the cap was a big red star. At his age he could not manage the climb down from the pontoon, and merely stared glumly at his colleagues enjoying the benefits of sitting down to good English tea and good Scottish bagpipe music. He declined a cup of tea with a brief wag of his head. After an hour or so of lively conversation, mainly about where lie the islands with the most beautiful women in the world, the two officials on board finally got around to stamping our passports and, in a most desultory way, leafing through our ship's papers. This was all done as a sort of resented nuisance, an unpleasant afterthought, and then we were officially in Yugoslavia. I told them I was glad to be back after sixteen years, and especially pleased to be in a country, at last, with its own sea coast. Now, I said, we might be able to speak in sailors' terms again, and perhaps get things done more efficiently and quickly. This pleased them no end. Then Thomas brewed another pot of tea. After a further hour's chat about Marco Polo being Yugoslavian the officials cheerily waved us good-bye and advised us to head for Apatin, to wait the night there. Navigation on the river was, they said, dangerous in the dark. I thought it wasn't too safe thereabouts in the daytime either, but said nothing and we left.

We reached Apatin, in the Autonomous Province of Vojvodina, just before dark. As darkness fell, I could see that in a nearby creek off the Danube there were a couple of cranes, with a lot of noise coming from that direction. On the main stream itself there was a small hut with a little pontoon directly below it. This we made for and, slowly crabbing sideways upstream with our bows parallel with the pontoon, found that there was sufficient water and very little current, and so tied up there. We found later, *Outward Leg* had arrived in the friendliest port of her whole voyage to date, all the way from San Diego, and one of the most friendly I'd ever been to in almost half a century at sea.

At Apatin we were treated like kings. There was not enough that the inhabitants could do for us. They brought us fresh water, they did our shopping, they washed our clothes and they wined and dined us regally. They even brought cooked lunches on board. Several people there speak good German, for this area was once colonized by Germans from the Black Forest. After the Second World War the Germans had been, we were told, either killed off or kicked out, and their places taken by Serbs shifted up from the south of Yugoslavia. In the district is also a large Hungarian-speaking element who also, in the main, speak some German. As soon as the youngsters from the local school knew we were English speakers, we were invited to visit the school. There the headmaster, whose English was about as good as mine, contacted people in Zagreb and Belgrade to arrange for our reception in the capital.

Here at the school and also in local homes (for he was often spoken of) we learned that one of modern Yugoslavia's heroes was the Scots soldier and diplomat, Fitzroy Maclean. He it was who had first brought Josip Broz—Tito—to the notice of Winston Churchill as an anti-Nazi fighter, in 1941. Tito's photograph was everywhere, even though he had been dead several years, and his memory was worshipped by old and young alike. As we progressed through Yugoslavia and saw no evidence at all of the Red Army or Air Force, we realized how clever and skillful a politician Tito had been. Of all the "great" men who had tackled Stalin only he, and he alone, had outwitted the Georgian monster.

The small hut above the pontoon where *Outward Leg* lay was the town kayak clubhouse. This was under the guidance of a large jolly man of generous disposition named Charco. He made our three-day stay in Apatin like being at home away from home. He guided us to the post office, the town bank, the food stores, the mechanics' shops, the shoe factory, and the shipyard. Charco made it seem that he was privileged to offer us all that he could. And he did all this without one word of anything but Serbian, which neither Thomas nor I understood at all.

The Croatians, of whatever descent, are a good-looking people, of a merry disposition. Every day, on the three days that we stayed in Apatin, the boat was crowded for hours by people, young and old, men, women, boys and girls. They were all very natural, and did not ask permission to come aboard. Why should they? I could enter their houses anytime. They were also very honest. Not one thing went missing at Apatin, even though we could not both be below and topside all the time.

Our next port of call after we left Apatin in the early dawn (to get away from the place before friends made us stay another day, and another) was Borovo, about forty miles downstream. On this stretch we found the buoyage improved and the channel quite clearly defined.

We also saw many garbage dumps on the banks. In every town and village of the Yugoslavian Danube we saw this. It appeared that garbage was trucked to the hills outside town and dumped over the river bank. Many, many, lovely hills and glades lay ruined and despoiled in this way. There was never any obvious attempt to hide the rubbish. It was dumped and left, the old paper and plastic to blow in the wind onto the river and then drift downstream obscenely, past the next garbage dump. The avalanches of discarded muck stank to high heaven as we passed them, whether there was a breeze or not.

Half a mile or so north of Borovo there was another kayak club with a pontoon. We found nine feet of water beside the pontoon, but were warned off by a supervisor with a red star on his shirt. So we shoved off, and headed downstream to Borovo itself. There were many small pontoons there, and a full-blown yacht clubhouse but no yachts. There we tied up for the night and reported to the local police station, as we were required to do everywhere we stopped in Yugoslavia.

Novi Sad, farther downstream, was one of the very few places, it appeared, on the Danube, where Soviet riverboat men were allowed to wander ashore. Time and again *Outward Leg* and her complement were photographed assiduously by large, dour-looking men in ill-cut, double-breasted suits. Never once, though, did they greet us, or talk to us in any way. Never once did they reply to my nods. They stared at the, to them, strange lines of our vessel, photographed her silently, and walked on their way. There was a "manufactured" look about them, as if they had been stamped out of a half-dozen factory molds.

Next day, 1 June, was a Friday. I did not want to reach the capital, Belgrade, late on Friday night, nor over the weekend, as "overtime" is charged by officialdom. So we delayed our departure until late morning, and took the day's passage slowly, or as slow as Old Father Danube would allow.

Our first stop was at Breska, about fourteen miles below Novi Sad. There, Thomas bought a live chicken for the equivalent of three dollars. This was to be our lunch, and as it clucked in Serbian we could not understand its protests when I stretched its neck.

At six o'clock in the evening we slipped away, downstream again, this time to Stari Slankamen, about six miles on. There was no pontoon there, and the approach to the town anchorage, across the mile-wide river, was fraught with shoals. But by first passing the town on the far side of the river away from it, then turning upstream and sideways like a crab and heading for the downstream end of obvious shoals, we made it through the intricate channels and anchored before the church, with its tower bearing southwest in eleven feet of muddy water, muddy bottom, current about a quarter of a knot.

On landing from the dinghy a little later, we were told in good German that our boat was the first nonlocal craft ever seen in living memory to arrive at Stari Slankamen anchorage. I was not surprised; I had been sweating during the whole difficult dusk approach between white-water shoals.

About half a mile from the anchorage we landed in the dinghy, downhill from a small, simple restaurant where we ate a small, simple meal for a small, simple price: $2.00 for the two of us. The meal was delicious pork medallions, cold potato chips and cold peas, with a cola drink. Mosquito repellent was, the waiter gave us to understand as he handed it to us, included in the price.

In almost pitch darkness we clambered down an awkward track, over tree roots, back to the dinghy, settled ourselves on its rubbery sides, and made our way back to our anchorage. I had brought a flashlight with me, as I always did when I went ashore. Jetty lamps were few. I shone the flashlight over the place where *Outward Leg* should be, as Thomas steered the dinghy. I shone it again. I shook it and shone it again . . . *our boat wasn't there!*

# 24

# *Beautiful and Bad; Charming and Repulsive*

Nights on the Danube were usually magic. After the afternoon wind, more often blowing downstream, had died down at sunset, the stars would come out and litter the clear sky in their thousands. Away from the few bigger cities the night air was clean and so clear that it would often have been possible to read a jetty notice, if we'd understood the language. At night the river was a wide strip of shining silver between black banks, coming, flowing, and going past us from one obscurity to another, while somewhere in the distance an owl would hoot, and around us, on the near banks, crickets chirruped.

Now and again there was a gypsy encampment not too far away by the river bank, and we could bask in the reflections of their firelight and hear their horses neigh and their dogs bark whenever some stranger wandered by. At fairly regular intervals river tugs passed, chugging away if they were heading downstream with a rough mumble if pushing against the current. We saw them approaching from miles away, far beyond the next bend, for their searchlights betrayed their presences long before we heard their engines or saw their navigation lights. The beams flickered in the night sky from one side of the river to the other, as the pilot and helmsman groped their way forward, skillfully navigating their barges with perhaps as much as 15,000 tons of cargo stowed in them, between the banks and shoals of the mighty, fast-flowing river. From afar, or from close by, it was always a beautiful sight to see the darkness of the nights defeated so.

Now at Stari Slankamen with our boat missing from her anchorage, we silently drifted, shocked, in our dinghy. I played my little flashlight on the site where *Outward Leg* had been anchored. There were, as

Thomas whispered hoarsely, several ships lighting up the blackness of the overcast night. I jerked around to peer downstream, and just as I did so a tug, God bless her, shone her searchlight on the western bank of the river. There, about a third of a mile away, was a ghostly light-gray shape, low in the water. It was low and squat and unmistakable, for we loved her. Thomas was too busy starting the outboard motor under my urgent pleading, to see her at all. Then, as the motor sprang to life, he leaned on the steering handle and we zoomed after our errant trimaran. All the while I prayed that both we and *Outward Leg* would not hit a hard shoal. Now and again the savior tug played its searchlight over us, and the brightness of it blinded us for long moments. I had grabbed the outboard steering column by now, half falling in the bouncing dinghy as I did so, and wound up with my false leg trailing in the river to one side for a few awkward moments. We lost sight of *Outward Leg* several times in our panic, but as our dinghy tore downstream she slowly emerged, first as a pale shadow, then as herself. As we zoomed alongside her I noticed that her anchor rode was still taut. That meant she was dragging and dredging herself slowly along the river bottom. Before we got alongside I had squirmed, somehow, into a half crouching position, and the moment the dinghy bounced along *Outward Leg*'s scarred starboard side I threw myself at one of her guardrail stanchions and twisted so that I was lying horizontal on our ama deck. Then, without even bothering to get myself upright, I rolled my body over and over across our deck until I was able to reach our cockpit coaming with my hands and drag myself bodily up to the edge of the steering position. There, somehow, I did a complete somersault and landed sitting on our cockpit deck. As I fumbled for the engine starter key I also dragged myself upright to the wheel, so that I was standing up. Then, as I noticed that Thomas was already at our bow and pulling our anchor line, I shoved Yannie into gear slow ahead and brought *Outward Leg* to a dead stop, bows against current. All this had been done without a word spoken between Thomas and me. Then I slowly moved her forward to help him bring our anchor on board, and we, shamefaced but intensely relieved, shoved real slow upstream, back to Stari Slankamen anchorage. We had to return there; the whole river-bed all about was, we knew, a nightmare of inlets, shoals and rocks, and in these circumstances it was "better the devil you know than the devils you don't know."

We soon had our own searchlight at play, and in ten minutes or so we were back at our original place. But we dared not both turn in, and spent the night at anchor watches, three hours on, three off. Of course we found the old general rule about anchor watches was still true—if they're set they probably won't be needed, but at least we could sleep in peace for our three hours each. As I dozed off I made another Danube resolution; never again would we anchor to one anchor without a bridle, and never again would both of us leave the ship at anchor.

Morning at Stari Slankamen brought the sight of a lovely old castle above the town, and below it, by the shore, an abandoned military watchtower. It was the first military watchtower we had seen in Yugoslavia, and I was pleased to see that it was rusty, deserted and even leaning over at a slight angle toward the river bank.

We weighed our trusty anchor from a very untrusty bottom at about mid-forenoon. It was still, we thought, two days too early to head directly for Belgrade, so instead we berthed alongside a kayak club at km 1173. We knew that Belgrade and the river Sava were at km 1170, so we guessed that the town above the kayak club pontoon must be a suburb of the capital. This turned out to be correct. After interminable discussions in sign language, someone turned up with a road map of Belgrade and showed us that the town we were at was Zemun. A short while later a German-speaking policeman turned up, booked us in as it were, and explained our mission to the kayak club members.

The first thing the kayakers did was insist that Thomas and I should go up to their clubhouse, where they poured something into a glass for us. When I knocked it back I wondered, through watery eyes, why the glass had not disintegrated as soon as the liquid hit it. That stuff was the closest, I think, I ever tasted to liquid nitroglycerine. Later, when the club, the riverbank and *Outward Leg* stopped whizzing round and round, the members showed me their kayak storeroom, which was an old Turkish cave running back a hundred yards from the cliff face beside the club. It was dry and cool and ideal for storing the lovely wooden canoes and kayaks, of which there must have been a hundred, all carefully propped up on high racks and lovingly cared for. They also showed me another storeroom. I wandered toward it a bit tired, but when the kayakers finally got the door unlocked I saw a sight which I'd never seen before, nor do I think I ever will again: there were trophies everywhere, piled on the floor, scattered over shelves and tables, dusty and encrusted with grime— and they were mostly silver and there must have been, Thomas agreed with me, a good five hundred of them, dating back to the early nineteen-twenties. I would have liked to find out more about this treasure trove, but unfortunately the German-speaking policeman, suitably fortified with liquid nitroglycerine, had left, and so we were back to hand signals, frowns, nouns and Serbian verbs which are not the most subtle way of communicating with me.

We found later that Zemun, for the more agile or well-off, was the best yacht-berth near Belgrade. The town was only half a mile or so away up over the hill, and all amenities were there, such as post office, shops, a fresh food and fish market. There was fresh water available at the kayak club in reasonable quantities and there were twelve feet of water alongside the pontoon. Taxis from Zemun to Belgrade city center cost about $7.00, but there was a frequent bus service, too, for pennies. These buses were usually crowded. For me on one leg they would have been too unsteady an undertaking.

By now we had been told that the Belgrade police did not, in fact, charge "overtime" on weekends, so on Sunday morning, 3 June, we slipped from Zemun and headed for the capital. It was a short hop, and I took an even shorter course than the recommended one. This was inside the pretty resort island of Veliko Ratno, which sat in the mouth of the Sava, immediately north of Belgrade. There was plenty of water in the channel. We were finding out that Belgrade was, in fact, a regular Venice of deep boat channels, all of them beautiful, all of them easily navigated.

As we turned the bend around Veliko Ratno island, the lovely old fortifications of Belgrade, on Kalemegdan headland, swung into view. It revealed itself as one of the most impressive sights we encountered on all of the wonderfully impressive Danube.

We had no river charts, but our road map showed us roughly where the center of Belgrade was, the Stari Grad or Old City. I headed for the nearest navigable-seeming water to it, and found that we were indeed correct to go there. It was the only place a foreign private vessel was allowed to go.

The policemen at the river-control post were, when we arrived, offhanded and slow, but not any more unfriendly than police are to strangers arriving unannounced in any cosmopolitan city. The berth we were directed to was noisy and dusty from working cargo craft close by, and overlooked by a docks-police post. There was also a bad swell from passing craft. On the credit side it was close to the tourist-ship landing, which meant that the outside world, as it left and arrived, saw us, and it was convenient to public transport to and from the city center.

Many Soviet passenger ships called at Belgrade while we were there. Always, when they were berthed near us, *Outward Leg* was the cynosure of all sly eyes and curious, on board.

The first thing I noticed when we reached the city center of Belgrade was that practically every male in the place between the ages of three and ninety-three continually spat. This was so even in the elegant pavement cafés of the Terraza. Sometimes they spat politely, little "thubs" on their tongues between tightly compressed lips. Sometimes, especially around the main railway station, it was great fruity gobs of green phlegm skillfully aimed between the feet of the milling passersby. At first I found this disconcerting but we soon became accustomed to it, and before long, whenever some man or youth that I was talking to spat, I did it too, to return his compliment, and in this way we got along fine with just about everyone we met in Belgrade.

The second thing that was immediately evident in the city was the number of uniforms about. They were everywhere, but there were no Red Army uniforms among them.

At the British Embassy, in the morning, at the loveliest old mansion in a city full of them, we were handed our mail. There were many good wishes from friends all over the world, but no payments for work done, yet. The most important thing we picked up was a package from New York. It was marked "Replacement clothing for U.S. Yacht in Transit." In it were twelve pairs of Levi blue jeans, medium size. These, by design, were to get *Outward Leg* most of the way from Belgrade to Istanbul. Apart from them, the only liquid asset in *Outward Leg* was $300.00 in notes.

I decided to cable Thomas' family for the $500 they were keeping for us as an emergency loan-fund. It arrived in Belgrade main post office two days later, but by the time we had it safely on board, converted from deutschmarks to dinars, and back to dollars, a week had gone by, and an almost unbelievable saga had taken place.

Most of the Belgrade taxi drivers we found to be helpful enough.

One of them in particular stands out in my memory. He was hoping to migrate farther, to the United States. He it was who gave us some of the first real clues as to what was happening in his country. He was virulently anticommunist, or rather anti-what-goes-for communism in Rumania. His tales sounded, even to me, like some kind of nightmare. Some of them we took with a grain of salt. We were soon to know better. I gave the Rumanian taxi driver, as we drove from one bank to another, tips about the taxi setup in New York. In return he refused to take one single dinar from me, even though I'd been in his cab for a good three hot, sticky hours.

At the Soviet Embassy the naval attaché claimed to know nothing of my application to make a detour to the Crimean coast of the Soviet Union. He told me, in parting, that while they might this time make me an exception to their rule that private visits to the U.S.S.R. are not allowed, he doubted whether it would be allowed on future occasions. "It's not our policy," he said, as if God had not made Russia.

The cheapest meals we found in Belgrade were at the main station restaurant on the Bratsva i Jedinstva Square. They averaged about $4.00 for two, for wiener schnitzel and salad with wine and coffee. But suddenly and for no obvious reason, the prices there started to rise at our table, and jumped in three days by one hundred percent. We reluctantly ranged farther afield for cheap meals, and found a Yugoslav self-service restaurant on the Nemanjina Avenue, which only charged $1.00 for as much food as we could eat, with a glass of wine and coffee.

Late at night gypsy families, on the move by rail for a change, slept under the lamplight on the station steps, covered in thick blankets under which couples made love, quite openly, while their children, or someone else's, slept peacefully close by, little thumbs in mouths. Large policemen, two by two and strangely benevolent-looking for Eastern Europe, strolled by, conversing quietly, ignoring everybody else.

Soon word about *Outward Leg* got around the media bush telegraph, and before many days we were heading up the forbidden-to-foreigners river Sava to a little restaurant under the trees on the island of Ada Medica. Mira Adanja Polak, a television interviewer famous in Yugoslavia, was with us. Her cameraman cluttered up the foredeck with his paraphernalia, too. We talked before the camera of our aims in *Outward Leg*, and of our voyage, and of the thousands of handicapped who were hearing of our progress and pinning their faith on us. She, who had interviewed many famous men, told me on camera that I was doing more for goodwill between Yugoslavia and Britain than all the British ambassadors had done since World War Two. I told her that that was probably because I had to; my boat was in the middle of their country. If I wasn't nice, I'd be in trouble. She laughed at that, but I was in deadly earnest. It was true. But *Outward Leg* was still, I was told, the first non-Yugoslav vessel to navigate the river Sava above Belgrade in living memory.

Before, whenever we had inquired about the Sava, we had met with low mutters. "It's a strategic waterway." The only thing strategic that I saw was that it might be a very good place to winter a yacht.

In the Belgrade that we visited from the river, beautiful, bad, charming and repulsive, like any other really great metropolitan city, not many people spoke English. Those who did were mainly youngsters, who said "Good evening" at noon and "Hello" when they meant good-bye.

The Belgrade adults seemed to be impassive until they were addressed. Then they livened up considerably, and their faces lit up like lighthouses on a dark night. They all had an almost overwhelming respect for a published author.

After the Mira Polak show had appeared on television the officials at the Pristaniste Sava Dock could not do enough for us and the policemen almost tripped over their bootlaces to help us fetch fresh water and fuel on board.

I wrote a note to the naval attaché at the British Embassy asking if he knew where I might buy charts for the lower Danube. There was, it seemed from the reply, no naval attaché as such; an RAF officer looked after the nautical side as well as, most likely, the air and land side of things. His reply was simple: there were no charts available, even though the Yugoslavs had been asking for them for years. He failed to point out that the Yugoslavs had been asking the Soviets, but that was the true case.

So, with our freshwater jerry cans full, our fuel tanks too, we set off, without charts, for the Iron Gates, to pass them and descend into the truly legendary lower Danube, to sail to the Black Sea, almost 750 miles away, and another near 300 miles beyond that to Istanbul, our nearest sure welcome. On board we had exactly $500.00 and twelve pairs of Levi jeans.

# 25

# *Last Outposts*

Once past Belgrade, the Danube, now fortified by the water draining from the whole of Yugoslavia east of its coastal ranges and north of the Macedonian mountains, changed yet again.

For about 125 miles, until his way was blocked by the narrow defiles of the Iron Gates through the Carpathian Mountains, he became deeper and wider, until at times the whole world seemed to be nothing but river and sky with, now and again, as incidental intrusions on the face of reality, small colonies of human existence.

On and on, for a dreaming infinity and an instant reality, the river flowed, unstoppable and omnipotent, sometimes as a torrent, half a mile wide, sometimes as a vast lake. Then he grew slow and ponderous, as if he had been poured over the face of the world by a calm purposeful majesty, and then changed once more to a dozen fast, dangerous streams scurrying between as many low islands which might be there that day and gone the next.

After Belgrade our sense of time and space changed. We were no longer passing through districts, countries, areas; *Outward Leg* was drifting, tiny and insignificant, through the vast reaches of a continent much the same as it had been for a billion years, except where man, with his undying impudence, had scratched the signs of his presence, fair and foul, on the eternal face of primeval nature. Often, where the Danube had overflowed his banks and flooded stretches of land as big as an English county, we saw what his gods thought of man's intrusions. Then the river was more like a sea, stretching away, farther than our eyes could see, a shining sheet of sinister, shallow silver, away to blue-gray mountains in the far misty distance. Sometimes a

235

thin, broken line of trees told us where the riverbank ought to be; often there was nothing to tell us anything, nothing but water and sky. Then we started to lose our orientation in the world as we knew it, and to look for small things, as we sometimes did on the wide ocean, to restore it. Then we turned to our compass, to what scrawled, homemade charts we had culled from rivermen, and to our music. They were the only things that made sense, that anchored us to the time we had been born into. So we held to the only dimensions other than water and sky that mattered then; and they were time and music.

Apart from the low purr of our Yanmar diesel engine, at few revolutions for most of the time, there were no sounds, except when Thomas and I spoke to each other, which wasn't often. We were each separately wrapped in our own cocoons of time and music. More often than not, this was Beethoven; only his compassion could counter the cruelty of such beauty passing before the ever-wondering eyes of us mortals. When we passed the rare villages and small towns, we let Mr. McPherson loose with his bagpipes, as a signal that we were coming and passing and leaving, and often in as much time as it took to think about it. When we passed the many flotillas of small fishing craft, mostly oared, we released Mr. McPhearson from his electronic prison, to rend the Danube air with plaintive strathspeys, so that the fishermen would be aware of our approach down their eddy-ridden stretches, and keep a lookout in case we or they were swept too close together. The fishermen thereabouts were mostly dressed in blue overalls, straw shoes and wide-brimmed hats. Their faces looked as weather-hardened as any sea fishers that I have seen. Mostly they fished at anchor and cast bottom lines, but often they drifted with the current, sometimes dozens of boats at a time, with a motor craft in attendance to tow them back upstream when their day was done, or later, to keep them from drifting too close to an invisible alien frontier line in the middle of the stream.

Lower middle Danube pontoons were few and far between. There were none that were not under guard. There were few that had any other facility on them or close to them except the chance of berthing *Outward Leg* for a mosquito-plagued evening and a bouncy night.

Most of the human settlements in the lower middle Danube valley were set well away from the river itself; sometimes as much as twelve miles away, because of the frequent flooding that occurred. On most of the pontoons only frontier guards and soldiers were in evidence, with now and again a few fishermen and their families. From Belgrade almost to the Black Sea, the Danube was like no other river that I know; it was a stream of odd, separate dimensions flowing through a real world which most of the time we were hardly aware existed, over the horizon. We could not often see or touch or feel the real world, and only now and again could we hear it, when a ship passed or when a plane might fly over a distant mountain; then its lazy drone would reach us, mingled with the bee-drones of the river.

Our departure from Belgrade had been twentieth-century enough; we had headed out from the Sava debouchment into the Danube, which was there about a third of a mile wide, passed under a road bridge and then past shipbuilding yards, factories, apartment blocks and suburbs. Finally came a few scattered cottages, and then we saw to our surprise that the river was suddenly over one mile wide. Here the scenery on the banks was as it must have been when the Romans first wearily and warily reached the Danube more than two thousand years before.

The channel was much deeper generally than farther upstream, before Belgrade. On average it was around twenty feet and reached apparently almost from bank to bank. But there were few or no buoys or markers, and those few mostly rusty, so we stayed about midstream, except where a sandbank, or a subtle movement on the face of the waters, told me there was some hazard. It was always easier navigating the Danube in the mornings and forenoons, before the wind rose. Then the surface of the river was as smooth as glass, and, by peering along it like a craftsman inspecting a newly filed metal surface, I could tell where underwater obstructions caused slight disturbances on the surface. But mostly it was a matter of hunches avoiding crunches.

The afternoon and evening wind, nine times out of ten, blew downstream. It didn't matter which way the river ran, in which compass direction, the wind took notice only of the river, and generally blew with the current. The narrower the channel, usually, the stronger the wind. Sometimes on a wide stretch it would be almost calm. Then the river would squeeze himself between two hills and the wind would increase, often to twenty knots; sometimes, in the defiles, to gale force. It was very predictable.

Thinking about the Turkish conquest of the Danube valley as far, almost, as Vienna in past centuries, I could only admire the Turks' and their vassals' sailing abilities. Their ships plied the Danube for centuries, helped only by oar power, courtesy of Christian and African slaves. No yacht nowadays could navigate upstream on the lower Danube without either a very powerful engine or a tow from some river ship. I would put the power-needed at about ten horsepower per foot of boat's length, to make a reasonable passage. It might be done with less power, but when the afternoon wind came up, the underpowered yacht was punching at very low speed. She would be stopped in the narrow stretches. There were no safe anchorages on the main stream itself, so the intrepid motor yachtsman would find himself eventually turned back, to look for a suitable place to drop his hook and to hold on until about midnight, when the wind dropped again. Which was all very well, except that anchoring in unprescribed places was officially forbidden. So that meant that our persistent upstream voyager, unless he was very lucky with his winds, might make about six miles a day. That would take four months, from the Black Sea to Belgrade; a wilting prospect for the most intrepid soul, I should think. Fuel and water supplies were very scarce and far between, and Christian and African slaves are hard to come by these days.

Until Zimonjic Ivanovo canal, at km 1136, the river was around half a mile to a mile wide on average, with few islands to divert the channels. When there were islands the river was fairly well buoyed and not too sparsely populated on the banks.

On the west bank of the river at km 1133 was the small town of Grocka. The speed of the current off the headland ran at about three knots in the morning, when there was no wind, and rose, windblown, to about six knots in the afternoon. I know that because we arrived in the afternoon and left next morning, and in between dragged anchor three times. We had not been able to lay *Outward Leg* alongside the pontoon, so had anchored stern to a barge already berthed. We had to anchor our stern to her bows, because the barge was loading sand over her side from a dredger's dumb barge. The first time we dragged was over supper. Some celestial anchor-drag organizer up yonder must spend all his heavenly time making sure that voyagers' anchors drag at the most awkward times. The second time we dragged was just as we were turning in. The third time was at some godless half-past nothing in the rainy middle of the soggy night. Each time, we had to start our engine, let go our stern lines, motor slowly forward, hold against the awesome current, and reset both our CQR and the Bruce anchors.

Smederevo, at km 1118, was an industrial town. I would have said "industrious," but we passed by it so early, to get away from Grocka's soft mud, that no one was yet out and about. It seemed to be all small factories, a large castle, looking brand-new in the clear air, a police station on the riverbank, and, half a mile downstream from the main town, a wonderful old town, completely surrounded, as we could plainly see, by its ancient fortifications.

We arrived at Ram at lunch time. At km 1078, Ram was unmistakable, and, we thought, unmissable. After miles and miles of flat, low hills on either side of the river, Ram rammed itself up atop a sudden steep peak jutting straight up out of the river on the west bank. Atop the peak was a fine old castle, looking so clean, as if it had just been built. There was a restaurant near the fort, off which we had anchored in slack water, but an honest and personable young man who worked there gave us to understand that the food there was terrible, and we'd be better fed if we crossed the river to Stari Palanka, where the DTD canal joined the Danube at km 1077. This we did, and were rewarded by the privilege of being gracefully served by one of the most civil and courteous restaurant owners I had met in Yugoslavia or anywhere else, one of the tastiest fish meals and happy wines I can remember in a long life of wandering. The meal cost exactly $8.00 for us both.

Stari Palanka was a tiny hamlet just inside the entrance to the DTD canal, a narrow waterway which joined the Danube with the great plain to the west of the Carpathian Mountains. I inquired as to the depths and widths of this canal, but no one could tell me anything much about it. I marked it down in my mind for some future gerontological exploratory voyage, some distant day, later.

Reluctantly, we weighed and carried on down the Danube. Even though the Carpathian Mountains were between us and the sea, she was calling to *Outward Leg* more and more. Only half a mile downstream from Stari Palanka, on the east bank of the Danube, was the frontier between Yugoslavia and Rumania. From thence on, for around 125 miles the frontier between the two countries followed the course of the river. From then on madness and paranoia exploded in converse relation to the voyager's closeness to salt water.

We had been lulled into complacency and a false confidence by the easygoing nature of the Yugoslavs. We had, until and below Belgrade, been sailing on an idyllic, if sometimes froward, river, through the charming, if sometimes distant, hills of Nirvana. When we told the restaurant owner in Stari Palanka we were heading for the sea, he said "Then you go through Rumania?"

"Yes," I replied, wondering where else he thought we could go on our way downstream to the Black Sea.

"Mmm," was that good man's pregnant reply. Then he changed the subject to how we managed to cook at sea in such a small craft as *Outward Leg*. I had noticed the little red signal in that "Mmm," but dismissed it as the usual Balkan intracultural jealousy. I should have known better. The man was far too good a craftsman at his trade to be jealous of anyone.

The frontier showed quite plainly on the low hill just south of Stari Palanka. Here there was another great wide scar, similar to the one on the Czech–Austrian border of evil memories. There were again tall, obscene-khaki watchtowers, again the small figures of young men standing around with the carrying of an automatic rifle as their only lunatic reason for being. There was again, even in that mid-June sunshine, emanating from the south side of that wire fence an air of resentment, bitterness, paranoia and foul intent. In my ship's log I made a note: *"Another fucking murderwire."* It was the only time I have ever used a curseword in my logs, in almost half a century of writing in logbooks.

Anyone who kills his own brother, or allows himself to be led into even contemplating it, is doomed, if there is any justice in Heaven, to eternal pain. As I stared at that gash across the hills of Carpathia, everything that the ocean had ever taught me about respect for life revolted, and I lost the best fish meal I had ever eaten, being sick in my cockpit bucket.

From where the Rumanian Tin Curtain excretes its murderous intent onto the fair and holy banks of the Danube, to Veliko Gradiste, our next port of call, was about eleven miles. On the frontier between Rumania and Yugoslavia there was little evidence of honest human existence on either bank of the river. On the Rumanian side low hills rose to the far Carpathians. They were for the most part covered in young tree plantations, and at every mile there was a watchtower with a soldier perched under its roof. On the Yugoslav side there was nothing but trees. Later in Veliko Gradiste we were told that many Rumanians had lost their lives trying to swim over this stretch of the Danube, most of them shot by sentries in the watchtowers. There were horrific tales, too, of Rumanians being half-drowned in their attempts, rescued by men from Soviet river ships, resuscitated, and returned to the Rumanian Frontier Police. They were, it was said, never seen again.

Veliko Gradiste at km 1059 was a charming little place, full of charming people. It also had a strong current, high winds at night, a bad harbor and a duty-free shop. It was a main Yugoslavian customs post. A sensible and friendly official there advised us to stay in Yugoslavia as long as we could, as far as Kladovo, below the Iron Gates, before crossing over into Rumania. He told us to stock up well with food, fuel and water at Kladovo. Noticing Thomas's by-now long hair, he sincerely advised him to get it cut, which my crewman did that same day, at a small shop near the harbor. The customs official told us that unless Thomas did cut his hair we would probably not be allowed ashore anywhere in Rumania. We didn't know whether to believe this or not at the time, but events proved him dead correct. Having long hair is a sign of individual choice. Behind the Tin Curtain that is a deadly crime against the State, for men and boys alike.

The policeman who met our boat in Veliko Gradiste warned us that taking photographs anywhere on the Danube from now on was forbidden. Not only on the river, but from anywhere within sight of the Danube. This, he intoned gravely, was a "strategic area." I looked over at Rumania, about three kilometers away. My eyesight is good, after years of necessitous gazing at sea. I could see nothing strategic at all except the watchtowers.

We stayed at Veliko Gradiste for three nights and days. The weather was rainy for the first two. A front was coming down from the north and breaking on the high Carpathian Mountains. The people of the small town treated us well. They were friendly, curious and helpful in many small ways. From the age of about nine up most of the youngsters wore blue jeans, leather jackets and large buttons which advertised "AC/DC" or "Rolling Stones." They all smoked too, and were forever trying to cadge cigarettes from us. Often the port police came along to chase the kids away. It was all in good fun, though; I love the company of young people. I find that if I treat them for what they are—themselves and not a reflection of us—they respond very well. If the kids at Veliko Gradiste made too much noise at awkward times, I shouted to them to pipe down, and tried to explain why they should. They piped down; not because I had frightened them or threatened them, but because they tried to understand why I wanted quiet.

Most of the time the youngsters asked us questions about our lives; they asked Thomas about his education and me about my voyaging. Our replies seemed to amaze them, namely that people could think of living freely, without depending on, or being shoved around by, some lumbering, clumsy, cumbersome, unthinking, central authority. I like to think that we sowed a few seeds in young, fertile minds in Eastern Yugoslavia.

During the course of our passage from Budapest we had heard vague rumors of two other yachts voyaging on the Danube. Both, it seemed, were German, and both were new vessels, being delivered from where they had been built on the banks of the Danube in Bavaria, to the Mediterranean Sea. At Veliko Gradiste we met up with one of these mysterious craft. She turned out to be *Karma*, a thirty-foot sloop being taken to the Aegean by her owner, a Bavarian about my age from Regensburg.

"Where," I asked him, "is the other German yacht?"

"He passed by here a couple of days ago, heading upstream again," was the good Bavarian skipper's reply.

"Upstream?" This was curious. Why would anyone turn against the Danube current?

"Yes," he explained "he's going home. He's fed up. He was well ahead of *Karma*. He got to Bulgaria and they tried to charge him for two weeks' hotel stay, even though he's living in his boat. There was an awful row, and the skipper got fed up. He couldn't fight the Bulgarians anymore. He's being towed back to Belgrade. Then he's going back to Germany, to haul his boat over to the Main and Rhine. He says it's easier than getting through to the sea this way. He's going to sail around Gibraltar!"

"Where's he bound for, eventually?" I asked, astonished.

"The Aegean, same as me."

"And he's heading over the Gap and around through the Mediterranean? But that's about eight thousand miles! He only had another five or six hundred to go to reach Istanbul!"

"He still says it's easier than getting through the lower Danube!"

I bore that conversation in mind when I was roused by a loud shout in English an hour later as I was resting in my cabin. I stuck my head topside through the companionway hatch. There, on the jetty, were two men, both middle-aged, and both unmistakably American.

"Hey," they shouted, "we're tourin' up the little old Danube in that there Rooshan boat, and we saw your "Old Glory" flyin' away here. We haven't seen any other American flag all the way up, so we thought we'd come on over and say hello!"

I stared downstream a few dozen yards. There, berthed beside the customs pontoon, was a big Soviet passenger ship, *Dnieper*. I knew her of old, for we had passed her several times on our Danube passage. I was pleased indeed to hear American English. "Hello," I replied.

The upshot was that Thomas and I were invited by the Americans, a group of working and retired lawyers from the Southern States, to dine with them on board *Dnieper* that evening.

Thomas and I turned up at *Dnieper*'s pontoon at about sunset. We were greeted vociferously by a large group of Americans. It appeared that a couple of them had read one or two of my books. I didn't know that, and to farther my cause and to try to safeguard the future of *Outward Leg* as much as I could, I took one of my short biographies with me. My purpose was simple. I wanted the Americans, when they returned home, to let their legislators know that they had seen *Outward Leg*, an American vessel, about to enter Rumanian waters. Then, if there were any serious incidents, and if *Outward Leg* did not report to the United States Consulate in Istanbul in reasonable time, perhaps some questions might be asked about us where it mattered in Washington.

The Soviet officials at *Dnieper*'s gangway, smiling all the time at their American paying guests, shot daggers from slit eyelids at both Thomas and me. They knew us all right, and they remembered the bagpipe music we always hurled at them as they passed by. No sooner had I taken out my biography, to give to the Americans' spokeslady, than it was grabbed by the "head steward" (impeccable English, beautiful manners, swift responses; they turn them out well at the KGB) and taken "below to show to the crew and take a copy for our passengers." If that biographical note was not in Moscow within the next few hours, then I am the keeper of the Eddystone Lighthouse. Their radio operator must have been a bit slow, because it took a good twenty minutes for the "copy" to be made, and even then it was not produced for the Americans, while I was on board *Dnieper*.

We had a wonderful couple of hours with the American lawyers, who wined and dined us like heroes or like condemned men. They were surprised that we were at all concerned about going into the Rumanian Danube in a small, frail vessel, just the two of us. They said they had been treated, where they had landed in Rumania, with much friendliness and politeness. But one elderly gentleman with the forthright tones of a good old Georgia boy, muttered sturdily "Well, of course, they want our money. They're sure after the dollars."

I didn't doubt either side of these comments. Not at all. But I also didn't doubt that the view of Western tourists traveling with Soviet guides in a Soviet passenger ship through the Soviet south-eastern European empire, to the places where they were shown, was profoundly different from the view of two people from the deck of a gashed and wounded ocean vessel wearing the United States ensign.

The next morning the Americans on board *Dnieper* and *Karma* had gone, and we in *Outward Leg* were once again alone with the silence of the river, and the Iron Gates and what was beyond them, ahead of us.

# PART THREE

## *Out*

The volume of water discharged by river Danube alone is about three hundred thousand million tons in an average year . . .

Marine life in the Black Sea is very poor in comparison with that in the Mediterranean . . . and extends to a depth of about 100 fathoms. Below this depth there is no life, and the water is charged with sulphuretted hydrogen . . .

Certain areas in [the Black Sea] are dangerous due to mines. Turkish pilots are forbidden to communicate to strangers descriptions or particulars of the fairways . . .

In the south central area [of the Black Sea] the relatively few ship's observations available do not agree well with the expectations based on pressure. Until more ships' observations are available there must be some uncertainty about the predominant winds. Winds of force 12 have been reported off the western coasts of the Black Sea . . .

Fog . . . in the Black Sea . . . unexpectedly high frequencies . . .

The Black Sea Pilot, 1969
British Hydrographic Department,
Ministry of Defence.


*The shore* [of Rumania] *sung of in the olden times by Ovid, the poet, as an inhospitable shore, represents today the marvellous Romanian Rivera . . . attiring thousands of visitors from the most far off sites of the world. . . .* in Summer the Romanian littoral turns into a vast stage, where wide-spreading cultural-artistic demonstrations take place.

Introduction to a map of
Constanta,
published by the International Tourist Agency,
Tomis Boulevard, Constanta, Rumania, 1985.

245

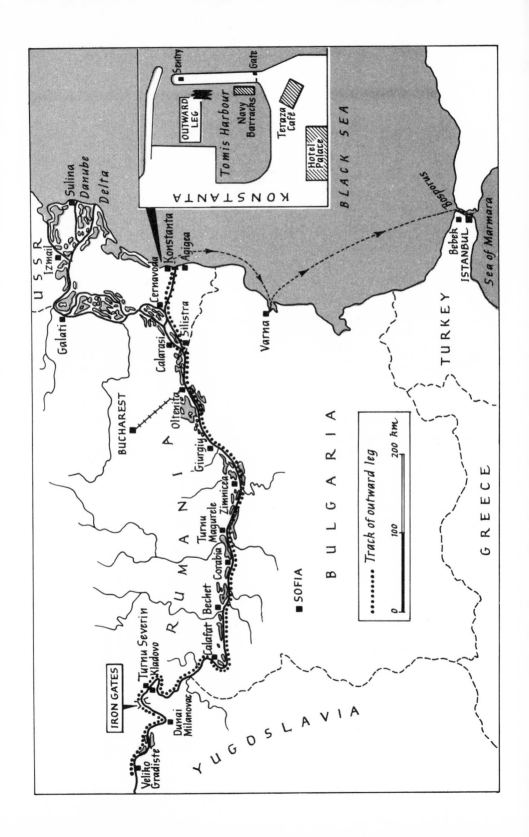

# 26

# *Through the Iron Gates*

A strong northerly wind, often over gale force, had been blowing for the two days and nights we were berthed at Veliko Gradiste. The locals claimed that this was not unusual. They said that the general rule was: the nearer the Carpathians and the Iron Gates through that mountain range, the stronger and more persistent the wind.

We had not been allowed to berth alongside the customs jetty. That was reserved for passenger ships, mainly Soviet and Bulgarian. They called in only for a few hours at a time, at odd intervals, and what money they brought was practically all that the town lived on. When the passenger ships arrived the town sprang to life; bars switched from plaintive, wailing Serbian music to country and western and the two small restaurants, empty and windblown usually, swiftly and magically converted themselves to places of culinary promise.

*Outward Leg* was berthed at the upstream end of the town jetty where the concrete platform joined the riverbank. It was an uncomfortable place, because the fetch of wind and sea (yes, *sea*) was long, stretching as far upstream as I could see. By the time the waves of the river reached *Outward Leg*'s berth, they were a good two feet high, so she and we bounced. We were moored stern to, with both our anchors out upstream. The river bottom was soft mud, and we dragged several times. This meant that one of us had to be on board at all times, and it meant broken nights. It also meant that parting from Veliko Gradiste was much easier than it would have been if our berth had been safe.

The duty-free store by the passenger-ship jetty opened only when tourist vessels arrived. We could, by regulation, use it only on the day of our departure. Buying "Kent" and "Marlborough" cigarettes, toothpaste and chewing gum was an operation which had to be well coordinated. These things were, so Thomas's hairdresser assured us vehemently, in very high demand in Rumania. He should have said they were worth their weight in gold. As it was, we spent $80.00 on them. A simple move downstream of a few miles would, it seemed, soon convert them to five times that value and more. He said nothing at all about the hazards of the move, but that was understandable.

*Outward Leg* had a job getting away from Veliko Gradiste. By the time we'd said good-bye to practically everyone in town, old, young, male, female and all gradations between, cleared police control and customs, and discussed soccer, Tito, Princess Diana, Marco Polo, Haile Selassie, Muhammad Ali, the methods used to rivet plane wings, the river Amazon and the day's weather with the customs chief, it was noon. The wind was blowing mightily at about thirty knots. It took a wet, cold Thomas a good hour of straining and heaving to get both anchors on board against that wind and a five-knot current, in two-foot seas.

When we at last were free of the ground and had turned downstream, we fairly flew, carried by both wind and current at a good ten to twelve knots. We covered, according to my log, thirty-one miles in just under three hours. We did this most of the way to the first defile with our trusty Yanmar switched off altogether, though ready to start instantly. The way we raised steerageway (enough extra speed to steer the boat efficiently) was simple; we merely lifted the dodger roof from its stowed position on the after cabin roof, halfway up, and wedged it there. This made an effective sail about ten square feet. With the wind, now reaching gale force, blowing right up our asses and the current sometimes racing around us in the narrows, sometimes almost making us hove to in the wide stretches of the Danube, we either sailed sedately or we tore along like a bat out of hell. A rather bedraggled bat, with her starboard side all abraded, a rather deep bat, with her freshwater and fuel tanks all full, and a rather musical bat, with her bagpipes blaring away over the foothills of the blue, beautiful Carpathian Mountains stretching away on both sides of the lovely Danube valley ahead of us.

At Veliko Gradiste Old Father Danube was about two miles wide. From there to the Iron Gates his width ranged from nearly five miles to a few hundred yards. Where the river was wide the current dropped to about two knots, but in the defiles it raged at anything up to fifteen knots. In the wide parts he averaged fifteen feet depth, but this could shoal down to seven feet in the channels. In the defiles, our depth meter often showed more than two hundred feet, and there the old bugger was very strong and knew it.

A few miles below Veliko Gradiste on both sides of the Danube, opposite each other, are the small towns of Pozezena in Yugoslavia, and Pojejena in Rumania. They had the same name in their own languages, but they were as different as chalk from cheese, and apparently as far away from each other, because of the Rumanian frontier guards, as I was from the planet Jupiter. Pozezena was a small, typical Yugoslav river town. Brown, mud-colored houses huddled by the riverbank, a couple of rusty old barges lay stranded on the foreshore, a few mangy dogs on the town jetty, some bare-assed kids swimming in the river where the water was slack, and above all, on a rise in the middle of town, an old church steeple. Just beyond the town, downstream from it, was the requisite garbage dump, with a wrecked old car upside down ontop of it.

Pojejena was what we would find to be the typical small Rumanian riverside town in those stretches of the river. It was set back well from the bank, its houses were aseptically clean and uniformly constructed. Instead of a church tower there was a big municipal water tower, gleaming silver with a huge red star atop it. Apart from the red star everything looked more like Holland than the Balkans. Except for one thing, or rather three: between the town and the river there was a long barbed-wire fence about ten feet high; at regular intervals along the fence there was a military watchtower; and atop the watchtowers, inside the little shelters with their roofs shining green, was a soldier with a machine gun. Despite the attractive appearance of Pojejena, Pozezena, with its garbage dump, mangy dogs and all, was far, far more attractive to me.

At km 1049 was the Rumanian city of Moldova. Its waterfront was one long line of working jetties with cranes and silos, fronted by a fleet of dumb-barges. There was no sign of any shops or cafés; no sign of anything except work and the means to perform it. This was to be the invariable case on the Rumanian Danube until the frontier line was left 430 miles or thereabouts downstream. There were never to be any signs of people *enjoying* themselves, never a fisherman on his own sitting quietly with his rod. They were always in groups, working at it under the supervision of an armed sentry in a tower.

On the waterfront of Moldova town, which stretches for one and a quarter miles, there were four manned military watchtowers. The docks were completely surrounded, as far as I could see, by a twelve-foot-high wire fence. Those are plain facts. We were close enough to see the tower sentries' faces, as they watched us pass by. They looked dumbfounded as we swirled by only yards away, all flags flying and Mr. McPherson blowing away hard on his bagpipes. The Rumanian sentries were all very young men, no more than twenty years, at a general guess. The many uniformed police among the workers in the docks were all middle-aged and older, and wore side arms.

The workers themselves were of all ages it seemed, and there were many women among them as they labored at loading or unloading the barges. Where there were armed guards, the workers either stared at us for a few moments, shyly, or ignored us ostentatiously. Where there were no guards they cheered us loudly and enthusiastically, all of them, without exception. This, too, was to be the case all through Rumania.

From Moldova downstream Old Father Danube showed us his true versatility. He widened into one stream, he narrowed into as many as six streams, he wound round sharp bends, he tore on for miles in straight stretches, he meandered through flat plains, he thrust through mountainsides, and he kept our eyes wide open for more beauty, more delights, more sudden twists, more surprises, more sudden dismay or even horror, and more hazards. It was as though the whole history of Europe, ancient and modern, was being swept before our eyes in one long, vast, fast panorama. He showed us everything in Balkan life, past and present. It was a moving feast, never ending, flowing on and on forever, it seemed.

On the Rumanian side there were no boat fishermen. On the Yugoslav side sometimes, not often, there were. I cannot, for reasons which will be obvious, tell you when or where one incident happened. I can only assure you that it is true.

As *Outward Leg* flew along somewhere on the frontier between Yugoslavia and Rumania with her engine silent and her jury sail helping the wind and current to thrust her downstream at twelve knots, I played a selection from Gilbert and Sullivan's *Mikado* on the tape player. Music on a river not only cheers the souls within earshot, it also serves, amplified when the need arises, as a very good siren, and alerts other small craft that a vessel is approaching them.

Somewhere along that long frontier I sighted a fleet of a dozen or so Yugoslav fishing rowboats. Every one of them was painted yellow and bore the Yugoslav flag painted on its sides, aft. All the fishermen were wearing the usual blue overalls and straw hats of the fishing communes along the river in those parts. They were spread over a good square mile of river, and were fishing away with bottom trolls as they drifted downstream. *Outward Leg* was passing them in the nine-knot current at a relative speed of about three knots. As I steered to pass between two of these small fishing boats, the tape player was sounding off with the song "Three Little Maids from School Are We." As *Outward Leg* passed by the stern of the forward boat of the pair, the man on it suddenly looked up and grinned hugely. His face was very dark and sunburned and he wore about a week's growth of beard. I was close enough to him to notice that his eyes were a pale blue and hear him, very distinctly and clearly, say in the very best Oxford English, "Ah, Gilbert and Sullivan; very nice too."

At first I merely nodded my head in agreement, as I would, say, on the Solent or on Long Island Sound. It was a second or two before I remembered where I was and where our boat was heading. I whipped round to see the man again, but he was fifty yards astern by now, and again leaning down over his lines, under the shade of his wide-brimmed hat. As we were in a straight stretch of Danube I kept staring round at the fisherman again and again, but soon he and his boat were a mere dot on the cool, uncaring face of the silver river, and then he was gone. There were then only the boat, and the silver river, and the green trees, and the brown hills, and the blue mountains, and the black wire fence to the east, and an insoluble mystery.

The scene at the Rumanian town of Pescari at km 1041 was almost a replica of the scene back at Moldova, only this time there were six military watchtowers instead of four and the wire fence was fourteen feet high instead of ten. But we were so fascinated with the view ahead of us that Pescari passed by almost unnoticed. Suddenly, from a great lacustrine stretch of pure silver six miles wide, the river forced his way through a rocky gap in the side of a mountain, which was no more than 550 yards wide. Heading for it with the wind at gale force astern and a ten-knot linear maelstrom under *Outward Leg*, and with eddies pushing and shoving our hulls this way and that, first to starboard, then to port, it seemed like trying to get one of Hannibal's war elephants into a mousehole. We shot through the gap at a good fifteen knots and the depth meter showed three hundred feet for some minutes, until we were about two and a half miles along a narrow defile overhung with high cliffs on both sides. It was all very dramatic, very sudden, a bit like the opening of a hangman's trapdoor, and for us, just as irrevocable. With that wind and that current, and that sea there was simply no way at all that *Outward Leg* could ever have turned back upstream alone. We were like a moth in a flooded street drain.

We had been so intent on entering the defile at Pescari that we had had time only to briefly glance at the lovely old castle at its entrance and wonder at the patience and stamina of the people who had constructed its teetering ramparts on the face of the cliff over such a raging torrent of water.

The first defile of the Iron Gates was about three miles long. Then opened up very gradually for about two and a half miles until it was again a more normal half to one mile wide. This stretch, all the way to the Iron Gates, about fifty-seven miles long, was the swiftest part of the Danube below Kielheim back in Bavaria, 750 miles upstream. In the old days river ships used to be towed up through here, first by slaves pulling on warps secured to mooring rings on the cliffsides, then by prisoners of war and of peace, then by steam engines, sometimes set on amazingly skillfully hacked platforms on the cliffs. In those days it took up to two weeks for a ship to pass from Kladovo to Pescari, accompanied, you can bet your life, by a whole lot of Turkish cursing and whiplashing.

Through the defile from Pescari to Kladovo was much of the finest river scenery I have ever seen anywhere in the world. It can only be described in superlatives. It was often overwhelming. Nature showed us what pygmies we really are and how futile our little thin wire fences.

On the Rumanian side of the long defile a road was carved out of the cliff bottom. The only cars we saw on it were two khaki-camouflaged vans. On the Yugoslav side, for the first half of the stretch, there was nothing but mountain, bare and stark, rising straight out of the Danube from hundreds of feet below his surface. There were a few stumpy bushes, but no trees, no flowers, no earth, no grass; nothing but stark, honest rock, from whose mighty sunburned boulders our playing of Beethoven's Ninth echoed resoundingly.

At km 1011 was another narrow defile. It was no more than 430 yards wide. This was guarded (on the Rumanian side, of course) by a single soldier bearing a machine pistol. He glumly watched us as we flashed by at all of fifteen knots right into the face of the mountain, or so it must have seemed to him. From there on, apart from the military road on the Rumanian side of the Tin Curtain, there were no signs at all of man's activities until km 1005. Then, on the Yugoslav side of the Danube defile, a new road, a couple of hundred feet above the river torrent, was being hacked out of the side of sheer cliffs which reached up for a thousand feet and more straight out of the riverbed. In the next few miles we counted more than *a hundred* bridges newly constructed over dizzy chasms for this new road. We were later told that this was a road being built by the national government to allow tourists access by land to the Iron Gates defiles. It will also, it seemed to me, give the Rumanian sentries, on their side, something to look at besides the face of the river or the corpses of their countrymen that they have shot while trying to cross it. If that's what the new road means, then long live tourism!

Km 1000, 620 miles from the estuary of the Danube, was a plain bit of rocky mountainside with nothing to show but the kilometer sign; yet, how significant it was, how very difficult to reach. Just below it, at Svinita in Rumania, there was another guarded pontoon in blackish water. From the fierce glares of the guards there no one but a nearsighted innocent, a raving lunatic or a defecting traitor whose approach was expected would even think of berthing a boat there.

Donji Milanovac at km 990 was the first town or place in Yugoslavia below Veliko Gradiste with a pontoon, but the wind was blowing so hard there that loaded river ships, anchored off the town, were rising and plunging seven or eight feet with each sea rolling downstream.

(Anyone who, like some yachtsmen we met up with in the Aegean, imagines that the Danube passage is "a cake walk" should read that foregoing paragraph again.)

I turned to anchor off the pontoon, then "crab" our boat in toward it to get a line ashore, when suddenly I noticed that just below the town there was a headland. I realized that this was where the Porecka river joined the Danube. I turned again downstream and headed for it, keeping well out in the channel so that we would not be rudely shocked by underwater hazards, which are not rare thereabouts, and which can severely damage a craft making ten knots or so, even with her engine in neutral.

In the Porecka river, about a third of a mile upstream against a three-knot current, we found first a Yugoslav river gunboat, with a friendly waving crew who dipped their ensign to our salute, then a very good anchorage in ten feet, thick mud bottom. The anchorage was just off a little restaurant which turned out to be a good place to eat. It also had a live gypsy band and was, it appeared, the rendezvous of every libertine and loose lady on or around the Yugoslav Iron Gates, and that's saying something.

The restaurant has a red, pagoda-style roof, so, to please the customers and to give the three gypsy musicians a break, Thomas clambered back on board and played for them our "Selections from *The Mikado*" by Gilbert and Sullivan. I was amazed to observe that one of the gypsies, an elderly gentleman, actually knew some of the music, and hummed it loudly.

The restaurant owner, a charming lady who spoke nothing but Serbian yet still managed to make herself understood, fed us while the local policeman was sent for. He turned up after a couple of hours, and booked us in and out again for Kladovo next day, over a game of chess with Thomas.

There was very little wind on the Porecka river, at least where *Outward Leg* lay anchored. The evening was lovely, viewed from under the pagoda roof of the little restaurant. The night was alight with stars and the river banks with the sounds of crickets chirping, the boat was in slack water, the holding ground was solid, God was in his heaven and all was right with the world. Before I turned in I stopped myself remembering the sights of the Rumanian shores and the dangers of the coming passage through that country. So I slept well.

The next day the wind blew on the Danube from twenty-five to thirty-five knots, and there was very little letup, even at the sharp bends of the river. That old northerly wind just kept blowing right on, following faithfully every turn and angle of the river channel. On average the seas were up to three feet high, so we were bouncing about quite merrily. The river width was from one to three miles on average and there was now a road on both sides of the river. There were two small hamlets on the Yugoslav cliffs, and nothing on the

Rumanian side but an empty road and an armed guard every half-mile or so.

At km 973.5 one of the narrowest defiles of the whole river Danube from the Black Sea to the foothills of the Alps was only about five hundred feet or so wide. The water from a good half of south, central and southeastern Europe poured itself through that gap, like floodwater down a drain. Our boat was picked up and swept through, touching, I am sure, well over twenty knots for brief moments.

At the downstream end of this mighty drain, which was two miles long, was yet another narrow gap in the mountain, this time the narrowest of all, only four hundred feet wide. Out of that one *Outward Leg* shot like a raving Valkyrie, at over twenty knots, all her flags ripping away in the forward speed breeze and Mr. McPherson blaring away at "Lament for the Old Sword." She was flung from between the cliffs and out into the middle of a huge lake. There she was almost stopped dead in the water, then, minutes later, was picked up at the mouth of yet another defile, almost as narrow as the one before it, and flung through again at a good twenty knots. It was all over so fast that it was as if it had never happened. We were borne through those defiles by a force so immense that anything but "almighty" would be too tame to describe it. The force transmitted signals incessantly, up through the rudder, through the steering cables, through the wheel, to my hand and brain, that it could, if it wished, swat and kill us instantly, like flies, anytime it had a mind to. The sudden feeling of forward movement, as the current lifted the keel and the hulls, was far more urgent and insistent than anything I had ever felt on a jet plane taking off, or in a train suddenly stopping at an emergency halt.

There was doubt about it. When I at last was in a position to check the course of the Danube defiles on a map I noted that the distance down the last two defiles before the Iron Gates Lock is about five miles, give or take a few yards. It took *Outward Leg* exactly fifteen minutes to cover the distance. That's twenty knots for the whole course. But for some few minutes she had been almost stopped in the great "lake" between the defiles. Inside the defiles themselves she must have been making, on the current with her engine just turning over in gear to maintain steerage way, *more than twenty-two knots* at times.

At km 964, at the downstream end of the last defile before the

Iron Gates Lock, engraved in the rock of the cliff face itself about eight feet above the edge of the torrent, was a Roman tablet, commemorating the conquest and subjugation of the lower Danube valley by troops under the Emperor Trajan. We passed close enough to it to read the Latin inscription, but too fast to note it down, word for word. On the Rumanian bank, a third of a mile opposite Trajan's tablet, a lone frontier guard nursed his rifle and stared as we shot past, playing "The Big Spree." It was a moment of utter incongruities.

The Iron Gates Locks themselves were tame in comparison with the defiles above them. Even though there was a forty-knot wind blowing straight down into the Yugoslav lock on the south bank, even though it almost made us collide with the great steel gates at the lower end, and even though it was only Thomas's agility and skill with his mooring warp, catching the very last floating bollard and holding the boat's forward weight on it, that saved us, it was still as child's play compared with negotiating the torrential rocky drains through the mighty mountains that we had just passed. In the lock, as we waited to descend, I felt as a dog must feel when he shakes himself after falling into a swift stream and has scrambled for the bank.

The Iron Gates Locks were immense, cavernous things, about a thousand feet long, about sixty feet wide by eighty feet high, when they emptied. There were two locks to go through, one after the other, and the total drop was 120 feet, or twenty fathoms.

The locks were crowded above us, as we dropped at a fathom a minute, with hard-hatted workers in various states of dress and, apparently, sobriety. A couple of the workers shouted some German, and they gave us to understand that they had never seen a three-hulled vessel before, nor had they ever seen any vessel wearing an American flag. All the way through both locks the workers crowded above us and gave us good cheer.

Inside the locks, none of the electric signal lights worked. This did not bother us. Only a moron could not see when it was time to move on, and beyond the last of the two lower gates there was nothing between us and the sea, we thought, but one more lock at Constanta. Now, as we emerged with Mr. McPherson playing "The Big Spree" for the jolly Yugoslav workers, we knew we were almost back down at sea level after almost eight months of climbing up and down across Europe.

Those were the thoughts in my mind as we made our way into

Kladovo. Six miles below the Iron Gates. That is, besides making out where the hell to berth the boat. The place was full of shipping; hundreds of river ships, tugs and barges, and it was a good two hours, after trying one place after another and having to leave for as many different reasons, that at last we drew up under the old castle, at km 934, and found a small customs post hidden away behind a fleet of waiting barges.

There was no way for me to get ashore in Kladovo. Even from the dinghy the only landing was fraught with obstacles and wet mud a foot thick, so we stayed on board that night, tied up next to a rotting old Soviet dumb-barge. We ate in the cockpit while our ragged, pale Stars and Stripes hung limply only a few feet away from the barge's ragged, pale red flag, with its hammer and sickle only just visible.

We turned in, ready to face entering Rumania next day.

# 27

# *The Lost Planet and the Void*

The river Danube below the Iron Gates was often like a sea. Here, he was wide, very long, and the fetches of wind and water raised seas that were as high, sometimes, as anything seen in the English Channel in any weather under a full gale. When *Outward Leg* headed out from the protection of the small spur of the riverbank that formed the "harbor" of Kladovo it was just such a morning.

Across the river, on the north side, was the Rumanian twin-town of Kladovo, called Schela Cladovei and, of course, it was strictly guarded by dozens of sentries in watchtowers. What brightened our eyes, though, was the sight of the first real sea-worn vessel since we had passed a Danish Baltic coaster on the Rhine eight months before. At first, to us who were accustomed by then to the size of river ships, she looked gigantic. We made over to where she was laid alongside. The rust streaks on her cliff-like sides told us their tales of stormy nights out on the sea lanes. She was black-hulled, with a grimy white superstructure and a white funnel with the horizontal red stripe of the Soviet merchant shipping fleet. There was a hammer and sickle of course, on the red stripe. Her name was *Bolshevik Karaev* and she hailed, I think, from Odessa on the Black Sea.

It wasn't quite the same as meeting the QE2 but on the Danube we couldn't be choosers, and the sea is the same for a Bolshevik as for a gammy-legged bastard, I suppose. Thomas and I waved at the few Russians on her stern rail cheerily, but were answered with glum silence. The size of the other somehow made *Outward Leg* seem smaller and very impertinent. There was an air about our boat that seemed to say, "I may be no longer Sea-Monarch of the Danube, but

259

don't tread on my tail!" As events turned out, that was the only attitude that she and I could have had, to push through to her true domain. In the old days we used to call it "stroppy swank." Some ragged-assed nippers on the British sailing barges had had it in full measure. They had been worked to death most of the time, they didn't have a penny to their names, but God help anyone who tried to bully them or so much as lay a finger on their scrawny but tough little shoulders.

Turnu-Severin, where we were to "enter into Rumanian waters," looked, from a distance, quite attractive. A big town, mostly of white buildings gleaming in the early morning sun, it covered an entire low hill down to the river's edge. In between the white buildings we could see dark green trees, long lines of them, and we guessed that these were wide avenues. We approached with Mr. McPherson doing his very best to alert any sleepy watchtower guards, their fingers more than likely on the triggers of their Kalashnikovs. The current upstream of Turnu-Severin pontoon was a mere three knots. I had the engine running "ahead" very slowly. I wanted to give the guards on the pontoon as much time as I could to inspect us through their binoculars and to become accustomed to the fact that we intended to berth alongside their pontoon.

Right beyond the pontoon on the river bank was a small office which looked very much like an old-fashioned British railway station. It was one-storied, its windows were either grimy or broken, and it had wooden decorations with peeling paint on them, all along the eaves. That, we saw later, was the harbor master's office and customs post. Next to that was, surprisingly enough, a big outdoor restaurant overlooking the river just upstream from the pontoon. Behind the restaurant was a large factory with huge red banners and signs festooned over its front fascia. This proclaimed that it was the local headquarters of the Rumanian Communist Party, whose Big Daddy was Nicolai Ceausescu.

I could read the sign on the building all right. Rumania derives its language mainly from the Latin and anyone with knowledge of Latin, Spanish, Italian, Portuguese or French can get the gist of any written matter in Rumanian, though imperfectly. Most conjunctives and common kitchen words are of Slavic derivation. This split in the composition of the language probably has much to do with certain facets of the Rumanian national character which, I eventually concluded, was definitely schizoid and certainly paranoid.

Far from having awakened the armed guards with our bagpipe music, I saw, as *Outward Leg* approached closer and closer, now turned with her bows upstream and "crabbing" toward the rough sides of the big pontoon, that we seemed to have sent them into a dumbfounded trance. There were about a dozen of them, all young, all in khaki fatigues, and they all wore filthy boots which reached up to their mid-calves.

The guards were supervised by two officers. One was a tall man in his thirties. He was fair complexioned and looked quite well groomed. He wore a light overcoat that reached down to his ankles, tied with a belt amidships. Him I named Yul because his head was shaved all over. The other officer was small, not more than five and a half feet tall, and *ancient*. He reminded me of Somerset Maugham, and so I named him Comrade Maugham. He was dressed in a plain gray uniform blouse, with a belt around his waist and another over his right shoulder. He wore riding boots which reached up almost to his knees, and they shone. His hair was very black, as though he had dyed it, and his skin, what I could see of it, was like creased parchment. Perched on his head was a peaked cap decorated with the customary red star.

By the time we had bumped slightly alongside, the pontoon was alive with guards now moving close to the boat to look her over. As the two officers scrambled on board, the onlookers were being chased off the pontoon by yet more guards who had run from the Party Headquarters, sleepy dogs moved off, disturbed from their mid-forenoon reveries, small piglets screeched as their grunting mothers pushed past the milling throng of humans, and clucking chickens were everywhere. It brought to my mind memories of arriving at Spanish railway stations back in the early fifties and was the first indication to me that we had indeed passed through a time warp. We were back in the fifties and would remain there, and even visit the forties, and thirties, dipping now and again into the twenties and the tens, and right back to the turn of the century, so that by the time we had reached the offing of the Rumanian coast we had almost forgotten that many parts of the rest of the world were, in fact, in the mid-eighties.

Comrades Yul and Maugham both spoke enough German for us to understand them. They were quite friendly in their attitudes to

Thomas and me, but later my crewman, who has a much more Central European and less innocent view of things than I, an ocean-man from an island, told me that he thought that had they found anything on board which, to their minds, should not have been there, they would have turned nasty very quickly, and God help us then.

As was our custom when arriving in an Eastern European country, we had already opened most of the lockers in our boat. All our secrets and "rudies" were exposed, for all the world to see. Both the ama hatches had been unscrewed, ready for instant opening should the officials demand to look inside the outriggers. Comrade Yul went forward with Thomas, where he inspected minutely the forward cabin.

Comrade Maugham stayed aft with me, and noted down the manufacturers' numbers of all equipment, radios, sextant, watches, satnav, cameras, weatherfax, typewriter, timer, clocks, rocket flare pistol, barometer, thermometer. He even asked the numbers of oil lamps. I invented numbers for them and he studiously wrote down "1066, 1805, 1815, 1914, 1918, 1939 and 1945." Thus our lamps were all given official numbers for salient dates in British history. Comrade Maugham's small side arm was in a gleaming leather holster. I kept, of course, a straight face.

Comrade Maugham then stiffly climbed up and knelt on my desk and reached up to my library shelf. He took down each and every book and riffled through it. He grunted *Palaya Buoy*. It took me a few seconds to realize that he meant *Playboy* magazine. I told him in English that I had given up masturbating several years ago, as it had started to affect my night vision. I offered him the *Oxford Book of English Verse* instead. He seized this avidly, as though it were a political catechism of the thoughts of Chairman Thatcher, but when he saw that it was merely verse lines, he thrust it away from him, not realizing that in it was far more powerful stuff than Nicolai Ceausescu could ever spout, and much more dangerous to any oligarchy disguised as socialism than any *Playboy* magazine could ever be.

When Comrade Maugham got around to inspecting my passport, which had been newly issued back in Vienna, he demanded to know why I had a new passport. "What is in the old one?" he almost hummed in anticipation of a catch.

I showed him my old passport tatty and full of stamps from a score of countries, from Bolivia to Finland, Alaska to Madagascar. When he saw the official stamp of the Soviet Antarctic Research Station in

Graham Land his attitude changed again, to one of almost-crawling respect. He politely handed my passport back and told us that we were welcome in Rumania.

"You must," he said, "only berth your vessel at designated places on the Danube, and you must not call in a Bulgarian port. If you do, the Rumanian visa in your passport will no longer be valid. Then you will not be allowed back into Rumania."

"But," I expostulated, "we would have to come back into Rumania, because we can't get to the Black Sea if we don't."

"I know," he replied, "but that's the law."

"Then, if we can't return to the Rumanian side, what can we do?"

"Either stay in Bulgaria forever, or return to Yugoslavia," was his reply.

"But we're on our way around the world!"

"We can't help that. Rumania didn't ask you to come," chimed in Comrade Yul. He was smiling, showing very good teeth. They reminded me of the Great White Shark. His head, now he had doffed his hat, was about the same shape, too. That spoiled his otherwise good looks.

"What about if I get another Rumanian visa in Bulgaria?" I asked.

"That's all right," explained Comrade Maugham. "Then we'd let you in, but you can only get it in Sofia, their capital, and that's a couple of days' journey from the river."

"So?" What was a couple of days' railway journey? I asked myself.

"Then you would have to enter Bulgaria as a tourist, and that means that they would make you pay two weeks' hotel fee, whether you need a hotel or not. That's *their* law," explained Maugham, distastefully.

Comrade Yul broke in again. "Here, in Rumania we treat foreigners much better. Here you only have to spend ten dollars a day each, in leus, and get certificates every time you change money! If we catch you changing money on the street . . ." He tapped his holster and grinned again. "And don't try selling anything from the boat!"

"Stay in Rumania, Captain, for your own sake. I generally don't like people who arrive here in yachts, but you earn your own way and you work hard at it, obviously," observed Comrade Maugham. "You remind me of the way some Rumanians used to be, when I was a boy, and I like your style. In different circumstances," he added mysteriously, "I think we could have been good friends." With that, he turned after briefly shaking my hand, and disappeared topside and ashore, back to the Party Headquarters. Comrade Yul stuck his cap back on the point of his bald head, grinned, and followed the ancient party official, like a storewalker following a department store manager.

"Well!" I murmured to Thomas when the Rumanians had departed. "Well, well, they didn't even notice the amas. We could have had ten spies in them!"

"Did they see the blue jeans?" asked my crewman anxiously.

"Old Comrade Maugham did. He was into every corner of my cabin."

"What did he say about them, is it all right?"

"Sure. He took out each pair, lovingly, and put them back again, wagged his head and clucked his tongue."

"Was that all?"

"No." I replied, "He said, 'You're going to be popular!' "

Thomas went ashore to change some of our money into Rumanian leus at the local bank. I waited for him at the restaurant overlooking the river. I simply did not feel up to walking any distance. Any nervous strain is just as wearing, for a one-legged man, as a physical strain. It was 8:30 in the forenoon when I clomped into the outside restaurant gardens. All about were workers, about a hundred of them from the shipyard nearby and from the river ships themselves, sitting drinking beer. Many of them were women, but I noticed that most of the women isolated themselves together in small groups at the tables. All the women, old and young, wore cloth headscarves. They also drank beer. I soon found out why they drank beer, when our two coffees arrived. Coffee was the equivalent of two dollars a cup, while beer was about twenty cents a bottle. Tea was nonexistent. So was food. This was, although we did not know it at the time, to be the case throughout all the Rumanian Danube, with one or two surprising exceptions.

After about an hour Thomas returned from the bank and from an unsuccessful attempt to buy fresh bread and vegetables. Even so, he was excited. "It's great here," he spluttered over his cold coffee. "It's like being in a museum, only it's a working museum. There's a steam engine just up the road pulling a long freight train."

This, at the time, meant nothing to me at all. I had been brought up among steam trains. It was only later that I realized that on the whole way through Europe, until then, of all the trains we had seen rushing along the Rhine, Main and Danube valleys, and around the towns and cities, not one of them had been pulled by a steam engine.

"It's just like an old movie," observed Thomas.

"How were the shops?"

"All closed, but there's a pharmacy that isn't. The shelves in it were empty."

"What about the streets, were they clean?"

"Much cleaner than in Yugoslavia. There are old women sweeping them." He sipped his coffee some more, then added, "All the shops have a big crowd of people outside them, waiting for bread or meat to be delivered from the government distribution centers."

"Couldn't you have waited a little while?"

"I asked a couple of people, those who could understand some German. They said that they weren't sure at all when the food would arrive. They might have to go on waiting an hour, maybe all day, and even then they were not sure that they would get any food."

"Jesus Christ."

"*Ja*, and we can't buy diesel oil here," he went on. "We have to buy tickets for it at the State bank. Then we can buy it with the tickets anywhere."

"Anywhere?"

"Well, not here. They don't have any. Maybe at the next town."

"Good. Great. *Maybe*. Well, get a ticket for fifty liters, Thomas."

My crewman took off to do as he was bid, and I walked slowly back to *Outward Leg*. Most of the people I passed were ill-dressed, the women in cheap-looking creased, shapeless dresses, the men in badly cut odd jackets, trousers and collarless shirts. It reminded me of the way people used to dress in Wales during the thirties depression. Most of the men wore the same kind of caps that Welshmen had worn then.

Soon Thomas was back with the government permits to buy fuel and we were off downstream, in Rumanian waters. We took off to the strains of the strathspey "Caledonian Canal," before the amazed stares of all the frontier guards, Comrades Yul and Maugham, gazing at us from the upstairs window of the Party Headquarters, and a hundred or so workers, who gawped silently at us until they were out of sight.

In Turnu-Severin, Thomas had tried to find river charts. He might just as well have looked for copies of Thomas Paine's *Rights of Man*. All he could find was a very poorly printed and small-scale roadmap of Rumania printed on gray-white paper, very rough to the touch. This showed the Danube as a grainy green line interspersed with white blotches which might, or might not, have represented islands. The details ended where Rumania ended, so that the rest of the world around Rumania was represented by a gray-white void. Even those bridges that were shown ended abruptly halfway across whatever river it was. The whole effect of the map, printed in Bucharest, the Rumanian capital, by a Rumanian government agency, was to make Rumania look like some sort of lost planet, covered with mountains, lakes, roads, rivers and railways, hurtling through the void of outer space. Ominously, one of the edges of the planet ran for seven hundred miles along the Danube, and it was along the edge of that void that *Outward Leg* would be voyaging. It turned out to be truly an edge, truly a void, and each time we rejoined the lost planet Rumania, it was as if we had landed from outer space. While we were out in the void between Rumanian ports there was no communication between us and the planet Rumania or anywhere else. We did not know what to expect when we arrived anywhere, and no one in Rumania had any idea that we were on our way. We might as well have been traveling down the Danube in the twelfth century. We had been warned against using our radios, and again, as in Czechoslovakia, we had been told we must have no communication with *anyone*, ashore or afloat, while we were under way on the Danube.

Each bend of the river, from Turnu-Severin on, was an exploration, each arrival at each frontier port was a discovery. We had no way of knowing what fuel or food supplies were available anywhere. Often, very often, the officials at one place knew absolutely nothing about the next place on the route. *Nine* times out of ten their advice or information was utterly wrong.

*Eight* times out of ten the destination, with no alternative within dozens of miles, was in a wind- and water-blown position, and also exposed to grave risk of damage from big ships passing by.

*Seven* times out of ten the "port" was miles away from the nearest village or shop.

*Six* times out of ten the "port" was directly in front of a huge factory complex, noisy and smelly, under arc light glares day and night.

*Five* times out of ten the Rumanian "port" was faced by an attractive Bulgarian riverside resort on the Danube, well lit and seemingly full of modern amenities, set among green rolling hills which fell to a beautiful river front.

*Four* times out of ten there was a water tap on the Rumanian pontoon, or close by it.

*Three* times out of ten the water tap, when turned, issued water.

*Two* times out of ten there were civilian fishermen or riverboat men near the pontoon, whose very presence seemed to ease the misery of the surrounding gloom.

*Once* out of ten we were received with smiles by the officials.

*No* times out of ten did we not play our bagpipes as loud as we could, when approaching or leaving a Rumanian pontoon.

But *ten times out of ten* each "port," each pontoon, each jetty, was guarded by armed youths in fatigue uniforms, and the boat was overlooked by other guards in watchtowers upstream, downstream, and directly over our berths. It was like cruising on the coast of some nightmarish penal colony.

Nowhere on the Danube where it fronts Yugoslavia or Bulgaria did we ever see a working Rumanian patrol craft of any sort until we reached Calarasi, about which more anon. There were official patrol boats at almost every "port," but these were apparently used only by police and party officials and their families for Sunday outings on the river. That was the only sign of any form of "water sports" activity on the Danube on the Rumanian side until we reached the sea. Often we saw, in the upper reaches of the Rumanian Danube where there were no humans in sight except soldiers and organized parties of rod-fishermen, women washing clothes on the banks of the badly polluted river.

At km 865 a new river lock was under construction. This lock was deserted, though I couldn't imagine why; it was a Thursday. Luckily for us it was open at both ends and we motored through with no problem. The depth inside the new lock was twelve feet. Out on the river, above and below the mysterious new lock, the depths averaged around fifteen feet, but there were shallow patches with less than seven feet, and one or two with less than six. The current varied from three knots to seven in the narrows. The channel width ranged from a third of a mile to several, and sometimes the maze of islands in the river was so wide that they stretched on both sides beyond the low horizon. There was much less shipping in the Danube below the Iron Gates than there had been anywhere above them as far as Regensburg. Most of the shipping we saw was Rumanian, Bulgarian or Soviet. There were very, very few Austrian or German ships in the lower reaches, but those that there were always gave us a cheer when we passed them. *"Alles gut?"* they hailed as they waved both fists, clutched together, aloft.

*"Ja, alles gut!"* we replied, holding our thumbs up. They were our only contact with the world outside Rumania.

On the way downstream to Calafat, our next port of call, as we passed along the Rumanian frontier with Yugoslavia, we saw dozens of concrete pillboxes set in the river bank at regular distances for kilometer after kilometer stretching over eighty kilometers. They were deserted, from what we could see, and a few of them had toppled over where the bank they had been built on had been undermined by the river. These sights made even me quite fondly disposed to Old Father Danube, because I too despise pillboxes, whether made of concrete or not, together with what goes in or comes out of them, whether human or otherwise.

The stretch from Turnu-Severin to Calafat is a remote area sparsely inhabited. Only by the very rare villages did we see any signs of human life other than sentries and passing ships. On one very remote stretch, as we were being overlooked by a half-stupefied armed sentry atop a high cliff, we were passed by a big Bulgarian tourist vessel named *Rousse*. She passed very close to us and we could plainly see the diners, more than likely Westerners, bent over their food and drinks in the brightly lit dining saloon. Not one of them could have seen the lone sentry, with his gun slung over his shoulders, up on the cliff in the cool darkness of the evening. I was very aware of the stark difference between our Danube and theirs, but I was not envious.

Lower down, evening was beginning to shade the light of the river. All around, wildlife was dashing about to make the most of the few remaining minutes of daylight. I was wondering as we were swept along, where the hell I was going to berth *Outward Leg* for the night. At about km 850 we saw a phallic-looking monument on the Yugoslav side and knew, from our atlas, that it must mark the frontier between that country and Bulgaria on the south side of the Danube. We passed it at ten knots. That meant that the bank on the far side of the river was Bulgaria. Other than the monument there was no indication that any frontier existed. There were no watchtowers, no sentries. Only on our Rumanian side did they show us that the Rumanian planet was still whizzing by us in our watery void.

Suddenly, from under the shady, dark trees on the southern shore, there was first a pall of blue smoke, then a roar as powerful engines started up. I was already expecting it when the Bulgarian gunboat raced over toward us, and the crewman uncovered its bow gun with one hand. I was already even expecting the tinny voice that hailed us over a loudspeaker in English. *"Stop your vessel!"*

# 28

# *Learning About Rumania*

By the time the voice from the Bulgarian gunboat had ordered me to "stop your vessel" I had already put the Yanmar gear into neutral. Thomas was already out on the starboard ama in case the gunboat should come alongside *Outward Leg*. I held both my hands up level with my shoulders to show the Bulgarians that I was not then steering, and to show them that I had complied with their order. Then I realized that they were in fact giving me an illegal order, for we were drifting in Rumanian waters, outside their jurisdiction. The gunboat was now about twenty yards off our starboard quarter, and drifting in the four-knot current.

"Follow me," the tinny voice ordered. I could see vague figures now in the wheelhouse. The man by the deck gun still leaning over the weapon, holding on tight. It looked similar to a Bofors 40 mm.

I shook my head, exaggerating the movement, so that the captain of the gunboat could clearly see my refusal.

"Follow me," the voice repeated the order.

I cupped my hands around my mouth and shouted "NO! WE'RE IN RUMANIA AND WE'RE STAYING IN RUMANIA." I also added, in a low voice, "God help us!" I shoved the engine into gear and steered our boat at right angles to the middle of the river toward the Rumanian shore. As I glanced around I saw that there was no one on the Rumanian bank. There was, for once on the whole Rumanian Danube, no watchtower, no soldier. "Just like bloody policemen," I called to Thomas. "Never there when you need them!"

"What?" He couldn't understand what I'd said. *"Was ist das?"*

"We're heading as close to the Rummy shore as we can," I told

271

him, "and if that Bulgarian bugger comes any closer or tries to get alongside, we'll run *Outward Leg* on the bank. If we do, you stand by to jump ashore as fast as Christ will let you, and head fast for the nearest watchtower and alert the Rummys what's happened. *Verstehen?*"

"*Ja,*" replied Thomas, but he was too busy being fascinated by the movements of the Bulgarian gunboat. She was following us, but steering downstream, on the Bulgarian side of the middle course of the river. Now one of the men who had been in the wheelhouse had climbed out on deck and was waving us toward the Bulgarian bank with his arm.

"What do they want?" asked Thomas. It was, I supposed, always more difficult for a German to disobey an order from someone in uniform in a government gunboat than it was for a Welshman.

"They want us to go with them into Bulgaria." I told him. "Then they're going to say we entered of our own free will. Then they're going to clobber us for two weeks' hotel cost. They're bloody *bandidos*, Thomas. That's probably what happened to the Jerry who turned back up to Germany. The bastards are waylaying innocent yatties! They can't touch us legally, because we're not under their jurisdiction, so fuck 'em. But keep your eye on her. Her gun's much bigger than our Very pistol." I shoved the Yanmar gear lever into full ahead, and *Outward Leg*, with a four-knot current under her, shot forward, made eleven knots over the ground. It was a very uneven ground, as I could tell by sweaty glances at the depth meter; the bottom depth varied from about twenty feet to less than five. We had no charts, and our only map looked like it had come from the inside of playwright Ionescu's toilet door.

Normally I would have followed the contours of the river banks around the long perimeters of the course like a racehorse on the outside track. That, usually, is where the deeper bed, scored by the faster current, runs. But with a Bulgarian gunboat following us, waiting to pounce on us if we so much as strayed over the middle of the river by one yard, we had to stay on the north, the Rumanian side of the stream, no more than a boat's length away from the bank. At that speed it was, with no charts, I imagine, like driving a mobile china shop through a herd of bulls. To say that my heart was in my mouth as we charged down the side of the Danube with our depth meter alarm buzzing every few yards would be an understatement. It didn't feel as if it was my heart, it felt more like my false leg, all of it, from toe to groin-buckle, not merely in my mouth, but rammed down my throat.

The chase lasted for a good half-hour as evening darkened all across the river. The Bulgarian gunboat continued to follow us, but she held closer to the Bulgarian bank. There were still no watchtowers, no soldiers on our Rumanian side. Only trees, trees, trees. Then, at last, at about km 836, two or three islands blocked the main river and split it into several swift-running channels. This was exactly what I had been hoping, praying for. I headed between the island closest to the Rumanian bank and the mainland. As the current swiftened, we lost sight of the gunboat behind the islands. We shot forward in the narrow, shallow channel like an arrow. We were three miles or so inside the passage between the island and the mainland when we saw a ship tied up alongside. She was clearly Rumanian, as we could see from her paintwork, white and black.

For want of a decent map or of a name for the place where the ship was tied up, I'll call it km 829. We tried to anchor there, but the current was too fast. It must have been around seven knots, and I could guess that the river bottom was not firm so, as soon as the anchor was down and the engine slowed down, we just went sliding on, away downstream like a leaf in a gutter. Eventually there was nothing for it but to tie up alongside the Rumanian ship. I could clearly see her name now, but because of our relations with that ship's crew then and later, I will disguise her name and call her *Memphis*, and say that she hailed from Galati. She may have hailed from there; she may not. I'm not going to say where she really came from because I don't want the skipper and crew to be in serious trouble with their present government, or what passes for "government" in that misruled, unhappy land. In short, they were good men and true.

In the dark, the crew of *Memphis* lit its lamps for us to get alongside their ship and helped tie up *Outward Leg*. Then they sent to the nearby village for the frontier guard on duty. He turned out to be a stubby young sergeant of about twenty-five, old for his occupation. He was surly and nasty-minded when he clomped on board with his rifle, but by the time we'd poured two or three drafts of Yugoslav *slivovitz* down him, he was quite merry and friendly. So much so that when he left the ship Thomas had to chase after the sergeant with his loaded Kalashnikov, which he'd forgotten and left on board *Outward Leg*.

The captain and crew of *Memphis* were a motley-looking lot, ranging in age from about sixty to eighteen. The thin skipper was in the middle range, about thirty-five. It was soon obvious that the party representative on board was the only crewman who spoke English. He was the mate. He was about twenty-eight, a big, friendly, comradely, strong, barrel-chested man. When we were alone with the skipper we found that he spoke a little German. We had a quiet, hurried conversation with him. He told us he was allowed only to navigate in Rumanian waters, and that his pay was the equivalent of about $60.00 a week. On that he kept a wife and three children in his home port. He asked about American wages for similar work, and when I told him that the captain of the tugboat in which I voyaged up the Mississippi river in 1980 was paid $1000.00 a week and owned two airplanes, he fell silent. Later he mentioned that he and the crew worked for three months and then had two weeks ashore on leave, but even then they had to work for some hours every day in the shipyard at their home port. The captain warned us of confiding in English-speaking Rumanians, but wouldn't explain why.

After we had eaten a simple meal with the skipper and the mate in the captain's quarters, which were very plainly furnished, the crew joined us. There were a half-dozen of them, and they were a good, merry company, who sang for us jolly-sounding songs. We had taken a couple of bottles of Austrian wine on board *Memphis* to share with them, and they provided some liquid dynamite of their own. The crew were all original characters, and I would normally have told all about them and what we discussed, but to do so might too easily identify them. Rumania being "governed" as it is, I dare not do that, for the men's sakes. I am not being censored. I am censoring myself, because if the favors that *Memphis* did for us then and later were known by the authorities in Rumania the skipper would probably be shot, or at least imprisoned for the next few years. But I know who they are, and what the name of their ship really is, and they and she will always be remembered in *Outward Leg*. One day, when the vicious oligarchy that at present rules in Rumania has been kicked out, I will tell the world the true story of *Memphis*. Later, much farther down the Danube when *Outward Leg* was in grave difficulty, *Memphis* turned up at a time and place which would seem implausible to any reader if written in a novel. She saved our bacon.

In the dawn light of the next day, 21 June, both Thomas and I experienced an optical illusion when the river widened downstream of the islands. The Danube appeared to be running downhill far more steeply than must have been the case. He seemed to slope to an angle of about ten degrees. It was either an optical illusion or the effects of the hard stuff on board *Memphis* the night before. On one side of us the rolling hills of Bulgaria were blue and green. Now and again there was a patch of yellow; wheat fields, we supposed. On the Rumanian side there was nothing but a watery, forested blue infinity, stretching from the silver river to the azure and pink sky in the northeast. On this stretch we were waved at by a few lone fishermen and shepherds on the Bulgarian bank.

At km 813 was a small fishing harbor, which was guarded by a watchtower and Rumanian soldiers. It might be used in an emergency. At km 811 there was a ruined mansion, which had once been very grand. This, we later discovered, was the "port" of Cetate. There was a concrete pillbox in the mansion gardens, right in front of the main door. Some wild flowers had climbed their way partly over the pillbox. Just downstream from the mansion was a stone jetty with a river ship alongside loading timber. There were six guards on the jetty, and a watchtower at the southern end. A cluster of fishermen were rod-fishing just downstream from the jetty, under guard. At km 795 was the port of Calafat.

Our arrival at Calafat was like a scene from between acts backstage at a comic opera. There were customs officials, soldiers, policemen, party youth leaders, boys, girls, ancients and babies, and the whole staff of the port captain's office on the pontoon to meet us. We were escorted, my crew and I together between coughing dogs, grunting pigs and fluttering hens, over a rough patch of muddy ground to the tiny customs office, which was hard by the ferry landing ramp. Ferries arrived and left for the Bulgarian side of the river about every hour, day and night. I noticed many Yugoslav, Bulgarian, Soviet, East German and even Czech cars waiting for the ferry, but by far the majority were Yugoslav and Soviet. Calafat was on the main route between U.S.S.R. and Belgrade, south of the Carpathian Mountains. There were no Rumanian vehicles, that I saw, using the ferry.

After an hour's desultory conversation, in basic German mainly about the "ill-treatment" of black people in the U.S.A. and Britain, we were allowed to visit the town of Calafat. The port was overlooked by a tourist hotel. These were, we knew, government-owned (as is everything else in Rumania) and they were, we had been told, found at most places where tourists pass through in any number. We were instructed to go to the tourist hotel if we wanted to have a drink or a meal. We were told that we also could change our money there. As this instruction was taking place in the customs office, I looked outside. A dozen dark-complexioned people were huddling under an old plastic sheet trying to keep away from the rain. The men all wore ragged clothes and fedora hats, incredibly shabby, and sacking over their shoulders. The women were all small and chubby with ragged clothing which would not be seen in any American or British community black, white, yellow, brown or sky-blue pink. The kids were small editions of their ragged parents. They were catching rainwater from the customs office roof in a tin can. Farther away several older boys garbed in rags were guarding three weatherbeaten caravans, and three animals that would, had their ribs not made them look like living skeletons, be mistaken for live horses.

As we left the customs office the big officer who had been our mentor waved the gypsies (for that is what they were) away perfunctorily and shouted at them. The gypsies scattered back to their caravans. He said, quietly, "Of course we don't have blacks, but we do have those swine."

I didn't believe my ears at first, and had to check with Thomas that I'd heard correctly.

Three of the youths who had been standing around the pontoon when *Outward Leg* had arrived then fell in step with Thomas and me and we started the long, for me, march to town. There were no taxis in Calafat. I was delighted to find that two of the youths spoke some English. They were students at the local college, and were anticipating, with resignation, being drafted into the Rumanian army in 1986. They seemed to think of it as I do of dying; as an unfortunately inevitable interruption to life.

They discussed Western pop music with Thomas, and knew the names of all the well-known groups. Throughout Eastern Europe wherever we passed, pop music was a common ground between youngsters from both East and West, and indeed, among some people not so young, too. In many places it was the only common ground, for Eastern youngsters' education about the West was very distorted indeed, from what I understood. Most of the Rumanian kids were taught and imagined honestly that people in the States and Britain still lived in the world described in *Uncle Tom's Cabin* and *Oliver Twist*. These lads said that the Rumanian television showed riots and disasters.

We walked up to the town of Calafat. It was very pretty, full of old villas and mansions, now taken over, as their posters and banners proclaimed, by the Communist Party of Rumania under its Great Leader, Benefactor and Teacher, Nicolai Ceausescu. On the main street there was a lovely old park of mature beech trees, with bench seats under their shades. The town was full of flowers. I sat on one of the benches and gazed at the colorful scene while Thomas and his new friends joined an ever-growing crowd outside the door of, apparently, the only bread shop in town. There were soon about 250 people, men and women and children, waiting for bread.

At the bottom of the wide avenue, when I hobbled down to check it, the paved roads petered out into clay lanes, muddy from the recent rain. The main road from the river ferry inland, unpaved and a sea of mud, passed the bottom of the avenue. There were no cars or other traffic on the road while I watched. There were two schools, one opposite the other, and a gasoline station. That was the only gasoline station that I saw, and it was around a mile from the river. Diesel oil was on sale there, for trucks only, or against "tourist tickets" such as we had.

The people along the avenue and among the hopefuls waiting for bread were dressed dully. Most of the women wore black, shapeless dresses and cloth headscarves. Some had black shawls on their shoulders. Some of the older folk had a terrible, mournful look in their eyes when they looked at me. It was as if they were trying to remember something that had happened long ago, and was now beyond recall. Now and again I saw one youngster who stood out, because he or she had made some attempt, natural in youth, of course, at elegance in their hairstyle or clothing. I mentioned this to one of our student friends. He told me that they had to be very careful; the police were everywhere, watching for any sign of Western-style "decadence." Alone, under the trees, one of the lads told me that even in the classrooms there were police informers. Students were instructed, even ordered, in schools, to watch for signs of Western mores or manners in their own parents. No foreigner could be invited to their homes; it was, simply, against the law. In Rumania there were very, very few escapes from state supervision at every hour of the day or night. One never knew for sure that what one talked about with anyone except a very few trusted friends would not be reported to the State Secret Police.

After we had waited an hour in the growing crowd for bread, it started to rain again, so I told Thomas that we would head for a café somewhere for a coffee or a drink. We found one at the top of the main street. It was a spacious place which looked as if it had once perhaps been a small theater. It was full of wrought-iron tables with fine wooden tops, all with four wineglasses set upside down on gleaming or once-gleaming white tablecloths. Alongside each table there was a wrought-iron bucket holder and a galvanized iron bucket just as there was in practically every public café I saw on the Rumanian bank of the Danube. It was eerie. It was a silent reminder of the omniscience of the Central Committee of the Rumanian Communist Party and of Big Daddy, who was watching sternly from a large, gold-framed picture on the wall. Nowhere in the restaurant were the ice buckets in use.

We waited in the café for an hour. Eventually my crewman rose and went over to ask a waitress to serve us. She came over to our table and, we understood, refused vehemently. Our young friends told us she refused because they were under eighteen, the legal drinking age. I protested that we were going to drink coffee. No matter, she still refused. The boys offered to wait outside. She still refused.

Once again, the youth told me that the waitress had often served him in the past, with soft drinks and such. Now she had refused solely because we were Westerners. This was the first time this happened to us in Rumania. It was to occur again a dozen times. It was segregation of the deepest hue, and for the worst of reasons. They did not know anything about our origin, our class background, our political beliefs. We were Westerners, and that was enough. They treated us in the same way as they treated their gypsies. We were as we were, and that was reason enough for them to treat us so. We might have been maniacal Trotskyites for all she knew; no matter, we were Westerners, and that was enough.

Later, inside the tourist hotel, we met a Bulgarian engineer who was on one of his frequent visits to the mayor of Calafat. His English was good, and we talked about yachting in Bulgaria. He said there was much interest in dinghy racing there. But he soon became very nervous, and stared around him continuously. Eventually the Bulgarian blurted out that he must take his leave because we were being watched by the secret police, and so he left. The boys had already gone. They had been warned to keep away from us by uniformed police, and had been sent home. Thomas and I had a meal in the tourist hotel, but found that the prices were comparable to those in any similar place in Austria or Germany, though the quality and cooking were nowhere near the same. From then we ate mostly on board until we reached Calarasi, except when we went for a day trip to Bucharest. Most of what we ate on board was canned food brought from Austria, for fresh food was almost impossible to find in Rumania, unless we "knew" someone, who could get it for us by devious means. Foodwise, it was worse than in Britain in 1945.

We returned to *Outward Leg* in Calafat port at about nine P.M., when the hotel restaurant and bar closed down and the lights were suddenly doused. There was not a soul to be seen anywhere near the port, not even in the silent watchtowers that overlooked everything. For the first time in Rumania there was not a policeman in sight while we were ashore.

The next morning, 22 June, we asked for permission to depart from Calafat at 8:00 A.M. It finally was given to us at 11:30, after the customs officers had again searched the boat thoroughly, but again missed the amas. Before we cast off, I asked the port captain where we might berth for that night. He told us to go to Bistret, at km 725—a run of forty miles. That, he said, should see us safely tied up before dark. Off we went, with Mr. McPherson rendering "Behind the Bushes" on his bagpipes for the benefit of any secret policemen who might be lurking on the bank. We were learning about Rumania. We wanted Rumania to learn a bit about us, and while we were at it—at times no more than a few yards from its shores—Bulgaria too.

At km 790, on the Bulgarian bank of the Danube, three gunboats were berthed. We dipped our ensign in *chutzpah*, New York style, but received in reply only stony glares from the crewmen. In daylight, with sentries all along the Rumanian bank, they could hardly apprehend our progress.

It was a fine day, but with a strong northerly wind and much cloud. The cloud shadows, as they passed over the surface of the river, gave the same shaded effect as shoals, so for both of us it was a lively day, figuring out which was cloud and which was shoal as Old Father Danube raced us along at about seven knots. The scenery was one of contrasts between the flat, dreary-looking Rumanian forest on one side, and the gently rolling, pretty foothills of the Bulgarian Stara Planina mountains on the other. We were now low on fuel, and I kept the engine at almost idling speed.

In the long, long stretches there were some little variations, and I noted them down as we sped along. It wasn't a case of spying along the frontier between Rumania and Bulgaria. Years and years of navigation on remote waters had instilled into me the habit of making navigational notes as I went along. Sometimes, I like to think, these notes have been useful to other voyagers who followed me, or might even, on more than one occasion, have helped them to get out of trouble. Even so, as we were on a frontier, I made sure, every time that *Outward Leg* entered a port, to hide the notes well away from prying eyes; the brainwashed mind behind them might think that I was noting down items of "strategic" value. I was taking a risk, I was fully aware, but I comforted myself that good habits will always outweigh inordinate risks or stupid regulations.

The average depth of the Danube between Calafat and Oltenita was eighteen feet, but sometimes there were shoals where the river was no deeper than seven feet, and often these were some miles long.

The port captain at Calafat had told me that an inlet existed at km 732. There, he said, if we got permission from the frontier police, we might anchor for the night. He said there was a watchtower by the inlet. Not only did the inlet not exist, but neither did the watchtower, which was an even bigger surprise. Where they were supposed to be, there was nothing but straight, rocky bank, overhung with trees, full of wild ducks and herons. Wildlife on straight river banks was all very well for the conservationists, but when it was our vessel we were trying to conserve, it was a very different story. Dusk was rapidly approaching and the current was running at six knots, so that no anchor would hold in the main stream.

At km 725, where the good port captain had told us a port existed, there was nothing either, on the Rumanian shore, although there was a big pontoon on the forbidden Bulgarian bank opposite. There was another Bulgarian pontoon at Dolni Tzibar, km 718, and one at km

707 too, but we could not stop there. We were not millionaires who could afford to donate two weeks' unneeded hotel fee to the Bulgarian government.

When we finally reached Bechet at km 679, I headed in for the shore, with Mr. McPherson's pipes rousing the Rumanian guards. It was a dreary place, merely a jetty with no pontoon, twelve feet of water alongside, two watchtowers, a dozen young soldiers, all armed, and a rusty but working timber loading crane. What made the place even drearier was the view of the Bulgarian town of Oriachov, only a quarter of a mile away through the light rain. In the dusk its town lights were being switched on in gaily colored profusion, and lively music wafted over the river. It was like running along a prison wall that overlooked a street of honky-tonks.

The only sign of life in Bechet for the first hour after our arrival, apart from the soldiers shifting their weights from one filthy boot to the other, was a small herd of goats busily doing their bit toward keeping Comrade Ceausescu's riverside grass as short as his soldiers' haircuts.

Someone at Bechet sent for the frontier "control," whose office was in Bechet village, a few miles away. As they had not turned up to "control" us by nightfall, I sent Thomas ashore to see if he could perhaps gets some bread at the village.

Even as Thomas reached the wire gate and told the sentry where he was headed, a motorcycle, with two officials mounted on it, arrived. They stopped and a frontier-police captain dismounted. He rushed over to Thomas and grabbed him by the shoulder. As the policeman weighed around three hundred pounds, arms and ammunition excluded, and Thomas weighed about a hundred, the ensuing denouement was inevitable. Thomas flew toward the captain, and the captain staggered backward for several steps. This maddened the captain. He grabbed his pistol. His friend, now off the motorbike, restrained him. He was an older man, I saw, as I gazed in silent astonishment at the scene from the cockpit.

Then the captain stood towering in front of Thomas, with his hands on his hips, and berated my crewman for a good five minutes. He shouted at Thomas in Rumanian at first, then in bad German. Then I heard him call my crewman a fascist swine, a German pig, a capitalist lackey, a running dog of Reagan, a fool, an idiot and a bastard to boot. Then he ordered Thomas to get back on board and tell me to move off, and get my filthy capitalistic boat away from Bechet.

Thomas, pale and shaken, did this. I, seething, clambered up on deck and planted my feet firmly apart.

The Beast shouted at me, *"Gehen Sie! Verschwinde! Schwein!"*

I stared silently at the Beast of Bechet, who now had marched over to the edge of the jetty; I looked him straight in the eye. I was trembling, but not with fear. It was with stark anger at this bloody, uniformed, poncing, son of a syphilitic bitch, bleeding, *fuck pig* who had *dared* to *shout* at my *crew*. No gentleman *ever* shouts at his crew ashore.

I silently studied his face. He was no more than thirty-five. It was a red face, and he had a black moustache and hate-filled eyes. The man, I saw, was merely a bully, and full of a bully's complexes. He fully deserved to be what he was and where he was, I thought.

I kept him waiting for about a second. His eyes flinched. Then I said slowly and loudly, very clearly, in German, *"NEIN!"*

# 29

# *Captains and Capitalists*

It wasn't easy to be defiant against the big bully of Bechet: I knew full well he had the power of life and death over everybody and everything on his side of the river, and the whole weight of a ruthless dictatorship behind him. He was standing there, with his young minions, armed to the teeth, all around him, and the only recourse I had, the only help, the only direction, was my own sense of what was *right* and a mind that despised him and all he stood for.

Now the Rumanian State Frontier Police captain was staring at me, his eyes wide open, his mouth working open and shut. He had obviously never encountered anyone who had simply said "No" to any of his whims.

Now he broke into Rumanian again, but in a much more faltering way than before. I stared him down. I thought of any Rumanian ships that might be in United States waters. Would their navigation be stopped if *Outward Leg* was arrested? How many were there? Three? Two? One? Would anyone ever know that we were in trouble? Would we simple disappear, as so many others had, into Big Daddy Ceausescu's prison camps?

He turned to me again and said something in Rumanian. I presumed it was the same order, to leave the pontoon.

I replied in English, "No. My vessel stays here for the night. You can order me to leave until the bloody cows come home, but I'm not leaving until dawn. Then I'll leave at first light. The river's unmarked, we've no charts, there's other traffic. Mister, you can take a running jump at yourself!"

At this the second officer, who wore a blue cap, chimed in. I almost fell over when he addressed me in fair English. "All right, Captain, my friend here little excited." He spoke rapidly to the Beast for several minutes, while the tension around us dissolved, then he turned to me. "All right, Captain, you stay until morning, but first light you go. Right?"

"I'll leave at first light, like I said," I replied.

With that the two Rumanian officers remounted their motorcycle and roared off, with Bechet-Bully-Beast glowering at me over his shoulder. I collapsed in the cockpit onto a seat and it was a full hour before I had regained strength enough to go below. I was still shaking with anger.

The soldiers on the jetty prowled up and down all night; we could hear their boots squeaking and the buckles on the straps of their automatic rifles jingling as we tried to sleep, and their low voices as they passed each other under the yellow light of the arc lamps. Before I turned in I gave one of them a packet of Kent cigarettes, so that they could smoke. He slyly smiled his thanks, but said nothing.

At a quarter to six next morning we were off, in silence. Soldiers stood silently around, rain ponchos thrown over their shoulders. They were not glowering at us through the morning mist. Now one of them even smiled as Thomas cast off and raised a desultory hand in reply to my wave of good-bye. Then we were off into the watery void again.

It was a ghostly morning. Thick mist hovered over the river from about a feet over the surface. Along the bank we could see wild ducks swimming about, but above them nothing but an ethereal white-gray mist, the same color as the void around our map of Rumania. Above the mist, now and again when it cleared, a tree raised its branches up into the sky, gray and ghostly. There was no sign of the Bulgarian bank, only a thick gray-mist blanket. Under us Old Father Danube gurgled and burbled at about four knots, although for all I knew it could have been a hundred knots or none. The depth meter sounded off almost continuously to give alarms every time the riverbed rose and the water shallowed off to five feet.

Later, at about 6:30, the mist began to clear, but very slowly, and it was ten o'clock before I could see both banks, but still vaguely, and only a few yards at a time. On and on we rolled. Then, toward eleven, as the sun rose, so the mist on the Bulgarian hills rolled back, revealing a pretty riverine scene with little villages and hamlets spread all along the bank, and plenty of lone rod-fishermen, sitting in meditation. I made a note in my log that morning. It said that "after being in Bechet, looking at the Bulgarian towns was like looking at the light." Each time I had headed out from a Rumanian "port" I had felt as though I had come out of the heart of darkness.

On this stretch in the mist, between Bechet and Corabia, kms 678 and 631, we passed many islands and shoals. The mist was, at first, too thick for me to take notes of the positions of the hazards, and anyway I was too busy peering about to keep clear of them. I saw that there was a good anchorage on the Rumanian bank at km 663 where a river joined the Danube. Fortunately the mist lifted enough for me to see a very dangerous shoal at km 649, and at ten knots I managed to avoid it just in time by swinging toward the Bulgarian bank. There the river was about a mile wide.

By the time the Rumanian "port" of Corabia had hoved into view the mist had almost dissolved and the visibility was about half a mile. The river was a confusing mass of channels ahead. Several islands and sandbanks cluttered up the stream. It was impossible to see which of the channels was deep enough to navigate. I decided to head in to Corabia to inquire as to the safe channels ahead. This is the normal thing to do on any uncharted river, fast or slow, anywhere on earth, when you reach an inhabited place. But we were not "on earth." We were in the void off the whizzing planet of Rumania.

On a river like the Danube, with a five-knot current pushing you inexorably toward unknown depths and with white water often stretching across the whole width of the river ahead of you, decisions have to be made and carried out quickly. If they are not, the river will push you on and on, fast, onto the shoals or past the point where the decision, good or bad, would be relevant.

At the time I had started to turn *Outward Leg* in the stream, to "crab" over to the Corabia pontoon, we had been too far upstream for me to see the armed guard on the pontoon. Now, as we slid downstream but with our engine "half ahead" to get alongside I saw that he was waving us away with his gun. It was too late for me to do anything else now; I continued going alongside. The sentry pointed his gun at me. I hovered, stopped in the river, only a yard away from the pontoon, and we stayed like that, against a five-knot current for an hour or more, while the local school headmaster, who spoke English, was sent for to ascertain what we wanted. While we waited we saw the local patrol boat, with officials and their families on board, leaving for a picnic trip upstream. We sighted them later a few miles on, under the trees on an island called Baloiu, with their picnic spread before them, and their kids terrorizing the lambs at play, just as capitalist kids would.

Having found out the safe channel (we stuck to the Rumanian shore, very close, between km 630 and km 626) we were swept on, and soon found that the natural order of the scenery was reversed; now it was Bulgaria that was low and flat, and Rumania rolling hills. Around kms 616 to 610 the Bulgarian bank was like a tropical forest. There were even a few palm trees to add to the illusion.

Turnu-Magurele, in Rumania, opposite Nikopol, turned out to be several pontoons backed by a long jetty supporting a dozen sentry boxes, four watchtowers, a few dozen armed youths and boys and three noisy factories. The factories of Turnu-Magurele belched smoke, white, brown, black and gray. This smoke was blown downstream by the prevailing wind and overcast the whole Danube valley for about twenty miles. As protests against pollution in Rumania would probably have been answered by firing squads, and as Rumanian television, we had been told, only showed riots against pollution in the West, I very much doubted if this would change in the near future, if ever.

At Turnu-Magurele, it being a Sunday, it was the customs officers' day off. The port captain, a thick man in every way, sent us off downstream to Zimnicea, where, he said, the customs would be on duty. This was another twenty-seven miles downstream. We shoved off and spent another four hours threading our way between islands, shoals, wrecks and other hazards, to Zimnicea. Sometimes, on this stretch, even in the clear air, the river was so wide that we could not see both banks at once. The afternoon wind raised quite a sea, about the same as the English Channel on a lively day. There were eight buoys that we saw, at kms 594, 596, 574 and three at 566 and two at 560. Three of the buoys were too discolored and rusty to make out what they marked. They all made a "bow wave" like a fast speedboat, as the current poured over and past them. They were shaped, as are many buoys on the lower Danube, like torpedoes, only thicker, and sixteen feet long and were surmounted by large radar reflectors, which seemed to be made of aluminum or galvanized iron, because they glinted in the sunlight as the buoys bobbed.

Zimnicea consisted of three pontoons off a fairly long jetty which supported six watchtowers, two dozen armed youths, six huge cranes and four factories, each one with smoke-belching chimneys. But the officials were fairly friendly, even though they temporarily confiscated our passports (illegally) so that we would not run away with one of their factories. By "fairly friendly" I mean that they did not order us off, as had the Beast of Bechet, neither did they shout at my crew.

Next day, early, we set off for Oltenita, from where our map told us a railway ran to Bucharest, the capital of Rumania. It was a fine day, and there was no problem with morning mist. This was a safe run, navigationally, as the river was wide and deep, except by the island of Batin, kms 532 to 522. There, the river was about two miles wide, and white water showed shoals just about everywhere. We were fortunate, for just as I was about to turn around and head upstream again, to somehow hang onto the bank until the wind died down and we might see the deep channels, a big Soviet convoy came heading up through and showed us where the channel was. We sighted only one rusty buoy around Batin island, and that was at km 523 and half submerged, so that it was most difficult to discern, and impossible to "read."

After that the river was only about half a mile wide. The average depth was eighteen feet. The scenery on the Bulgarian side was very pretty, with the small village of Stilpiste taking the prize for attractiveness that day. Half a mile downstream from Stilpiste there was a high waterfall on the Bulgarian shore which scattered water from the cliff from about three hundred feet up so that the water drops falling looked like millions of diamonds against the green leaves of the cliff bushes. It looked idyllic, just the place to anchor for a few hours; but the current was very strong below the waterfall, almost seven knots. As we passed the waterfall, hundreds of wild geese flew by in perfect squadrons.

Heading down the Danube in the watery maze downstream from the Iron Gates, all the way to the Dobrudja, there was a tremendous feeling, when we were under way, of freedom from the familiar restrictions of space, time and human custom. It was not like being on a wide ocean, nor even on a sea; we were always conscious that unless we were very careful it could be the mighty river, and not we, that was in control of our destinies. But it was a certain, unique kind of freedom, in that we had chosen to be on the river. It was our choice, and not the river's, and that separated us from the vast majority of mankind.

Once forced, by political circumstances, to be alongside Rumania, as we were, we felt as surely imprisoned as anyone on Death Row. Ours was an insane schizophrenic exercise in escaping the hazards of Rumania by dodging the hazards of the river. Each was equally dangerous; each, in its own way, equally menacing and threatening. But of the two sets of menaces we always chose the river's, for then it would be our own stupidity or lack of concentration that sent us to our swift disaster or even deaths, and not the mindless, moronic, robotic machine of paranoid repression that rumbled on and on ashore, in every nook and cranny of the frontier.

God help anyone who looks, as we did for days and weeks, to the shores of a client state of the Soviet Union as a passable haven from an even worse state of affairs. Yet this is how we felt, as we passed by Bulgarian pontoons.

At least, we knew, Bulgaria let some light in from the outside world, no matter how dim it might be after filtering through the Kremlin windows, but Rumania was as black on the frontier as the hole of Calcutta, and just as stifling, at least to me.

At km 511, on the Bulgarian bank where there was a green meadow along the shore, a tall boulder stood all alone. It must have weighed all of a thousand tons, and it puzzled me as to the enormous forces which must have brought it there. It was shaped like a Celtic dolmen, like one of the pillars of Stonehenge. There were no other boulders or bare rock as far as I could see, which was about five miles.

At km 499 we passed, with Mr. McPherson rendering "The Big Spree" on his pipes as loud as he could, the important Bulgarian Danube port city of Ruse. This was where many of the Bulgarian Danube tourist ships hailed from. Several of them were in port, turning round for passengers, and all of them hailed us and sounded their sirens for *Outward Leg* as she passed. On the five pontoons many people, crew, passengers and plain townsfolk, from what I could see, waved us on our way.

Before we arrived off Ruse we managed to get hold of some diesel oil, but I cannot say from where or when. We got twenty-six gallons, which was as well, for at the time we were down to two gallons, and there was no sign of being able to get any more until we reached the sea. This had worried me greatly. There was no telling where we might find some fuel. It was very scarce in Rumania. Gasoline was almost nonexistent.

The pontoon at Giurgiu was another dreary place, below a long line of factories, noisy and smoky. We decided to press on for Oltenita. There was a strong wind, but now it was from downstream for the first time since leaving the Iron Gates. Its general direction was from the southwest. I could smell the salt in it, all the way from the Adriatic Sea, four hundred miles away. Thomas thought I was fancying that, but I was sure of it. It was the first sniff of salt-water air I'd had since Holland, almost nine months before, and there was no mistaking it. As I gulped it in, it made my blood race. I didn't imagine it; I could feel it like a fever.

The wind against the current set up a heavy sea. By midafternoon the waves were about three feet, from trough to crest, and short with it, no more than about nine feet or so. This made for a good, wet pounding to windward all the rest of the day, but slowed us down little, for Old Father Danube was just as anxious as were we to reach the Black Sea.

On leaving Giurgiu we passed under the only bridge we had seen on the Rumanian Danube until then. This was a railway bridge, and very high above the river. A train passed over it as we passed under, and practically every window on the train had hands waving from it.

Just below the bridge we were astonished to see a hydrofoil ferryboat fly up the river and steer straight for us. It must have been making thirty-five knots against the current. It missed us by only a couple of feet. Everyone on board the hydrofoil, the Bulgarian *Meteor 3*, was cheering and waving at us like crazy people as she shot past us. From then on, this was to be a regular occurrence, all the rest of the way downstream off Bulgaria. Not only *Meteor 3* cheered us, but also *Meteor 1, 2, 4, 5* and *6* did, as well as every plodding river ship that sighted us. It was very soon plain that everyone afloat on the Danube knew of *Outward Leg*, what she was, where she hailed from, what she was doing, and where she was bound. It was, must have been, all word of mouth. Now the passing river ships plodding upstream and flying downstream did not merely greet us with waves from the helmsman or crew; now they blew their sirens, each and every one of them, even the Soviet ships. It seemed that everyone on the river was a well-wisher, except on the Rumanian pontoons. There, as a rule, we might just as well have landed from some strange planet on the other side of the constellation of Alpha Centauri, and were instantly and automatically suspected of evil intent.

There was a lot more shipping on the Danube below Ruse, so our navigation was made much easier by following the tracks of the ships coming and going. This meant that with our catch of diesel oil, we could now go faster, and we were covering ten miles an hour. The only safe-looking havens we saw for a craft in distress, except for pontoons, which usually were occupied, were on the Bulgarian shore, near a fishing camp at km 454, inside a narrow creek, and at km 441, between two low islands covered with waving, long grass. Otherwise, there was a strong sea everywhere, and very little lee from the wind.

By this time I had figured out one of the reasons why the sight of our arriving seemed to send the Rumanian frontier guards into fits of manic, almost lip-frothing aggression: it was the khaki shirts that Thomas had worn. They were ex-West German Army surplus shirts and had been given to him by some kind soul back in Passau, who had taken pity on his pale, frail, shivering frame in the colder spring evenings. I told him to hide the khaki shirts, and don a white (or white-ish) one. He did so, and the change in the attitudes toward him was almost miraculous. Rumanians, we found, were very "knee-jerk" people. If we could make the right "taps" we got the right "knee-jerks." That was very important when the owner of the knee carried a Kalashnikov rifle, or was behind a machine gun atop a watch-tower, or could order the shooting of anyone within miles, innocent or not. That was, we were fully aware, day and night, the kind of darkness through which we were voyaging.

At Oltenita astonishingly, we met the most civilized and cultured harbormaster it has been my privilege to encounter in many a long year, in any commercial haven. He was a large, elderly gentleman who spoke good French. It is not so often that French-speakers are so good-natured. In between discussing modern yacht-building techniques he tended the required tomato plants in the small garden outside his cottage. He in turn was attended by his mate, a youngish man with a large and noisy family. Between them they managed to buy for us the first fresh food we had seen since we had entered Rumania (God, was it only four days before?).

The harbormaster at Oltenita spoke with uniformed armed youths on the jetty and arranged that they would at last have something to guard, namely *Outward Leg*, while Thomas and I visited Bucharest for one day. There were no taxis in Oltenita, naturally, so we made our way into the pretty little town, about three miles from the port, by means of a haulage truck, which had been hailed down by the harbormaster's mate. Its passenger seat was covered in wet clay-mud, which soon virtually smothered me.

In Oltenita we headed for the main square where stands the town state bank, to change a few more of our diminishing deutschmarks. We were met at the door of the old building, with its peeling walls, by six men who looked, dressed and sounded exactly like the type of men I had seen at the counters of betting shops in Belfast and Glasgow. They, without a word, after inspecting us, escorted us to the teller's counter and watched us closely while we waited for half an hour for the first-ever, it seemed, foreign currency exchange to be made in Oltenita. They did not say one word, either to us or among themselves the whole while. All of them were unshaven and wore collarless shirts, filthy round the collar. All had muddy shoes. These were the town's secret police, we were later informed.

The bank interior was one of the dullest places I have been in in a life sometimes perforce spent in dull places. It was very dusty, had very high ceilings, and was staffed by twenty-eight people, besides our party of eight. There were men and women of all ages behind the counters. There were no seats or tables in the public area, and there was no public, except Thomas, me, and the six silent secret policemen. The only decorations in the place were a large picture of Big Daddy Ceausescu, Teacher, Comrade and Benefactor, on the wall, in full regalia, and a stuffed fox on a lower shelf. I thought the pair would go admirably well closer together. All the rest of the bank interior was drab stone and marble. It looked such a hopeless place that I was astonished when we were handed, by a mousy-looking young woman in pebble glasses, a huge roll of leus notes. For our 200 deutschmarks they looked a very generous exchange, but when Thomas counted them they were, indeed, the correct amount, but all in notes of one and five leus, the lowest dominations. I'm not saying the bank had to send out to the town for enough leus to buy our deutschmarks, but it certainly looked like it. Our arrival and request gave rise to many whispered conferences behind the teller's counter, and much passing back and forth, through the back doors, of practically all the bank staff before the roll of leus was assembled for us and tied with a length of rough string into a bundle as big as a boot. The whole roll was filthy, almost as grubby as the shirt collars of our escorts.

At last we emerged into the surprising sunlight outside the bank. We had to rush through the town square, a pretty place of shady old trees, to the railway station opposite. The steam train (which again excited Thomas) was already blowing what sounded like a thin rendering of "On Top of Old Smokey." There was neither roof nor platform on this railway station, nor were there on any others on the forty-mile run to the capital, which took five hours to cover. This was the only occasion on which I ever traveled in a train which was slower in progress than the boat I was voyaging in at the time, so I was quite pleased with its slowness. It was all jerky starts, swift, rumbling passages and shocking halts. Then long waits.

The train was crowded with peasants and shipyard workers when it left Oltenita, and at the dozen or so stations en route to Bucharest it picked up at least five hundred more country passengers who were, for the most part, heavily loaded with bundles of small farm produce they were taking somewhere. The Rumanian people on the train were not, it seemed, at all miserable. They were simple people who treated both Thomas and me with every consideration. Once away from uniforms they laughed and joked among themselves, and greeted each other as if they had not met in years. They were very much like Latins in South America or southern Spain. They were polite and curious about us, but too polite to tire us with too many questions. There were many obvious gypsies on the train, but they mostly kept to themselves, usually in the clattering spaces between one carriage and the next.

On arrival at Bucharest we were surprised to find that the train did not enter the city at all, but stopped in the middle of an open field some miles outside town. The field was surrounded by factories festooned with huge red banners proclaiming that they were the property of the Rumanian Communist Party under the Leadership of its Great and generous Benefactor and Teacher, Nicolai Ceausescu. Massive pictures of Big Daddy stared out from every wall. Armed soldiers lined the side of the railway track where the thousand or so passengers, Thomas and me among them, alighted in the middle of nowhere. If Thomas hadn't been a decent German I would have told him that this must have been very much like arriving at the gates of Auschwitz.

At last, after trying to inquire, in the midst of the milling throng, our way to the city center, we were directed by an incredibly scruffy but polite little man to the local subway terminal. This was about two miles toward town along a very roughly paved highway, down which streamed a continuous procession of trucks carrying workers from somewhere. Another line of trucks carried workers apparently *to* somewhere. The workers being carted around were all in the same type of overalls and all wore hard, white plastic hats. They all seemed to take it for granted that being trucked around in overalls and plastic hats was a normal thing.

The descent into the Bucharest subway, down an escalator, revealed the most beautiful, efficient, and certainly the quietest and most law-abiding underground transport system I have ever seen anywhere. The passages and vestibules were marble and granite, all very new-looking. There were marvelous frescoes on just about every wall. I was so taken with inspecting the surroundings that I don't even know if we paid for our rides or not.

The subway carriage was half full of students on their way to college. The boys and girls were all dressed in exactly the same uniform, blue, with a red scarf, and the boys all wore a blue peaked cap. The girls and boys sat or stood separately. One young lady stood to let me sit, but I gently refused her offer. "Olympics, Olympics!" I told her, and she laughed. Little did she know.

Somehow, Thomas, who is good at making his way without speaking a word of local languages, piled himself and his skipper off the smooth subway train at some open space surrounded by tall buildings. In the open air, we sat on a nearby low wall for a few minutes so that I could rest. Rubbernecking on one leg is not the most relaxing way to while away the hours. The noise of traffic and people passing was too loud for us to speak much to each other, but there was something very different about this city. It took me a minute to realize what it was. There were very, very few shops on the streets, and no advertising, not even on the roofs of the buildings around the city square. The only sign said, simply, "Ceausescu." I thought it odd that they should advertise anything already so ubiquitous.

A short visit by Russian-made taxi to the Hotel Intercontinental revealed that one Bucharest taxi driver was just as prone to cupidity, avarice and greed as any London or Paris counterpart. The "Brasserie" in the Hotel Intercontinental was full of Third World visitors and students taking refuge among the cola dispensers and syrupy Muzak from the hard reality outside of the Marxist vision of the future offered to their own countries. Most of the Asians and Africans in the Brasserie spoke French, I was pleased to hear. It's not often that I am pleased to hear French. It usually heralds a speaker wrapped up in solely his own needs and ambitions to the exclusion of anyone around who is not female, young and desirable. That is, except for the harbormaster at Oltenita, who was at the town station at midnight to meet us when we finally returned on the train, weary from our visit to Bucharest.

On the way back to the Bucharest railway terminal in the open field outside town, the taxi driver silently pointed out to us a line of cars waiting for their gasoline ration. It was *three miles* long. The taxi driver, by signs and odd words we understood, told us that while taxis, all owned by Big Daddy, and party cadres, likewise, could obtain gasoline as they wished, lesser folk might take as much as three days to get to the head of the gasoline line, and by then supplies might have run out for another week. We knew that Rumania had its own oil fields and its own oil refineries. We wondered into which of Big Daddy's family pockets the profit from the gasoline shortage, chronic all the time we were in Rumania, was going.

Bucharest was the fourth European capital we had visited on the continent on this voyage. We couldn't take our boat with us this time. The canal between the capital and the Danube, already started, was not due to be finished until 1995. We couldn't take our boat to Bucharest, but we did, I think, take her spirit.

We stayed in Oltenita for two more days. One day for me to get over the effects of the difficult and arduous clambering around on trains, subways and streetcars in Bucharest, and one day to get over the effects of having lunch in the huge old mansion, now converted to a restaurant for workers, at Oltenita.

This old mansion was one of the most unkempt, untidy, filthy and unlikely places to eat well, but we did. The meat, rare in Rumania, was grilled on a barbeque spit outside the fine but ruined old front doors. Soldiers, workers, police, customs officers and ocean sailors, all now accustomed to each other, stood around, eating with their fingers and drinking like earls. Among us, large dogs and noisy pigs chased their young toward the river. This lunch was also one of the most expensive I have ever had, for four people (we had two guests for the only time to date), thirty dollars equivalent in leus. We could ill afford that rate of spending. I would have offered blue jeans in barter, if there had been anyone there I could trust, but there was no one, except Thomas, and he was broke.

As *Outward Leg* finally departed from Oltenita she passed by the big shipbuilding yard. We had Mr. McPherson playing "Lament for the Old Sword." When they heard us, over the din of their tools, *every one* of the thousand or so men and boys working on the ships downed tools and cheered us to a man. They danced up and down and waved their shirts in the hot sunshine. Above them big red banners streamed silently, futilely. "*America, America.*" they shouted, over and over and over again, all the way to the downstream end of the mile-long yard. Many of them held their two joined fists over their heads.

Finally we sighted the Bulgarian city of Silistra and, just beyond its pontoon-lined jetties, a long scar across the hills which showed where the Bulgarian-Rumanian frontier finally left the Danube and headed across the Dobrudja toward the Black Sea. The expected and long-awaited scar of raked earth was, of course, overlooked by a long line of watchtowers on the Rumanian side of the high fence which followed it.

Opposite Silistra, on the Rumanian bank at km 376, was a pontoon. Behind the pontoon were the usual watchtower and soldiers, but there was something else, too, and that was very unusual for Rumania. There was a hotel right by the pontoon. This was where the harbormaster in Oltenita had told us to go, before heading farther into Rumanian-only Danube waters.

No sooner had I turned the boat and neared the pontoon than sure enough, a soldier ran down to the water's edge and waved me away; then he aimed his gun at me. A voice from the hotel windows shouted in good English, "Keep away!" then "It is forbidden!" then I saw a man waving an arm downstream. "Go to Calarasi. It's the next turning to the left!" He shouted good English with, I thought, a Scottish accent.

I bore off and headed for Calarasi. We found the town at last up a narrow, winding stream, the Borca, about seven miles off the main river. It was a Rumanian holiday resort, full of vacationing workers, most, it seemed, from a half dozen factories in Timosioara, up in northwestern Rumania.

On the way up the narrow stream to Calarasi, we passed by a bathing beach, the first we had seen in Rumania along all the six hundred miles from its frontier with Yugoslavia. Indeed, it was the first place I had seen in Rumania where people were quite obviously enjoying themselves. The beach was crowded with mostly fat men and their mostly chubby wives and families. There were some rowing boats and even a few "Optimist" sailing dinghies with youngsters at their helms. There was a long line of modern cars parked behind the beach, and multi-colored parasols scattered everywhere, like butterflies stuck on a fly-ridden honeypot. There was an air of affluence about the beach.

I'm not saying that this beach was for small-time Party Bosses, nor for favored technicians or functionaries of Big Daddy Ceausescu's One-Party Oligarchy, but it was most certainly, compared to what we saw later, a *very* upper-middle-class-looking beach. I was quite sure, as I stared at the frolicking families, that neither Karl Marx nor Fred Engels would have in the least approved, especially considering the rocky nature of the lower order's "beach" farther upstream, among the oily effluvia of the berthed river ships, right beside the discharge of the town's main sewer.

The harbormaster at Calarasi, a friendly, gushing, excited old ex-sea captain, amazed at our appearance, welcomed us and told us to stay as long as we liked. He (illegally) took the passports and ship's papers from us, to keep in his office until we were ready to leave, as was the custom in Rumanian ports.

We walked, Thomas and I, along the pleasant riverside park and, after waiting for two hours, we ate at a holiday restaurant crowded with vacationing workers, in all states of ebriation and inebriation, then we turned in fairly early. Everything closed at nine o'clock, even in a holiday town.

Next morning, to get out of the way of a departing barge, we moved downstream, alongside a river passenger ship. The skipper, bless him, gave us some fish and hares and fresh plums for our breakfast. We had just set to on these, when the clatter of boots topside told us the Calarasi "control" had arrived, perhaps with our passports and papers, so that we might depart.

The Calarasi control arrived all right. They poked two automatic-rifle muzzles down into my cabin. "Don't move!" a loud voice ordered in German. *"Sie stehen alle unter Arrest!"* "You're all under arrest!"

# 30

# *Hulls, Hells and Highwater*

It's almost funny how, when things are tense indeed, even one little mundane occurrence can break the tension. As Thomas and I, in the dead silence that followed the announcement, gawped up through the hatchway, the galley-kettle whistle blew.

Aloft, in the cockpit, were two Rumanian frontier police troopers pointing Kalashnikovs straight at us, while above them, on deck, was a frontier police lieutenant and a sergeant, both holding pistols. In the galley, the kettle blew.

Thomas needed no urging from me to interpret what was being shouted at us. "Don't move!" they yelled, all together, then the lieutenant screeched, "Your boat is under arrest! You are in Rumanian strategic waterway. You have purposely left the international waterway of the Danube to spy!" The lieutenant had a piping voice. I guessed his age as about twenty-two. "What have you to say?" he added, his voice almost breaking.

I felt a complete fool as I said to Thomas, in reply to this tirade, "Ask him if you can go in the galley and turn off the stove before the kettle burns itself out." Thomas passed on my question to the stupefied lieutenant.

The noise of the whistling kettle had shaken the two soldiers too, and they eased their rifle muzzles up out of the hatchway. The lieutenant looked very puzzled for a moment, then, with a cluck of dismay, he brusquely nodded his head. Thomas walked forward into the galley through the engine-room passage. As he reached the galley and I heard the kettle stop whistling, I said to him, "And ask these blokes if they'd like a cup of tea?"

When Thomas relayed this, the lieutenant gasped and gestured violently for me to go topside. I purposely made my clambering up on deck even more cumbersome than it usually was, and stumbled against one of the soldiers in the cockpit. He laid down his automatic rifle and grabbed my elbow to help me up. Then the sergeant leaned down to give me a helping hand, too, while the lieutenant's eyes almost fell out of his head when he saw my false leg. It was, as usual, in a sandal, and painted white so that I could see it below me in the dark at nights on deck.

The lieutenant obviously was at a loss what to say or do. On the passenger ferry alongside us quite a cargo of people had collected, and they were all leaning over the guardrails, watching us silently. I glanced up and guessed there were at least a hundred passengers and crew watching the proceedings.

"What do you mean, under arrest?" I asked the lieutenant, through Thomas, who was now at my side. I suddenly heard in my head, clearly a sort of "*déjà vu*," and remembered that I had spoken that line somewhere else quite recently. It was like an old record track being played over again, only that I was making the sounds. The lieutenant was a studious-looking, slim, smartly uniformed chappie, with rimless spectacles, looking rather like a younger, more modern edition of Heinrich Himmler. He even, I saw, had a cut-away chin, the same as old Heinie. Now he had put his toy gun away and was holding his briefcase in front of him with both hands, as if he were defending what virtue he might have with it.

"Your boat is in strategic waters," he repeated. Then he went on, "You must start your engine and follow us." He gestured at their patrol craft bobbing alongside *Outward Leg* in the wake of a passing ship. Their boat was tied up to ours with only one mooring line, and its long wooden fender was bumping against *Outward Leg*'s gunwhale. I turned to Thomas.

"Get another line on that there bloody boat, Thomas," I ordered, "and stick a fender between us." Then I turned back to the lieutenant.

"Our passports and papers are not on board," I said. "Before I move my boat anywhere I must have them on board. We deposited them with the harbormaster last night. He said he'd return them to us when we were ready to sail. I'm not leaving this berth without them."

As Thomas interpreted this the lieutenant's jaw dropped. He turned and stared at his sergeant. His sergeant looked nonplussed. Then the lieutenant said to me, "I have your papers and passports here in my briefcase. I will keep them with me safe in our patrol boat. You must follow us."

"No," I wagged my head. "Not without my ship's papers and our passports in my custody!"

"Follow us!" The sergeant piped up.

I ignored the sergeant. Always aim for the top. I carried on speaking to the lieutenant. "This is a United States registered vessel. The deck that you are standing on is United States territory. I am a British subject, but I am the legally appointed captain of this vessel. My crew is a citizen of the German Federal Republic, but he is legally employed by me. The ship's papers of this vessel are the private property of people who have broken no law that I know of, Rumanian or otherwise. Our passports are the property of the governments of our countries. You have no right to hold either our passports or the ship's papers. I will not move my vessel that much . . ." (I held up a finger and thumb an inch apart) "without our papers and passports on board in my custody."

The lieutenant stared at me throughout this, as if he could not believe his ears.

I went on, "Now, you can do what you like, Lieutenant, but until I have my passport, and my crew's, and my ship's papers in my hand, if you want me to move this vessel anywhere at all you must get in touch with the embassies of the United States, Great Britain and West Germany, in Bucharest, and then, when their representatives turn up, if they advise me to move, I will. But until then, *no!*"

"But you must move for the passenger ship to leave," faltered the young man.

I knew I had him. "Not until you hand over my ship's papers and our passports."

"But I have them safe in my briefcase, and we will not run away if you follow us," he whined.

"No."

"But my chief told me to hold onto these . . ." he moaned.

"Bring your chief here. He can hand me my documents," I replied.

I stood on deck with my back to the Rumanian ferry, but above my head and behind me I could sense the tension in the crowd of passengers. Of course they would not understand the German and English, but they would know that some battle of wills was taking place.

There were a few moments of dead silence. Then the lieutenant said, in a low voice, "Then you won't follow us without your papers?"

"No. Certainly and irrevocably, *no*. Not one *inch*," I replied, quietly.

The lieutenant turned to his sergeant, who was staring at me in amazement. Then he bent down, opened his briefcase, put in his hand, and extracted *Outward Leg*'s blue folder with her ship's papers in it. He proffered this to me, with a weak smile.

"And the passports, too!" I demanded, then added, "Please."

The lieutenant looked at me through his spectacles again. He seemed to want to cry. "Then you'll follow me to my chief?" he pleaded.

"If I have all my ship's and crew's documents in my custody, yes."

He dived his hand into his briefcase again, pulled out Thomas's green and my blue passports and, with a bow, handed them to me. Now he tried his English. "You must stay close my boat," he murmured. "Many . . ."

"Shoals," I added for him as he fished for the word.

"Exactly," he agreed, as I clomped down into my cabin to put *Outward Leg*'s documents in our strongbox. Alone, below, my hands shook.

Back topside, I saw that the passengers on the ferry, all of them, men, women and children, were talking among themselves and staring at me and Thomas as though we were the boxing champions of the world. They were obviously amazed that we had actually had the temerity to challenge, stand up to and outface someone in uniform, armed with a gun. They shuffled about and waved their hands, smiling at us. I gave them a broad wink. The ferry skipper grinned hugely.

I looked over at the patrol craft. It was now let go, and was standing out in the stream only a yard or so away from *Outward Leg*'s side. The sergeant, expressionless, was on the wheel, the lieutenant was peering at us through the wheelhouse door, while the two soldiers still grimly pointed their automatic rifles at me.

Thomas, with an astonished grin on his face, stared at me. I grinned back at him and winked. "Shall I let go from the ferry?" he asked.

"No. In a minute. First shove Mr. McPherson on the tape player!"

But my crewman was already swinging down the after hatch and in a few seconds the strains of the strathspey "Delvinside" were joyfully, defiantly and, I hoped, inspiringly wafting over the town of Calarasi, its narrow stream, the ferryboat, all its crowded passengers, and the Rumanian frontier police gunboat hovering alongside. No sooner had the first notes of the pipes blared than all the ferry passengers burst into clapping and cheering as loudly and merrily as they could. Soon the cheering and clapping was taken up by people on the ferry pontoon, on the riverbank, and on the park benches beyond. In three minutes, as we let go of our mooring lines and parted from the ferry, everyone within sight was shouting and waving at *Outward Leg* and even the soldiers on the gunboat held their rifles up vertically and were grinning their heads off.

It was an achievement so unusual, to have outfaced the authority of Big Daddy Ceausescu's gunmen, it was a little victory so complete and so deep, that it filled the air all around us as *Outward Leg*, with her Old Glory fluttering, our British ensign and German burgee waving, and our Red Dragon eating the breeze as we sedately followed the gunboat as slow as I could ever possibly manage, upstream, back the way we had come downriver the previous evening, that we could smell it, feel it, and even *taste* it. By now, even the frontier police lieutenant was smiling as he too recognized the little victory, and wanted his share in it. I gladly let him have it, too. Magnanimity in victory is never a loss.

We were "guided" six miles upstream, past the bourgeois beach and back into Old Father Danube's main stream. It was a lovely day and even the river seemed to share our little victory as he gamboled along, wide and deep. Then we headed slowly against the four-knot current directly for Silistra town, which didn't make sense to me, because Silistra was Bulgarian. For a few minutes I was worried that we might have been, in fact, hijacked into Bulgarian waters, or that these Rumanians were exiling *Outward Leg* so as to be rid of her incipient threat to "law and order."

But soon we found that we were being taken to the Rumanian customs post which controls traffic passing along the river into and from the solely Rumanian stretch of Danube, from Silistra to Galati.

There, at Galati, we were told, was another control for traffic coming and going into the last stretch of the Danube which Rumania shares with the U.S.S.R. as he at long last debouches through his great estuary, into the Black Sea at Sulina.

The customs control post we were taken to was at a pontoon only *one yard* inside Rumanian territory just inside the Bratul Ostrov, which joins the Danube at km 375 on the Silistra bank immediately above the town river wall. The pontoon was so close to Bulgaria that we could see Bulgarians eating in their flats in the high-rises only fifty feet away, behind a twenty-foot-high wire fence. The wire fence was *just* inside Rumania, guarded, of course, by a Rumanian watchtower every few dozen yards. The Bulgarian city stopped dead at the wire, and on the Rumanian side of the fence there was nothing but soldiers, customs officials, pigs, hens and mud.

It took a couple of hours for the customs chief and the chief of the Rumanian frontier police in those parts to arrive at the boat. During that time I was able to figure out where *Outward Leg* had gone astray. I could plainly see the pontoon on the north side of the Danube at km 376, where we had been warned off the previous evening by the rifle-toting soldier and told to go Calarasi by the man who shouted to us in a Scottish-sounding accent; but this pontoon, right slap-bang next to the Bulgarian city of Silistra, on the Bratul Ostrov river, was where he should have told us to go.

When the customs chief and police boss finally showed up they were quite obviously in their very best bibs and tuckers and also on their very best behavior. The police boss was a bit cool and offhand, as he should be of course, but the customs chief, a little old man dressed in a uniform so gorgeous that he looked as if he should be standing outside the Victoria Palace Theatre in London, was both impressed by our morning performance and disposed to be friendly. He listened patiently while I gave him instructions on erecting a big sign at the pontoon across the river, at km 376, to show passing vessels where the real customs control post was. I even drew a sign for him. A big, pointing finger ten yards long directed straight across the river. This interested him, and he asked me to write down on the sign words that would direct future yachtsmen who might pass that way to the correct place. I wrote "Hey! It's over there, schmuck!"

The little old customs chief carefully placed my signpost design in the side pocket of his lush blue uniform and gravely shook my hand, assuring me that the sign would be erected as soon as ever possible, i.e., as soon as it was approved by the Minister of Trade in Bucharest, to avoid future unfortunate incidents such as had taken place through simple errors that morning.

Later I learned that the customs chief had kept his word. That was the only bit of graffito left by *Outward Leg* on her whole two thousand three hundred and seven mile voyage from London across Europe.

By the time the customs and police chiefs, with their entourages, had climbed onto the pontoon and picked their way over the pig-shit-littered track to a convoy of official cars waiting nearby, it was lunch-time. But we decided to eat our meal under way and shake the dust of Calarasi and Silistra off my foot. To the rousing cheers of farewell of practically the whole of the frontier staff of the Ostrov district, *Outward Leg* shoved off with Mr. McPherson rendering the march "Lochaber Gathering" to face our very last day's run down the mighty Danube.

Between Silistra and Cernavoda, our next port of call, there were no pontoons at all in the forty-six miles. The river was fairly wide, between a half and four miles, and well marked by buoys under the usual Danube rule of "Green to Green Heading Downstream." The land on both sides was Rumanian, and there were many signs of watersport activity, now that we were away from the frontier. There were a few people on the banks fishing and swimming, and most of them cheered and waved to us as we rolled by. We were going at a good speed now, with Yannie pushing along at three-quarter revolutions, because with each mile I could smell the salt tang in the air more and more. There were a few villages, and occasionally some empty dumb-barges either waiting for cargo or in reserve for more prosperous times on the river. On these there were usually gangs of youngsters frisking about and diving or swimming. These youngsters, boys mainly, always shouted at us, *"Chingo! Chingo!"* This word was a mystery to us until we reached Cernavoda where some young lad explained, in halting English, that it meant "chewing gum!"

Like American cigarettes, chewing gum was looked upon by most Rumanians as an almost invaluable treasure, and was often used as a bartering medium. We had gradually learned about the value that Rumanians placed on such little things as foreign cigarettes, lighters, ballpoint pens and such, but it wasn't until we reached Cernavoda that we realized that all the way down the Rumanian Danube we had been riding on board what was, in effect, a floating gold mine, at least in those parts. We could have lived for a year on the barter of my two hundred ballpoint pens alone.

There was a small-craft harbor at Cernavoda, but foreign small craft were required to tie up at the pontoon immediately outside the entrance to the recently completed canal that linked the Black Sea with the Danube.

All the way across Europe, we had known about this canal, although most of what we knew had been culled from brief reports from ships that had passed by its confluence, or from hearsay or vague rumors. I had even seen a film about the opening of the canal by Big Daddy Ceausescu, several years before, while I was back in Germany.

Apart from these rumors and guesses, very little was known about the canal. For this reason, and because I longed to be back in sight of the sea—any sea—we had decided to turn off the Danube at km 300 and head along the canal for forty miles, to Agigea, where it joined the Black Sea.

Cernavoda turned out to be, for us, the happiest place in the whole of Rumania. It was the only place where we were not under continual armed guard, except for the short stroll we'd had in Salafat town, the train journey from the river to the capital, and the trip up the "strategic" Bucea river to Calarasi.

Being unguarded was such a pleasant change that we decided to stay at Cernavoda for a weekend while we negotiated with the Black Sea—Danube Canal authority for a passage through their waterway. The port captain and the civil policemen on the control pontoon were just that—civil. They let us come and go on board and ashore as we pleased, at all hours. They spent most of the weekend entertaining their families and friends, all party members, so that most of the evenings it was more like a floating nightclub. In the afternoons they used their official patrol boat to take their families on trips out on the Danube. Best of all, they left us alone.

The riverbank at km 300 to km 299 was the pleasure-ground of the good people of Cernavoda. From dawn until dusk, and sometimes until nine o'clock in the evening when all the town lights were doused and only soldiers and policemen roamed the streets, they could be seen fishing, hundreds of them, men and women and kids. It was some time before I was told that these people were fishing for food for themselves and their families. They never saw meat. Most of them were in rags, and even the best dressed among them would be thought of as shabbily dressed by any Western standards. There was a distinct separation of the sexes along the Cernavoda riverfront. Crowds of boys and youths gathered right by the boat to beg "chingo" and to puff their fists in front of their faces for cigarettes, but there were very few girls or young women. They were mostly at home, doing housework, as we could see.

There was a bridge over the Black Sea–Danube Canal a little farther inside the waterway. Over it, day and night, heavy trucks roared by. In between the trucks, gypsy wagons, colorful and "picturesque" and poverty-stricken, their drivers and riders in rags and tatters, their animals fit only for the knacker, wended their own ways from nowhere to nowhere.

Navigating our passage through the Black Sea–Danube Canal was an anticlimax compared to our previous experiences on the river Danube. We had been told we would not need to have a pilot, and that the passage would cost $25. The canal passage was straight, dull and dreary, what we could see of it under the arc lamps, for we were allowed to navigate it only at night, at a moment's notice, and then, only with a pilot on board. He had no sense of humor. He was a convinced communist and an utter bore. He was rigorously polite, "Nothing to port, Captain," and, "Easy to starboard, Captain," when we were under way and would not sit down in the cockpit despite my repeated indications to him to do so. When we were stopped he talked like a phonograph record and took no notice at all of my ripostes or arguments. I was happy to see him clamber cumberously ashore in Agigea.

As we took off from Cernavoda about two hundred people turned up to see us depart. Most of them were poor and the vast majority were youngsters. I like to think that they still remember *Outward Leg* and all it stood for, as pointing to a future where fear of "authority," omniscient and omnipotent, would not rule their every living minute, thought and action.

It took from 9:30 in the evening of 1 July, until 5:30 on the morning of the following day, to traverse the Black Sea–Danube Canal. It was forty miles long in all. This meant a mean speed of four and a half knots, with the engine, while we were under way, of full revolutions. There were two locks on the canal, one at either end, and at the first lock, close to Cernavoda, at km 59, the total drop-down was about three inches.

Between the locks the canal was ninety-eight yards wide most of the way, and the bridges had a uniform height over the water of about twenty-seven yards. The depth of the canal throughout was twenty feet, with here and there a variation of only a few inches.

Like most modern constructional works, the Black Sea–Danube Canal looked as if the designers had not had the human race in mind when they dreamed it up, but only machines. It was a long concrete ditch, bordered by extensive tracts of muddy clay, interspersed with a few jetties on which stood monstrous cranes lit by cold arc lights at night. On each side of this water-filled trench of concrete, artificial hills of mud had been thrown up to a height of about a hundred feet, so it was impossible for us, in *Outward Leg*, to see what lay beyond them. It made me feel like a germ being drawn through some monstrous alimentary tract.

We arrived at Agigea just before dawn broke in the east. Thomas soon turned in, dead tired. I waited up for a few minutes to see the sun peer over a straight, horizontal shadow of a line far away in the distance. The line was low down, beyond the nearby lock gates. Then silently, I bent my head, satisfied that I had again seen the sea, and humbly thanked God for it, with all my heart. After that, I slept.

# 31

# *Thalassa!*

Half an hour into the forenoon I woke again. It was a fine, dry, sunny promise of a day and apart from the frontier guards crunching gravel with their heavy boots on the dock above our heads, quiet. Stretching myself, I stared again over the canal to the southeast, to reassure myself that what I thought I'd seen a couple of hours earlier had not been imagination. There was a pale blue line across the horizon, low down over the immense dock gates. It was the sea all right. I tapped Thomas on the shoulder and poked my beard in its direction.

"*Thalassa,*" I said, quietly.

"*Was ist das?*" He was holding a cup of tea, freshly brewed.

I'd forgotten, he was nearsighted without his glasses. "The sea, Thomas, *der* frigging *see*, you know, what *du* steer *sein* bloody U-Boats *unter* . . . What old ladies piss in 'cos every little helps . . ."

Thomas dived below and donned his glasses, then, after he had slid topside again, he stood for a good five minutes in the cockpit staring out at the thick, hazy blue line far away. We both stared at it, until I glanced at Thomas. He was gazing at the sight like a good Catholic before the Eucharist. It was for him, it seemed, a holy moment for longing, adoration and thanksgiving. "What did you call it?" he asked suddenly, quietly.

"*Thalassa.* It's Greek. It's what the immortal ten thousand, or their remnants, shouted when they saw the sea after the march across Asia Minor in the *Iliad*, you know, Homer . . ."

"*T'alassa, t'alassa,*" Thomas murmured, over and over again, quietly, as if to himself, as he stared to the southeast. He never could pronounce "Th."

"That doesn't sound like Homer to me," I joshed him. "More like Oscar Wilde!"

At nine o'clock, after a breakfast of porridge and pears, courtesy of the Calarasi ferryboat skipper, we made our way, both Thomas and I, to the Agigea port captain's office. The port captain was a fat, corrupt fop, who kept in his locked desk drawer a carton of "Kent" cigarettes and a bottle of "Johnny Walker Black Label" whisky, probably purloined, I calculated, from the West German yacht *Karma*, which had passed through the canal two weeks before *Outward Leg*.

The port captain of Agigea, Rumania's intended super-port, was in a uniform which must have cost a small fortune. It was smothered, practically, in gold braid. It looked almost like a *gold* uniform with *blue* braid. It was made of blue doeskin serge and the gold braid looked real gold to me. There must have been a kilo of it. On his feet, which he folded in front of him as he lounged beside his desk, he wore black shoes with white tops, the kind we used to call "brothel-creepers," and he looked more as though he should be in charge of a Buenos Aires whorehouse than a multibillion-dollar ship canal. He was fattish with dark, greasy hair and he moved his fingers, ring bedecked, like amebas, and his body like a great jellyfish. When he spoke, it was with a false deliberation.

First he wanted to know why we had come through the canal and not carried on down the Danube, all the way to the sea. He spoke fair English.

"Because I wanted to visit Constanta," I half-lied, "to see the famous casino." Now I was really laying it on. We had $200.00 in the whole wide world to get *Outward Leg* from Rumania to Rhodes, including hoisting her mast and sorting out any small losses to the dozens of rigging-fittings. As soon as I'd said this I realized I'd made a mistake. Now the fat bastard thought I had money. I wasn't wrong in my realization. His little black eyes lit up as he cleared his throat under his treble chins and tapped his gold pen on his blotter. Suddenly he smirked from amid his gold braid and said, "The charge for your canal transit is $475.00. I'll take it in any Western currency, but dollars if you have them."

For a moment I was staggered. Back in Cernavoda we had been told the charge would be $25.00 without a pilot, if we followed another ship through, and $45.00 with a pilot on board our boat. There was no way we could pay $475.00. For forty miles that worked out at $13.30 a mile!

"But we've just come over twelve hundred and fifty miles down the Danube and the transit hasn't cost a cent!" I expostulated.

"The river Danube was not constructed by the Rumanian people," he replied, still smiling.

"But why were we not told of this charge in Cernavoda?" I asked him.

"Those people don't know anything about it," he scoffed. "This is where the canal is run from, right here!" He tapped his blotter again with his gold pen.

"I can't pay that much," I told him "I earn my money writing, and sometimes I don't get paid for work performed for months . . ."

"Then you'll have to wait here for months, in that case . . ." He said this in a mincing tone as he hoisted his fat body out of his chair and waddled out of the room, lugging his kilo of gold braid with him.

Thomas and I returned to the boat to try to figure out what to do. My leg stump was red-raw from all the clambering about, and I had to rest now and again on the way over the dried mud along the dock road. It was soul-searing to be so close to the sea and yet so far still. Beyond the great lock gate, shut tight, closed at the far end of the last lock, we could now plainly see the sea, and ships at anchor at Constanta roadstead, only a mile or two away.

All around us the canal, brand-new and the uglier for it, was still and silent, except for parties of people marching along the dock tracks with shovels over their shoulders. These caught my attention and held it, and it was a minute or two before I figured out why. Then I saw that none of them had, by the looks of them, ever done any manual work before. All of them, men and women, had the soft, gentler—not necessarily flabby—look of sedentary workers. The walk and the stance of office workers are, to me, unmistakable from a mile away. For one thing they keep their arms closer to their bodies than do manual workers, and the men walk more from the hips than from the shoulders. These Rumanian people of all ages, all carrying long-handled shovels over their shoulders, were silent. They were all clearly, if a bit shabbily, dressed in ordinary city summer clothes and shoes. They stared at us while they marched by out of step, under the escort of two armed guards to each party of about twenty or so. When I told

Thomas that they were office workers, he asked me how I could be so sure.

"I can't be absolutely certain," I told him, "but if they are not office workers or shop attendants, then I am the target ring on the helicopter platform of a North Sea oil rig."

Sure enough, when we had made friends, warily at first, then fonder, with our Kalashnikov-toting boy who guarded *Outward Leg*, and played him some country-and-western music, he explained to us, mostly in sign language, that the shovel carriers were groups of people from the cities. By order of Big Daddy *every* sedentary worker in Rumania had to spend a few days each year shifting mud-clay with a shovel on the Black Sea–Danube Canal. It was called "National Recreation," and it went on day and night, winter and summer. Everyone in Rumania *must* work, be in the armed forces, or starve or be in jail. That was the law, he said.

The upshot of our enforced wait was a stalemate. The canal authority, in the person of the uniformed poof, wanted $475.00. I didn't have $475.00. I told his minions I had $100.00, and part of that was for re-hoisting the mast and getting to Istanbul. There was much going back and forth by various gentlemen from the canal authority, from the police, from the frontier police, from the Constanta docks authority, from the Constanta tourist office.

Next morning, early, the price had been brought down in $25 stages from $475.00 to $350.00, each change in price involving a long, painful hobble from the boat to the port captain's office and back again, and an agonizing clamber up and down the dockside ladder of twenty feet or so. So the day wore on, a helpless, frustrating confusion, until one helpful soul from the canal authority, an ex-merchant-ship officer, Severin Anastis, slid on board and told me that there was a loophole through which *Outward Leg* might sail, all three hulls of her. If I could prove that the vessel was an "experimental craft," then we might get away with paying only *forty-one dollars!* Quickly I rifled through my filing cabinet, an old biscuit box. There it was, a Certificate of Incorporation of the Atlantis Society, "*to research ways and means of making ocean sailing in small craft a viable proposition for severely handicapped people*," under the laws of the State of New York, President, Tristan Jones. "*Present assets, nil!*" I mentally and mournfully added.

"What have you experimented with?" asked Severin Anastis.

I showed him our pride and joy; the enlarged handhold in the after cabin companionway, made wider so that I could jam my foot in it while I wedged myself on top of the cabin top, to take sextant sights at sea.

That was far as my resources on this voyage had allowed in the way of "experiments," so far, since October 1983. It had cost at least fifty cents. For the rest, I'd never had the time or money to experiment, only to get on with the job of staying alive, writing and moving.

But there was no time for reflection. As I handed over the frayed Certificate of Incorporation of the Atlantis Society, Inc., New York, to Severin, I comforted myself that every writer and sailor must be either crying or laughing, and there wasn't much difference between the two, so I laughed as he went up the ladder.

Severin was back in a few minutes, puffing, and two colorless canal authority clerks were with him. Within a few more moments they had taken my $41.00, given me a receipt, and stamped my ship's papers. Then they left the boat. In another ten minutes, with a young and jolly pilot on board, the last lock gate slowly opened and *Outward Leg*, with Mr. McPherson playing "The Big Spree," passed into the salt waters of the Black Sea.

I asked Thomas to dip a bucket in the sea and bring it to the cockpit. He did. I dipped my hand in it, captured a little of the water in my palm, lifted it to my mouth and gulped it. *Salt water! Outward Leg had conquered Europe! We'd done the bastard!*

I sent Thomas below for the one bottle of good Franconian wine remaining on board. He opened it and poured out two fingers in four glasses. I handed one glass to our wandering pilot, one to Thomas, and poured the odd glass into the sea, through my cockpit toilet drain (which is operated by gravity, being a vertical pipe, straight up and down, open at both ends). I took, then, my glass in my hand and in Welsh I toasted the sea all around us, to the four cardinal points of the compass. *"Euchi Dda!" We'd finally done the bastard!*

*Outward Leg* had made the crossing of the whole continent of Europe for the first time ever, by a United States registered vessel from any ocean, by way of the rivers Rhine, Main and Danube, a total of 2179 nautical miles.

Thomas and I had taken the very first American ocean vessel to Bavaria, Austria (post-1918), Czechoslovakia, and Hungary (post-1918). We had taken the first American or any other ocean vessel ever to the hearts of three European capital cities, Vienna, Budapest and

Belgrade. *Outward Leg* was the first ocean trimaran of any nationality to make the crossing, and we had done it all, the haul across Bavaria excepted, on *less than $10.00 a day!*

More important, I thought as we motored five miles along the coast, now in a sea surge, now with depths of a couple of hundred feet, we had been seen by hundreds of thousands of people, many of whom had never before seen an ocean multihull, and visited by many hundreds, including eight hundred or more handicapped people, mostly youngsters. Eight hundred out of 450 million handicapped people in the world was only a drop in a big bucket, but it was a start.

As the flat coastland south of Constanta passed slowly by and as *Outward Leg* steadily rose and fell to the sea's urging, I comforted myself that we still had left in our kitty $159.00. With any luck, we'd reach Istanbul with some of that still on board.

The docks of Constanta were huge by any standards. The great seawalls were being extended south and west for yet more miles. Yet all the five days we had spent in the Black Sea—Danube Canal we had watched no more than five ships pass through. Now, at the exit from the canal, a harbor was being built that would be extensive enough to contain all the world's merchant ships, and room besides. From horizon to horizon there was little but monstrous walls of concrete slabs, cranes, heavy trucks and dredgers, all working away. As we passed them I remembered the little ragged lads in Cernavoda stealing food from waste plates. There must have been enough money being spent during the hour that we alone passed through Constanta Bay to have fed all the starving kids in the Balkans, let alone Rumania, for a year. Some would say that the new docks will help to feed the kids in the future. That would be wrong, because those docks were being built on sand, and the first big storms would probably sweep them onto the shore. Even on a dead calm day, with a sea in the offing as flat as the top of the Agigea port captain's head, there was a surge coming into Constanta Bay like a roller coaster. The whole Black Sea–Danube Canal complex is a Lloyd's Registered, first-class disaster and should have been constructed miles farther north, so that the exit joined the sea through Lacul Sinoe, north of Constanta, in more protected waters.

The "Tourist Port" of Tomis was the old, small harbor of Constanta, built originally by the Phoenicians, and ever since used by small fishing craft coasters. It consisted of a mole behind a high seawall, a pillbox and an armed guard on the end of it, a naval barracks constructed on an old barge which floated at the root of the mole, and several Rumanian fishing trawlers. There were fifteen feet of depth alongside most of the mole. There were a few bollards, and some mooring rings, but most of the mooring rings were either strained, bent or broken. The wide mole was dimly lit at night until nine o'clock, when the streetlamps, except around the Rumanian Naval Headquarters and the pillbox, were extinguished. In north winds, there was a bad surge.

I had intended to hoist the mast on 4 July, American Independence Day, for *Outward Leg*'s sake. But the winds were too blustery on that day. Besides, if we were to do it by hand we would need assistance. There were no hands available except through the good offices of the port captain of Constanta, and he would have to consult with the local Communist party bosses before they could be provided, we were told.

"What about a crane?" I asked.

"The same thing there," I was told. (I have to be very careful about "who and where" here. Some people could be shot.)

While we waited for the wind to drop so that we could get the mast up reasonably safely, Thomas and I explored the area around Port Tomis. At the end of the mole, through the sentry-guarded gate, across a wide plaza, there was a café with outdoor tables called Tomis Teraca. It served mainly beer and some wine to officials and small-time bureaucrats who turned up usually in Russian-made cars with official plates.

Above the Teraca café was the Hotel Palace, which was a hotbed of wheeling and dealing. The toilet in the hotel lobby was a full-scale money-exchange office during the afternoons, and "forbidden" foreign goods like blue jeans, cigarettes and music tapes were bought and sold in the evenings.

The city area above the port had an air of seedy disrepute, but it was not unpleasant. It looked as if every door would creak, every window jam, but as if interesting things were happening behind them. There was, all about, an ambience of steady, silent intrigue, for good or ill. Women who passed, young or old, kept their faces downcast. Young couples seemed to take their courtships very earnestly. There was very little laughter. Every effort, every request, every demand, seemed to cause either maximum confusion or outright denial. Nothing was ever easy or convenient or willing.

Farther north of the city was the holiday resort of Mamaia, full of hotels reserved for foreign tourists. One evening Thomas and I visited two hotels in Mamaia. The area was like another world from the real Rumania we knew. There were no uniformed armed guards, no officials in a dozen different menacing uniforms, and what secret police we detected were all in Western clothing, with long hairstyles on the men. Prices, too, were very Western. The roads crawled with police cars. We couldn't recognize them as such, of course, but our Rumanian companion could. Because our companion was Rumanian we were refused service at one hotel. At the next we were served only soft drinks, because it was after nine o'clock. The taxi driver, who returned us to the docks, was an avaricious scoundrel. He overcharged us almost double. I liked him for that. Any sign of personal enterprise, in Rumania, should, I felt, be encouraged to the hilt. As we'd sold another pair of Levis for a small fortune in leus, I handed him *three* times the normal fare. There was nothing else to spend it on and we couldn't take it anywhere else.

Thomas told me that the supply of food in the shops was remarkable for its paucity. Only carrots, onions and spinach were available. He had managed to get hold of a loaf of bread, though, because he had passed a State-run bread distributor the moment it had opened. There had been a rush and a crush for five minutes, as the townspeople fought for their loaves, and then the shop had shut again, to the silent despair of a hundred or so housewives and old people.

"Where's the loaf, then, Thomas?" I asked him. He didn't seem to have one.

"Oh, I gave it to an old lady. She was so old, and could hardly walk . . ."

That evening, when we returned on board, we found a bundle wrapped in newspaper in the cockpit. It was wet from the falling rain. I scrambled it open, and sure enough, it was a loaf of bread. There was no message. I thought, "That's ordinary Rumania in a nutshell."

With the naval sentry at the dock gate we stopped for a while to exchange pleasantries. Soon he returned with a uniform shirt to exchange for "Kent" cigarettes. Soon some of his mates turned up, full of banter now that we were becoming "part of the furniture." The

evening ended with Thomas exchanging two packets of "Kent" cig-
arettes for the full uniform of an able seaman in the Rumanian Socialist
Republic Navy, shoes, belt, shirt, cap and all. It's all still on board
*Outward Leg*.

The following day the boat was visited by two hundred aspiring
students at the Merchant Navy Training School in Constanta. The
visit was not arranged and certainly not intended by Big Daddy's
minions. The aspiring cadets had been taken to sea in navy tugs on
a short "seasickness" test. As they waited to be carried out into the
lively offing, they could hardly avoid seeing *Outward Leg*, nor hearing
her bagpipes. Within minutes, despite the hard stares of their su-
periors, they were all crowded round the boat, exchanging conver-
sations with Thomas and me. The wonder in those kids' faces when
we told them what we were and who we were and where we were
bound, and how we did it all, was something to behold. We left many
a grain of a thought well planted among that lot.

Later that day, as a mobile crane trundled up the jetty, we knew
that the party bosses had sent it to raise our mast. The cost, the
foreman said, would be "about $50.00" but a final cost would be fixed
after he had seen what time and materials would be used. That was
fair practice anywhere, except that the cost seemed to me a bit steep.

The foreman was, he gave me to understand in very basic English,
of Armenian descent. Although he continually commented on the
shortages of materials and the cumbersomeness of Rumanian Communist Party bureaucracy, he never criticized it. He spoke of it as if
it were the most natural thing in the world for us to have to go to the
city of Constanta Communist Party Secretary General's desk for permission to raise a boat's mast, and for the wherewithal to do it. He
accepted that split pins could not be bought for love nor money in
Rumania, and that those we needed had to be manufactured by ourselves out of brass wire, to buy which we had to go to the desk of
the Secretary General of the Constanta City Communist Party . . .
and then head for the main docks storehouse with *twelve* forms in
*triplicate*, each of which had to be signed and stamped at four different
desks in eight different offices, all widely spaced apart in the Constanta dockyard. It had taken us five days to make the jury-split pins.
There was no phosphor bronze or aluminum available.

Soon the small mobile crane's jib had picked up the mast. Then
four dock laborers clomped on board and helped lift the mast by a

strop secured about halfway up. In vain, as the crane kept lifting and lifting, did I try to explain that the mast should be laid down again and the strop moved farther up the mast so that it would hang more vertically. There was no holding the Armenian, no telling him what needed to be done; he shouted and bawled, the crane driver was confused, but he was a good party man, the laborers were carrying out orders; Thomas and I were powerless. One of the hulking brutes from the dockyard grabbed the mast heel, lined it up, with two of his comrades mauling the swaying mast as he did so, and he rammed the toe-holding bolt through the tabernacle and the mast.

Then the mast was grasped at an angle of about eighty-five degrees from the horizontal and five degrees from the vertical by the small crane, and held by its toe to the tabernacle by the stainless-steel, half-inch bolt. All that needed to be done was for someone to haul on the topping lift, rigged as a temporary backstay, to bring the mast fully vertical so that I could slip in the small heel pin to fix the mast-foot firmly square and upright in the tabernacle. Gasping, as I tried to help the mast upright against its tremendous forty-foot leverage, I shouted to the Armenian to order his laborer on the after deck to haul away on the topping lift, to get tension on the swaying masthead. Instead, the Armenian probably ordered him to let go, because that's what the moron on the after deck did.

I stared with horror at the feet of the slowly falling mast which was, we later realized, pushing the small mobile crane *back*, away from the boat. I heard the awful sound of breaking metal as the aluminum tabernacle slowly started to tip itself asunder. Aghast, as our mast moved inexorably forward and down, I waited for the bang of our tabernacle being ripped out of our deck, and the mast heel exploding upward, taking my head and the upper part of my body with it, out over the surging waters.

# 32

# *Victorious, Happy and Half-Knackered*

As I gawped, my eyes riveted, horror-struck at the mastfoot, as big and round as an elephant's, still creeping, crawling and slowly tearing our tabernacle, half-inch-thick cast aluminum, to shreds, a voice broke the silence behind my back. It spoke English. It was very clear, very real English. It was an English voice, a deep voice, an Englishman's voice. "Do you need a hand, old chap?"

It was kind and civilized, and I was hearing it in this Rumanian hellhole deep behind the Iron Curtain, bereft of rational, sensible, human minds for miles and miles and miles, while my heavy mast was slowly, so slowly, inexorably falling over sideways, and not a decent repair facility between me and the Aegean Sea.

"Thomas, nip up the crane jib. Eddie," I yelled at the Armenian, "you go back aft and show that dimwit back there how to pull the topping lift. For Christ's sake steady the mast, hold her, *hold her*," I heard myself yelling.

Above my head, as I glanced up, the forty-foot mast was shaking and shivering, teetering and tottering. Then Armenian Eddie had a purchase at last on the line led aft to the stern deck, and for a few minutes the mast was reasonably safe, as long as no other craft entered or left the harbor and set up a wake. If that happened, as sure as two follows one, the surge set up would bring the whole ton and a half of tottering weight aloft crashing down on the foredeck, taking half the midship's deck with it, and smashing the foredeck to splinters. Then, *Outward Leg*, to all intents and purposes, would be an unsailable wreck.

The worst thing about all these proceedings, for me, was not so

319

much what was happening, as the fact that I couldn't move myself, on my one leg, anywhere fast enough to do what was needed. It was a matter of trying to send signals fast enough and loud enough so that they could be rapidly understood in German (Thomas) and Rumanian (Eddie). I was doubly, trebly handicapped by the language problem.

*"Having some problems?"* the English voice asked behind my back.

By this time Thomas was at the very end of the swaying crane jib and securing another strop farther up the mast, so that the crane might get another purchase and further steady our mast. Then we could haul down on the shrouds and make it safe. Now the strain was off the tabernacle and it had stopped tearing itself asunder. By this time I had slithered over to the starboard ama and somehow tied a line onto one of the upper starboard mast shrouds and hauled the line down hard. Then, with the topping lift bowsed down aft, the second crane purchase taking the weight, and my shroud rigging screw connected and screwed home, I could look around.

The sweat was pouring down my forehead. I knew my stump groin was bleeding. I peered at the place where the English voice had come from.

There were two men, both fairly young, both more prosperous-looking than anyone else around. They were dressed in sports jackets and gray trousers. One of them had a badge on his jacket pocket, a moustache, and a camera case slung over his shoulder.

"Good morning," I gasped at the moustache. "What can I do for you?"

The moustache grinned minutely, and the blue eyes above it lit up. "Well, good morning. We're from BUP Press Agency."

"Oh, God," I thought, "they even get here!" But what I said was, "BUP? What are you doing here?"

"Well, we're covering the visit here of HMS *Naiad* . . ."

*"What????"*

"Yes, Maggie thought she ought to send one of our frigates on a sort of 'show the flag' thing in the Black Sea. It's in the main dockyard now. The lads don't like the place. They can't wait to get to Istanbul . . ."

He told me that this was the first visit of a British warship—or indeed any Western powers' warship—to Rumania for years, and that HMS *Naiad* had pulled into Constanta only hours before. "What can we do for you?" asked the moustache.

"Ask the Engineer Officer in HMS *Naiad* to come on over here to Port Tomis and see me, for Christ's sake!"

And that's how, miraculously, we got a steel bracket made which would temporarily hold the mast toe down on the deck-bedding plate of the tabernacle long enough, and in some quite heavy winds at times, to get *Outward Leg* to the Eastern Mediterranean where a new stainless-steel tabernacle could be made and fitted.

As soon as our mast was securely held down by the stays and shroudwires, and the crane strop was taken off the mast, Eddie sidled up to me with his bill. He had scribbled it down on a piece of brown packing paper taken out of his pocket. It was for $100.00!

"What the hell's this, Eddie? *A hundred dollars?*"

"Yes, you had the crane for over an hour, so we have to charge for two hours. Don't worry about paying the workmen. I'll see to that."

I said, "But that's bloody banditry, Eddie. You've caused a good three hundred dollars' worth of damage! You almost wrecked the mast and cabin top, and the foredeck! Christ, a hundred dollars!"

The upshot was that I managed to beat him down to $80.00, but he was adamant for that payment. The party would be upset as it was, he said. With the $10.00 that Thomas had spent the day before, that left us with $49.00 in the world, for I had nothing, that I knew of, anywhere else. We had three tins of Hungarian corned beef in the boat, and some rice.

That afternoon, after the jury bracket had been fitted and our sails shipped for the first time in nine months, and after chasing about for several miles from one office to another, I finally got permission to take our boat out into the offing for a short sailing trial, to make sure that everything was working properly before we finally took off for Bulgaria and Istanbul. I was allowed to sail up and down immediately outside Port Tomis harbor for exactly fifteen minutes, no more. Then I had to return under the eyes of the armed sentry at the end of the mole. To make sure I did return I had to leave my Dunlop dinghy and outboard motor with the sentry.

It was miserable, this penal, probationary sailing, but once we were out in the offing I let Thomas scoot her around like a frisky colt in a steady twenty-knot northeaster while I watched the new tabernacle bracket like a cat watching a canary. Before we knew it, our fifteen minutes were up and we had to come back into port, feeling as though we'd hired our boat from Big Daddy Ceausescu himself, for a few very expensive and unforgettable minutes of utter freedom. We collected our dinghy and outboard motor and were safely under the guard of a Kalashnikov again. I gave the guard a cigarette and got him to show me the breech mechanism of his automatic rifle. There was no ammunition in it!

The rest of that week was taken up bringing the boat in line for the three-hundred-mile leg to Istanbul. A new spare log impeller was fitted, our roller headsail gear was adjusted and freed, all our blocks were overhauled and our sheets were reversed. Thomas did the one-hundred-hour routine on faithful little Yannie. Then he fitted the safety nettings between the bows in case he should fall over himself at sea, checked lamps and radios for batteries while I overhauled and adjusted my sextant and dug out our seacharts for the Black Sea and the Bosphorus.

All this we did at the time almost insensible to the wonder with which the Rumanians watched us. We were aware only vaguely that we were free men while they were not. They never used the word "emigrated" or "went," when they talked of anyone leaving their country, it was always "*escaped*," even from party officials, when they spoke English. To them we were "escaping" from their country. The look in their eyes as they watched us was tragic.

On 6 July Thomas and I were invited on board HMS *Naiad*, to dine in the wardroom. This was a great occasion for both of us, but especially for me, for I'd never dined in a wardroom before, and never had I wanted to. But my memories of Royal Naval officers were far removed from the present day reality that I saw and felt in HMS *Naiad*. These officers were not, except in courage, as their forbears had been. They were highly trained technicians, and literate. Their relations with the lads below decks were obviously vastly different from those of their forbears. Now there was much more mutual respect and far less disdain on the one hand and outright resentment or even fear on the other. This cheered me enormously. I enjoyed the first decent meal I'd had in weeks. I also enjoyed the "Nelson's Blood" with which the officers, all far too young to have been in "my" navy, regaled me. Their rum was not out of a barrel, as, of course, had been ours in the old days. It came out of a bottle, but by God it was a good old brew and soon had me in fine fettle. As Thomas and I left the ship and walked away from her bright lights into the gloom of

Rumania, an armed, uniformed moron rushed up to me and brusquely demanded something in a rough way.

"What's this fucker want, Thomas?" I asked my crewman. I could hardly see straight. All I could see was yet another uniform, yet another gun, yet another of Big Daddy's bully-boys. He was about thirty, with fat jowls.

"He want to see your documents, Tristan."

"Documents is it, you bastard?" I said softly as I glared at the face over the gun.

The face glared back at me and the man growled something, then he barked at me.

"Documents?" I yelled at the policeman, "I'll give you five of the best bloody documents you'll ever see . . ." and with that I hit him right in his flabby jowls. It was a good square punch, and I brought my fist back to "draw him another goffer," but, I was told later, was restrained by the ship's doctor and engineer officer, who had rushed down their gangway when they saw me go for the copper. I don't know what happened after that; only that we were left in peace to return to our ship like good, honest, law-abiding sailors should be.

The next morning I awoke to a thick head and a certain little satisfaction. I'd had a stomachful of bullies and thick-headed moronic bastards shoving people around right, left and center. Our mast was hoisted now. The sea was only a hundred yards away.

That night, well fortified with yet more of the hard stuff, Thomas and I watched the throng arrive at the Teraca Tomis café. There came dozens of party officials and functionaries with their wives and offspring. They parked their Russian cars and sat at the tables over their beers and wineglasses. I made sure that my walking stick was handy and safe, then I stood up. I knew full well we were being watched by every eye in the place. As I stood on my foot, a dead silence reigned for a full minute and I let it reign.

I said, "Good evening, ladies and gentlemen, comrades and the rest!" I paused briefly, "I think many of you know who I am, and I think I know what you are, and what your purpose in life is . . ." Thomas was pulling on my jacket hem. I shoved his hand away. "On behalf of my crew here, and of myself, and of my boat, *Outward Leg*, which will soon, God willing, be heading out to sea again, I want to thank the people of Rumania for all the little kindnesses that you have shown us."

I hesitated for a moment, then bowed and said, "Thank you."

At this a few people burst out clapping. They were soon followed by most of the others. Only a few red-tabbed officers glared at me. I took another swig of hard stuff, whatever it was. Then, when the clapping had died down and all were silent again, I continued: "I think that the people of Rumania are among the kindest, the most helpful in many little ways, the most colorful and certainly among the most attractive people in the whole of Europe if not the world!"

At this there was another enthusiastic burst of applause. Again it died down. Now everyone's attention was directly on me. Now even the red-tabbed officers were, if not smiling, at least not scowling.

I went on quite slowly, in measured tones, "I also think that the Rumanian people are the most downtrodden and misgoverned that I have encountered in the past ten years. I love you. I want to be back with you some day. But I also think that your present government is corrupt, inefficient, brutal and ignorant. I believe that society must rest on justice and love. Anything else is organized wrong. I think the Rumanian government is an oligarchy, and I say that its slogan should be 'Jobs for the Boys!' *I think it is fascist!*"

Now all the red-tabbed officers, except one or two, rose and swiftly left their tables. A few civilians followed them but a good ninety out of the hundred functionaries remained. Their eyes were almost as wide as their mouths. A few were very slightly nodding their heads. One woman clapped her hands, until they were grabbed by the man with her. Somewhere a baby cried, but was soon hushed.

"Rumania, I love you!" I cried.

There was another burst of clapping. Someone shouted *"Bravo!"*

"But your government stinks to high heaven!" And with that I sat down. They could do what they liked now, I thought. I'd said what I felt, and the truth of it was all that mattered to me.

There was dead silence all around on the café terrace as I picked up my stick. People stared into one another's eyes. No one moved. Not a soul in the place stirred and no one looked at either Thomas or me as we left for our boat in silence.

Next morning, as I hobbled around on my morning exercise walk along the seafront avenue to the old casino, a dozen people came up to me, complete strangers, and silently took my hand to shake it enthusiastically. We had no more problems with armed soldiers stopping us for documents. Now, obviously, everyone knew who we were and what we were. I was just in time to see HMS *Naiad* steaming out of harbor, her "flag-showing" visit over. I silently stared after her and wished her the best.

On 12 July I had intended to sail at daybreak, but "control" did not show up until midday, to clear us out of Rumania. Eventually they did this with good, if slow, grace.

Soon *Outward Leg* was again curtseying to the gods of the sea, dingle-bobbing down the Rumanian coast, about three miles offshore. There was a weak northerly breeze, no more than fifteen knots all that afternoon. I was too busy watching all the sailing gear, checking it, testing it, to feel much emotion, even relief, at being back at sea. After so long in inland waterways, even on rough ones like Old Father Danube, our vessel needed to be wet-nursed a great deal when she finally headed out to sea, and just about every nut and bolt and cat's whisker was checked and re-checked. We rigged the running poles and hoisted the genniker. We handed it again an hour later when the wind shifted over the port quarter. We hoisted the twin headsails and let them have their way for a while. We rolled them up and hoisted the spitfire, just to see that it was in fettle, then the storm jib, and the trys'l. After that we took all the reefs in on the main, then let them out again, so that *Outward Leg* herself must have felt like a lady finally released from a sickbed, trying all her dresses on, changing her hairstyle a dozen times in the same day. We adjusted the Aries self-steering gear, and let *Outward Leg* have her head for many a long stretch and stride on each *point* of sail, but always we returned to our course, away from Constanta.

Midnight saw us about twelve miles southeast of Cape Mangalia. The light was, surprisingly, working. We slowed down for the night. There was no point in fetching the Bulgarian coast in the hours of darkness, and anyway, I knew that in the Gulf of Varna the wind piped up at breakfast time and blew onshore, so we could get a good lift then. But we still kept deck watches, Thomas and I, for the area was thick with shipping heading every which way.

At 2 A.M. we rounded Cape Shableh. That was as it should be, and at four-thirty, just as dawn was shaking apart the trembling blackness of the night, we sighted dark Cape Kaliakos, fine on the starboard bow.

Breakfast saw us whizzing along at ten knots, with the Bulgarian port of Varna clearly visible a good twenty miles away. By ten-thirty we had passed the breakwaters, stooged around a bit looking for a lodging, and been ordered to tie up at the Varna Yacht Haven just inside the breakwater.

After Constanta, Varna was an anticlimax. Anywhere would be, I suppose. We missed all our Rumanian friends greatly. Varna could never hope to affect us both in the same way that Constanta had, in every way. It was more modern for a start. There were far fewer uniforms about, although no doubt there were just as many officials. The harbor immigration and customs officials were correct and polite, but the questions were much the same as they had been in Rumania: Who were we meeting? Did we know anyone in Varna? In Bulgaria? Were we intending to stay ashore anywhere? Where? Did we intend to use our radio? Were we in touch with anyone else by radio? But the Bulgarians were much more sophisticated than the Rumanians. The iron fist was there all right, but it was well disguised under a fairly thick velvet glove.

The only remarkable thing in Varna was that people nodded when they said "No."

In our berth, right opposite the Bulgarian presidential yacht, a monstrous Italian-built gin-palace of a craft with a full-time crew of six hulking young men, we worked at adjusting *Outward Leg*'s wind instruments and refixing the compass light. These were the only two defects we had found in our first leg back at sea. That wasn't bad after ten months inland, all the while with the vessel unrigged.

In Varna, miraculously enough, the printer's proofs of my book *Outward Leg* were waiting for me at the post office. The lady at the Poste Restante counter gave me the first smile I got in Bulgaria. I corrected the proofs in one all-day and all-night session, and returned them to London the next day. The lady gave me the second smile I saw in Bulgaria, apart from Thomas's, and her smile was also the last smile in that country. It seemed to me that the average Bulgarian had the demeanor of an undertaker's apprentice.

We went ashore together for a visit into Varna town. There were many more small shops there than there had been in Rumania, and consumer goods were in profuse supply, but they were not, by any means, cheap. They seemed to be about the same price, taking the rate of currency exchange into account, as they would have been back in Western Europe. I can't say anything about the quality, for we had no money to buy anything except one meal.

At the restaurant, we were lucky to be served. When Thomas started to order sausage and potatoes, the waitress asked him where he was from. Her English was nonexistent but we caught her gist.

*"Deutschland,"* replied Thomas, as innocent as ever.

*"Ost oder west?"* shrieked the good lady in café-German. We were nearing the Mediterranean all right, where most local women have voices like parrots.

"West," replied Thomas. At which the good lady threw her head in the air and marched off grimly, nodding her head.

A man sitting at the next table, who said he had worked in West Germany, intervened and persuaded the comrade-waitress to serve us a meal of cold, greasy sausage and even colder spuds, which she slammed in front of us, neglecting to give us knives, still nodding her head.

I phoned the Soviet Embassy in Sofia, to ask for the naval attaché. I wanted to chase up what was happening about my application to visit the Crimea. We were told he was "on holiday" and that they "did not know when he'd be back."

Later, inside the city, which was crowded with Russian Navy soldiers all sitting around in shady parks drinking beer and staring at the passing women, we entered a large café. All the staff were sitting around a table drinking coffee.

"Coffee?" we asked.

"No coffee." They grunted at us, and went back into their huddle.

We returned to our boat. It was late evening by then. The long rows of advertisements on the walls of the docks fascinated me. They were all arc-lit, and were the first commercial advertisements we had seen since we left the Yugoslav frontier. They showed cars and re-frigerators, and all the other paraphernalia of "modern living" that was on offer in The Bulgarian People's Socialist Republic. There were no hammers, no sickles evident, and the only red stars were on the caps of policemen and Soviet sailors.

We from *Outward Leg* were much more aware of the tight fist that controls Bulgaria than the average tourist might be. We could not shift the boat one inch without informing "control." We could not even go ashore without reporting to the "control" tower which over-looked everything in the port, ashore or afloat. There was not a minute of the day or night when a dark shadow did not stand in the tinted windows of the high "control" tower, watching us. If we had wanted to invite anyone on board we would have had to inform "control." Bulgarians were not allowed on board under any circumstances. That had been made very clear within five minutes of our arrival in Varna.

Several of the Bulgarian yachts in the haven had Bulgarian crews on board. They never greeted us, they never even smiled or nodded at us. They rarely even looked at *Outward Leg*, although the haven director did say that she was one of the first trimarans ever seen there, if not the first. I am not sure if this Bulgarian yachtsman's coldness was caused by *Outward Leg*'s size—she took up the space needed for two monohulls—or because of our American ensign. I suspect it was the latter.

Passing "civilians" on the seawall walk stopped and gazed at our boat, sometimes for an hour or more, and talked among themselves about her. But the Bulgarian yachtsmen behaved as though we did not exist. It may have been simple prejudice or bigotry, nationalistic or nautical, but it may also have been because of that shadow behind the tinted glass of the tower.

On 16 July we sailed from Varna after having been questioned closely by the immigration officials and police about where we had been and who we had seen, after they had searched the boat. What for, I cannot imagine. Apart from seven pairs of blue jeans and some Rumanian cigarettes, our only assets were twenty American dollars, and we couldn't have fed a starving cat, let alone a stowaway. They missed the amas again. As we left Varna we were shadowed all the way out to five miles offshore by an Immigration Service launch. Then when she saw we were really heading away, she left us alone, with the immensity of the sea and our memories, both fond and bitter.

The Black Sea showed her temperament that night. First there was a very steady north wind, until about the first dog-watch, then it swung right round to the south and diminished until there was a calm with a sloppish sea. We started Yannie and slogged our way in a miserable jerky motion for a couple of hours, then the wind swooshed down again from the north, force-six for an hour, dropped to nothing in another hour, then smashed in from the east for a while, before it finally sulked and hid itself, muttering, leaving us with about seven different sea fetches coming from as many different directions, but mainly from the south.

Off the Bulgarian shore the sea was shallow right out for several miles, often no more than sixty feet, but then it dropped off in chasmic suddenness. It was a nasty sea, the Black Sea. I headed out for the middle of the sea where the current is supposed to run south, straight toward the Bosphorus, and sure enough, by sun sights next day, found that we had gained about two knots of southing that way. Another reason for keeping to the middle was that close inshore on the Bulgarian-Turkish frontier there were said to be minefields, old and new. This was common gossip among the coastal fishermen of Rumania and Bulgaria whom I spoke with, but no one else seemed to know about it, or if they did know, they weren't telling.

Just after noon on 17 July, I sighted land. It was at first, as almost always, vague and ghostly in the horizon haze. An hour later a line of position showed it to be Cape Rumelia on the west side of the northern entrance to the Bosphorus. A few minutes later we piled on sail to get into the Bosphorus before the north wind, up our tail, blew too hard for comfortable steering. It raised a hellish sea by teatime usually, we were told later.

By 2 P.M. we were well inside the narrow Bosphorus Strait and were hailed by the Turkish customs control vessel off Sariyer. I turned *Outward Leg* into the wind and hove her to. "Here we go again," I thought, imagining yet another dozen heavy boots trampling through our boat, rifling through all our lockers and cupboards, another third-degree questioning.

There was none of that. The Turks skillfully tied up alongside, invited Thomas onto their vessel with our ship's papers, stamped our crew list, and waved us on our way with a smile.

I was dumbfounded. I stood, like an ox at a crossroads, staring at one Turkish officer for a full minute as the boat nodded and the jib fluttered in the wind. He was small and darkly complexioned.

The officer started to let go of his boat's lines from our cleats. I felt a strange panic. They were leaving us!

When at last I managed to shout, I called, "But . . . but . . . where shall we go? Where shall we anchor . . .?"

The Turkish officer looked up. Then he unbent and unfolded his hands before him, until his arms were outspread wide. He smiled broadly, showing brilliant teeth under his black moustache. "Any-where!" he shouted.

I couldn't believe my ears. I called out again, "But . . . where shall we go?"

"Go anywhere you like, Mister. You have the whole coast of Turkey; it's all yours!"

I shoved the wheel over, but steadied it again until the mist cleared from my eyes. It was the first time that we had not been ordered into a place where we *must* go since we had left Austria, seventy-eight days before, and one thousand two hundred and fifty miles back.

*Outward Leg* had three ice-damaged hulls, a weakly held mast, a severely wounded side and $20.00 in the world. But she was *free*.

We headed for Istanbul . . . but that's another story.

# List of Ports of Call

## on Outward Leg's *voyage across Europe*

### Britain

1 London, St. Katharine's Dock
2 Hole Haven, Essex

### Holland

3 Ijmuiden
4 Sixhaven
5 Amsterdam
6 Utrecht
7 Arnhem
8 Rheden
9 Nijmegen

### West Germany

10 Wesel
11 Homburg
12 Düsseldorf
13 Cologne
14 Remagen
15 Koblenz
16 Lorchhausen
17 Assmannshausen
18 Rüsselsheim
19 Frankfurt
20 Obernau
21 Faulbach
22 Gemünden
23 Markbreit
24 Schweinfurt
25 Hassfurt
26 Bamberg (3)

27 Erlangen (2)
28 Furth (2)
29 Nürnberg (2), Gebersdorf
30 Ingolstadt
31 Neustadt
32 Bad Abbach
33 Regensburg
34 Straubing
35 Passau

### Austria

36 Obermühl
37 Linz
38 Grein
39 Ybbs
40 Weittenegg
41 Tulln
42 Vienna (City Center)
43 Deutsch Altenburg

### Czechoslovakia

44 Karlova Ves
45 Bratislava
46 Hrusov
47 Komarno

### Hungary

48 Komarom
49 Esztergom

50   Nagymaros
51   Vencermaros
52   Budapest (City Center)
53   Romai
54   Lupazig
55   Adony
56   Mohacs

*Yugoslavia*

57   Batina
58   Apatin
59   Borovo
60   Vukovar
61   Novi Sad
62   Breska
63   Stari Slankamen
64   Stari Banovici
65   Zemun
66   Belgrade
67   Ada Ciganlija

68   Grocka
69   Ram
70   Veliko Gradiste
71   Donji Milanovac
72   Kladovo

*Rumania*

73   Turnu-Severin
74   Calafat
75   Bechet
76   Corabia
77   Turnu-Magurele
78   Zimnicea
79   Guirgiu
80   Oltenita
81   Calarasi
82   Cernavoda
83   Agigea
84   Constanta
85   Varna

*Bulgaria*

Passed close to the following ports on the river Danube: Novo Selo; Evdokia; Vidin; Lom; Kuzudoi; Oryakhovo; Nikopol; Svishtov; Ruse; Ryakhovo; Tutrakan; Popina.

*Turkey*

86   Istanbul (Bebek)

From Istanbul *Outward Leg* sailed a thousand miles through the Sea of Marmara, the Dardanelles and the Aegean, to Rhodes and Kastellorizo. This book was written in the latter island in twenty-eight days flat.